INSTANT BIBL[...]
FOR SMALL [...]

By Barry L. Davis, D.Min.

www.barrydavis.org
www.pastorshelper.com

GodSpeed Publishing

Copyright©2013 Barry L. Davis

Table of Contents

INTRODUCTION

I am so glad that you have invested in this Instant Bible Study guide. I have been leading small groups for 20 years and know the value of good Bible Study material.

That is why I have painstakingly written each one of these guides with you in mind – while I don't know you, I do know how hard it is to come up with good questions that will really cause people to dig into God's Word. So I have tried extra hard, with God's help, to produce material that will lead you and your group closer to Him.

There are four main parts to each study:

1) **Open It** – this is an icebreaker question to get people to feel more comfortable with each other.

2) **Dig Into It** – this is where you discover what the Bible actually says. This is the analytical part.

3) **Reflect on It** – this is where you apply what you have learned to your life.

4) **Pray About It** – this is where you take the time to pray for each and every need within your group. **DO NOT SKIP PAST THIS PART!** It is vital for your group that you connect in prayer.

In Christ,

Barry L. Davis

LESSON 1 – DOES GOD EXIST?

Romans 1:18-25

OPEN IT:

What do you think is the biggest reason that some people question the existence of God?

DIG INTO IT:

1. *Read Romans 1:18-20* and answer the following questions:

   a) Name some specific examples of "godlessness and wickedness" people use in our culture to "suppress the truth"? (v. 18)

   b) How does the creation reveal God to humankind? What attributes of God can be known by observing the world around us? (vv. 19-20)

   c) Is this enough evidence for God to leave humankind without excuse? (vv. 19-20)

2. *Read Romans 1:21-25* and answer the following questions:

   a) How would refusing to recognize God lead to futile thinking and darkened hearts? Examples? (v. 21)

   b) Why would a person choose to worship the creation rather than the Creator? (v. 23,25) Do people do this today?

   c) How might giving "them over" to the evil activity they desire be a punishment? (v. 24)

REFLECT ON IT:

1. What is the most compelling argument that you've heard that God *doesn't* exist? That He *does* exist?

2. Have you ever doubted the existence of God? Why or why not?

3. A friend tells you that they can't believe in God because they lost a child and believe that if there is a God, He is to blame ...What would you say to them?

4. How is God demonstrating His existence in your life right now? Is there something you can share with the group?

5. Has God ever been more real to you than He is right now? If so, how can the group help you to draw closer?

PRAY ABOUT IT:

"Nothing tends more to cement the hearts of Christians than praying together. Never do they love one another so well as when they witness the outpouring of each other's hearts in prayer."
~ CHARLES FINNEY

LESSON 2 – CREATED AND CARED FOR

Psalms 139:13-15; Luke 15:4-10; 1 Cor. 13:12

OPEN IT:

Do you think it would be a blessing or a curse to be an identical twin?

DIG INTO IT:

1. *Read Psalms 139:13-15* and answer the following questions:

   a) What does the phrase "inmost being" refer to? (v. 13)

   b) What level of involvement must God have had in the process of your creation to be said to have "knit" or "woven" you together? (vv. 13, 15)

   c) Do you think God literally knew you before you were born?

2. *Read Luke 15:4-10* and answer the following questions:

   a) Who does the lost sheep and lost coin represent? Who do the shepherd and the woman represent? (vv. 4-10)

   b) Why would all of Heaven throw a party when someone repents and turns to Jesus? (vv. 7, 10) How does this demonstrate each person's uniqueness before God?

   c) To what extent will God search for a person who is lost? Are there any limits? (vv. 4-10)

3. *Read 1 Cor. 13:12* and answer the following questions:

a) How well does God know us as individuals? Does He know us better than we know ourselves?

b) Does this bring you comfort or fear? If comfort, in what way? If fear, why?

REFLECT ON IT:

1. Do you normally think of yourself as a unique individual created by God, or as just one of the vast crowd of humanity?

2. What is your reaction to the fact that God was intricately involved in your creation? What does it cause you to do or say that you wouldn't otherwise?

3. Were you ever lost and then found by God? Tell the group about your experience.

4. Do you feel loved by God at this very moment? Can you share with us why or why not?

5. If you could ask God one question about why He made you the way you are, what would it be?

6. Would you say that God did a good job when He created you? Why or why not?

PRAY ABOUT IT:

"Prayer is not only asking, but an attitude of mind which produces the atmosphere in which asking is perfectly natural."
~ OSWALD CHAMBERS

LESSON 3 – SUFFERING AND INTERCESSION

Romans 8:18-27

OPEN IT:

Of all the people you've ever known, who has suffered the most and what did they suffer from?

DIG INTO IT:

1. *Read Romans 8:18-21* and answer the following questions:

   a) Why are our "present sufferings" not worthy to be compared to the "glory" to be "revealed in us"? (v. 18)

   b) At what time will the creation and the "sons of God" be revealed? Who are the sons of God? (v. 19)

   c) Why and how is the creation in "bondage to decay"? (vv. 20-21)

2. *Read Romans 8:22-25* and answer the following questions:

   a) How does the analogy of childbirth correspond to the redemption we await? (vv. 22-23)

   b) If we are adopted and redeemed when we accept Christ as Savior, is there a future adoption and redemption to look forward to? Explain what you think it is: (v. 22)

   c) What exactly is it that we hope for? (vv. 24-25)

3. *Read Romans 8:26-27* and answer the following questions:

a) In what way does the Spirit intercede for us? Why? (v. 26)

b) Who all is involved in this intercession?

REFLECT ON IT:

1. Has there ever been a time that your suffering, or the suffering of someone you knew, led you to doubt the goodness and mercy of God?

2. Has suffering ever caused you to draw closer to God? Please explain how and why.

3. Do you ever "groan" (vv. 22-23) as you wait on Jesus' return? Are you patient as you wait?

4. What do you look forward to the most when Jesus returns?

5. Have you ever been so distressed that you could not pray and the Spirit took over for you? What brought on the pain?

6. What are you suffering from right now that the group could join with you and the Spirit in prayer?

PRAY ABOUT IT:

"The Spirit, when He prays through us, or helps us to meet the mighty "oughtness" of right praying, trims our praying down to the will of God..." ~ R.A.TORREY

LESSON 4 – DEALING WITH LONELINESS

Gen. 2:18; Eccl. 4:9-12; Matt. 27:45-46

OPEN IT:

Can you remember any popular songs about loneliness? What stood out about them?

DIG INTO IT:

1. *Read Genesis 2:18* and answer the following questions:

    a) Why wasn't it good for man to be alone?

    b) God said he would find a helper "suitable" (lit. "corresponding to") for Adam. How important is it to have "suitable" people as our companions in life?

    c) Would it be accurate to say that the first problem for humankind was that of loneliness? What does this tell us about our own need for companionship?

2. *Read Eccl. 4:9-12* and answer the following questions:

    a) What four practical benefits for companionship are listed here?

    b) Are there emotional and spiritual benefits that aren't listed here? What are they?

3. *Read Matthew 27:45-46* and answer the following questions:

    a) In what way was the Son forsaken by the Father?

b) What do you think Jesus was thinking in this moment?

c) Do you believe Jesus can fully relate to our loneliness? In what ways can He help us to overcome it?

REFLECT ON IT:

1. Can you be lonely in a crowd? If so, how?

2. Is loneliness sometimes beneficial? Why or why not?

3. In what period of your life would you say you have felt the most alone? What, if anything, did you do about it?

4. How does knowing God's desire to fulfill humankind's need for companionship make you feel? Does it help?

5. Do you believe that God really cares about you right now, at this very moment? How do you know?

6. What would you do and/or say to help someone that is living in a state of loneliness right now?

7. What is one thing we could do for you as a group that would make you less lonely?

PRAY ABOUT IT:

"Prayer is not monologue, but dialogue; God's voice is its most essential part. Listening to God's voice is the secret of the assurance that He will listen to mine." ~ ANDREW MURRAY

LESSON 5 – OVERCOMING SIN

James 1:13-15, 18; 1 John 5:4-5; Rom. 8:8-9

OPEN IT:

What was one of your biggest struggles as a teenager?

DIG INTO IT:

1. *Read James 1:13-15* and answer the following questions:

   a) What is *sin*? What synonyms for sin can you name as a group? List them:

   b) Where does our personal sin find its origin (in other words, *who is to blame*)?

   c) Explain in practical terms the process of conception and birth as it relates to sin? How does it compare with the "birth" language in James 1:18?

2. *Read 1 John 5:4-5* and answer the following questions:

   a) Is this "overcoming of the world" in the present, future, or both? Explain your answer:

   b) Does Jesus give us the power to overcome; does He overcome for us, or both? Please explain:

3. *Read Romans 8:8-9* and answer the following questions:

   a) Do we choose who/what we will be controlled by? How or how not?

b) What would be some practical examples you could give of a person living under the control of the Holy Spirit? (Hint: Gal. 5:22-23)

c) Is it possible to be partly controlled by the sinful nature and partly controlled by the Spirit? If so, explain the type of turmoil a person would go through in this type of condition?

REFLECT ON IT:

1. Knowing the incredible price Jesus paid for the forgiveness of our sins, how do you think He feels when we continue to sin?

2. Do you think we take sin as seriously as God does?

3. Has there ever been a time in your life where you no longer felt the struggle between committing sin or living in righteousness?

4. How has God equipped you to overcome sin in your life?

5. Share with us a time when God has helped you to overcome a particular sin in your life? How did He do it?

6. Do you describe yourself as a *sinner saved by grace*, or as a *saint who occasionally sins*? Why?

PRAY ABOUT IT:

"We can be tired, weary and emotionally distraught, but after spending time alone with God, we find that He injects into our bodies energy, power and strength." ~ CHARLES STANLEY

LESSON 6 – DEATH AND THE AFTERLIFE

2 Corinthians 5:1-10

OPEN IT:

Have you, or anyone that you've known, claimed to have an "out of body" experience when close to death? What do you think about such claims?

DIG INTO IT:

1. *Read 2 Cor. 5:1-5* and answer the following questions:

a) When and how will our "earthly tent" be "destroyed"? (v. 1)

b) Can we know for certain we will have an eternal home, or is it just something we think *might* happen? (v. 1)

c) List some ways that we "groan" in our present bodies: (vv. 2-4)

d) In this context, what is the purpose that God made us for? (v. 5)

e) What synonyms can you think of for "deposit" in relation to the guarantee of the Spirit? (v. 5)

2. *Read 2 Cor. 5:6-10* and answer the following questions:

a) Is it true that we would rather be with the Lord than in our present condition? Why or why not? (vv. 7-8)

b) What specific goals can we list for pleasing the Lord while still in this life? (v. 9) Name them:

c) What determines what we will receive at judgment? (v. 10) Is the reference here to eternal destiny or to reward?

d) Does the Christian face judgment in the same way that a non-Christian does? See John 5:24; 1 Cor. 3:13-15)

REFLECT ON IT:

1. If you could choose at this very moment to be with God for eternity or to stay on this earth for another twenty years, which would you choose and why?

2. If you only had 24 hours left to live, what would you do or say in the time you had left?

3. When you think about the afterlife, which of the following words best describes your feelings and why? *Excited, Fearful, Worshipful, Apprehensive, Other…*

4. Do you know without any doubt that you will go to heaven when you die? If so, explain how you know. If not, explain why not.

5. Describe a perfect day for you in heaven. What would it be like?

6. How can the group pray for you today?

PRAY ABOUT IT:

"Prayer at its highest is a two-way conversation and for me the most important part is listening to God's replies."
~ FRANK C. LAUBACH

LESSON 7 – SINGLE OR MARRIED

1 Corinthians 7:1-9

OPEN IT:

What was the worst dating experience you have ever had? Tell us about it.

DIG INTO IT:

1. *Read 1 Cor. 7:1-2; 8-9* and answer the following questions:

   a) List some benefits of not being married:

   b) Are there things you could be more effective at in the Kingdom by being single? Name them:

   c) In what way could being single lead a person to live an immoral life? Is this always the case with single people?

2. Read *1 Cor. 7:3-5* and answer the following questions:

   a) Why would a husband or wife choose not to fulfill their "marital duty" to their spouse?

   b) Are there behaviors or actions that would lead a spouse not to desire intimacy? What are they and how can they be overcome?

   c) Is ownership of the other spouse's body something that is forcefully taken or willingly surrendered? How could this text (v. 4) be misinterpreted and/or misapplied?

   d) What negatives things could happen to a relationship where one spouse sexually deprives the other?

e) When would be an appropriate time to refrain from sexual intimacy in the marital relationship? What benefits would be derived from it? How long should this continue?

REFLECT ON IT:

1. What advice would you give to a young person considering marriage? Is it advice that you personally follow?

2. How has marriage or singleness helped or hurt your devotion to Christ?

3. In what ways could you compare marital intimacy to intimacy with God? In what way is it similar and in what way is it different?

4. If sexual intimacy became impossibility in your relationship what other type of intimacy could take its place?

5. If married, what can you do to make yourself more desirable to your spouse (let's not get too graphic!).

6. How can we pray for your marriage or singleness today?

PRAY ABOUT IT:

"God does not delay to hear our prayers because He has no mind to give; but that, by enlarging our desires, He may give us the more largely." ~ ANSELM OF CANTERBURY

LESSON 8 – MARRIAGE GOD'S WAY

Gen. 1:26-28; Eph. 5:21-33

OPEN IT:

What do you admire most about members of the opposite sex? What confuses you the most about them?

DIG INTO IT:

1. *Read Gen. 1:26-28* and answer the following questions:

   a) Notice the singular use of "man" yet the plural use of "them" both describing Adam and Eve. What can we assume to be true of their relationship as God intended it?

   b) What does it mean to be made "in the image of God"? Do male and female reflect different aspects of that image? If so, how and why?

2. Read *Eph. 5:21-33* and answer the following questions:

   a) Why is mutual submission necessary? (v. 21)

   b) How does submitting to her husband fulfill a need in the life of the wife, or does it? (vv. 22-24,33)

   c) How is the term "submission" often misinterpreted?

   d) To what extent is a husband to love his wife? (v. 25)

   e) How does loving his wife to this degree fulfill a need in the life of the husband, or does it?

f) Should the instruction given to husbands and wives be a difficulty or a blessing? What determines which type of experience they will have?

g) In what way does the relationship of marriage correspond to the relationship between Christ and the Church?

REFLECT ON IT:

1. As a group, list some notable differences between men and women and discuss the positives and negatives of those differences:

2. In what positive ways can you build on the differences in your relationship?

3. Name some practical and God-honoring ways a couple can be in submission to one another:

4. *For those who are married:* Do you feel like you are living out your God-ordained role in the relationship you're in?

For those who are not married: How can you help those who are married live as God intended?

5. How can we pray for you today?

PRAY ABOUT IT:

"Worship and intercession must go together, the one is impossible without the other. Intercession means that we rouse ourselves up to get the mind of Christ about the one for whom we pray."
~ OSWALD CHAMBERS

LESSON 9 – AN ATTITUDE OF GRATITUDE

Psalms 95:1-7; Col. 2:6-7

OPEN IT:

What are the two things you are most grateful for and why?

DIG INTO IT:

1. *Read Psalms 95:1-7* and answer the following questions:

    a) What two specific expressions of praise does the Psalmist encourage? (v. 1)

    b) What five titles are given to God?
    v. 1a _____
    v. 1b _____
    v. 3a _____
    v. 3b _____
    v. 6b _____

    c) In what specific ways do these titles themselves (above) express thanksgiving to God?

2. Read *Col. 2:6-7* and answer the following questions:

    a) Pay close attention to the phrases "just as" and "continue" (v. 6). What is the connection here?

    b) How does living for Christ demonstrate an attitude of thanksgiving to God? (v. 6)

    c) Who strengthens us? Is it God, ourselves, or perhaps a combination? (v. 7) Explain your answer:

d) What practical steps can be taken to be "rooted and built up" in Christ? (v. 7)

e) In what way can practicing these steps lead to an overflow of thankfulness to God? (v. 7) Is it automatic?

REFLECT ON IT:

1. Do you ever literally *sing* and *shout* Thanksgiving to the Lord? Why or why not?

2. Is it easy or difficult for you to remember to thank God on a regular basis? What do you thank Him for most often?

3. What do you do to keep your expressions of thanksgiving from becoming just a dry, boring routine?

4. If you could see yourself through God's eyes, do you believe He would feel that your life and your words were an adequate expression of thanksgiving to Him?

5. What do you need to do differently in your life to demonstrate that you are truly grateful to God?

6. As a group, take the time to pray for each other's needs, but also take time to express your thanksgiving and praises to God:

PRAY ABOUT IT:

"I have lived to thank God that not all my prayers have been answered." ~ JEAN INGELOW

LESSON 10 – DEALING WITH CONFLICT

Prov. 20:3; 21:9; 26:21; James 4:1-3; Phil. 2:1-4

OPEN IT:

How did your family handle conflict growing up? Did your parents ever fight in front of you?

DIG INTO IT:

1. Read *Prov. 20:3; 21:9; 26:21* and answer the following questions:

a) Why does quarreling have such a devastating effect on a family?

b) Why are those who are "quick to quarrel" considered fools? (20:3)

c) Is this problem more common in men or women?

2. *Read James 4:1-3* and answer the following questions:

a) What is the root cause of fighting and quarrels? (vv. 1-2)

b) In what way are fights and quarrels the result of refusing to submit to God? (v. 3)

c) What should the first step be toward resolving conflict? (v. 2b, 3) How is this passage often taken out of context?

3. Read *Phil. 2:1-4* and answer the following questions:

a) In what way are humility and unity related? (vv. 1-3)

b) What is the center of agreement that would cause us to be "like-minded, etc..."? (v. 3)

c) If there is a disagreement between two Christians (esp. in marriage), whose interests should have priority? (v. 3)

d) How can you look after both your own interests and the interests of others at the same time? (v. 4)

REFLECT ON IT:

1. Do you think of yourself as a "fair" fighter when it comes to quarrels with your spouse? Why or why not?

2. Are your fights usually resolved quickly, over a long period of time, or not at all?

3. How should being a Christian affect the way that we resolve our differences?

4. If God were to come to your house in the middle of one of your fights with your spouse, what do you think He would say and/or do?

5. What can you do personally to make the atmosphere of your home more peaceful? In other words, is there something that you need to change?

PRAY ABOUT IT:

"A man may study because his brain is hungry for knowledge, even Bible knowledge. But he prays because his soul is hungry for God."
~ LEONARD RAVENHILL

LESSON 11 – GOD IN A MANGER

Luke 8:2-20

OPEN IT:

Go around the room with one person answering the first question, the next person the second question, etc…

1. Where were you living when you were seven years old?
2. What was the weather like around Christmas time?
3. Who did most of the decorating of the tree?
4. What special tradition did your family observe at Christmas?
5. What is your earliest memory of a Christmas morning?
6. When did you open your presents and where?
7. What Christmas present stands out in your memory?
8. What brought you the most joy at Christmastime?

DIG INTO IT:

Read *Luke 2:8-20* and answer the following questions:

1. Why do you think God chose to announce the birth of His Son to shepherds?

2. What did the angel's message and the rejoicing of the heavenly host say about the importance God put on the birth of His Son?

3. What do you think the good news, "A Savior has been born…Christ the Lord," meant to the shepherds?

4. Do you think Mary and Joseph realized the cosmic significance of the child she had just given birth to?

5. Luke says, "Mary treasured up all these things and pondered them in her heart." (v. 19) What kind of thoughts do you think were running through her head?

6. What one word would best describe how each of the following felt that day? Mary, Joseph, Shepherds, Angels.

REFLECT ON IT:

1. How do you think the story of Christ is received in our culture?

2. Describe how you would have felt if you had been there when a "great company of the heavenly host" appeared?

3. Do you think you are as receptive to God as Mary, Joseph, and the shepherds were? Would you be if a host of angels came and appeared to you? Would it make any difference?

4. Have you ever had an experience where you felt God was making Himself known to you?

5. How would you describe your relationship to God right now?

6. How can we pray for you today?

PRAY ABOUT IT:

"The amount of time we spend with Jesus – meditating on His Word and His majesty, seeking His face – establishes our fruitfulness in the kingdom." ~ CHARLES STANLEY

LESSON 12 – RESPONDING TO JESUS

Matthew 1:18-25; Matthew 2

OPEN IT:

If you could have personally witnessed one event in history, what would you want to have seen?

DIG INTO IT:

1. Read Matthew 1:18–25. Matthew highlights Jesus' birth in these verses. What do they tell us about his origin and destiny?

2. What does it mean to say that the child in Mary's womb, "is conceived…from the Holy Spirit" (v. 20)? Explain:

3. Read Matthew 2. In this chapter Matthew portrays Jesus' initial reception by the world. How does Jesus the heavenly King contrast with Herod the earthly king?

4. There are many traditions and myths in church history about the wise men which may or may not be true. But strictly from the information in this passage, what can we discover about them?

5. Jesus was born during the time of King Herod (v. 1). From your reading of this chapter, what was Herod like?

6. On hearing of Jesus' birth from the searching Magi, Herod also begins a search for the newborn Christ. How does his search compare with that of the wise men?

7. God is the unseen actor throughout chapter 2. In what ways can we see his behind the scenes" actions (vv. 6, 15, 18 and 23)?

8. If you had never heard this story before, what would stand out most to you in this birth narrative?

REFLECT ON IT:

1. Is Jesus more "real" to you during the Christmas season than at other times of the year? Why or why not?

2. The responses of the wise men and Herod are typical of the ways people respond to Jesus today. What factors might cause people to respond to Jesus in such radically different ways?

3. The Magi not only found Jesus, they worshiped him and witnessed to the entire city of Jerusalem concerning his birth (2:2-3). In what ways has your search for the Lord resulted in worshiping Him and telling others about Him?

4. How has knowing Jesus involved you in a search or journey? Tell us about it:

5. If you could ask God for one gift this Christmas, what would it be?

PRAY ABOUT IT:

"If Bible Christianity is to survive the present world upheaval, we shall need to have a fresh revelation of the greatness and the beauty of Jesus.... He alone can raise our cold hearts to rapture and restore again the art of true worship." ~ A.W. TOZER

LESSON 13 – EXAMINING THE SCRIPTURE

2 Tim. 3:16-17; 2 Pet. 1:20-21

OPEN IT:

What is the best book you have ever read, other than the Bible? What made it the "best"?

DIG INTO IT:

1. *Read 2 Timothy 3:16-17* and answer the following questions:

a) In your own words, explain what "God breathed" means as pertaining to the Scriptures.

b) Is Timothy referring to the Old Testament, New Testament or both? Explain your answer:

c) List the four areas Scripture is "useful" for:
1. _____ 2. _____
3. _____ 4. _____

d) In which of the four above areas would you say Scripture has been most helpful to you and why?

e) In what practical ways does God "equip" us through His Word?

2. *Read 2 Peter 1:20-21* and answer the following questions:

a) What role did the prophet play in writing Scripture?

b) Would it be more accurate to say – "God literally wrote every word of Scripture" or "God oversaw the writing of Scripture through men that He chose"? Explain:

c) Did the Holy Spirit include the individual writer's personality, style, etc…in the writing of Scripture? Explain:

d) What does it mean to be "carried along" by the Holy Spirit?

REFLECT ON IT:

1. What is the greatest benefit that Scripture has had for you personally? What is the detriment?

2. Do you find it difficult to spend time reading the Bible? Why or why not?

3. The Bible claims God as its origin. When you read the Bible do you feel as if God is literally speaking to you?

4. If all Bibles were suddenly taken from the face of the earth, how long would it take you to realize yours was missing? What would be different about your life?

5. How can we pray for you today?

PRAY ABOUT IT:

"The greatest thing anyone can do for God and man is pray. It is not the only thing; but it is the chief thing. The great people of the earth today are the people who pray. I do not mean those who talk about prayer; nor those who say they believe in prayer; nor yet those who can explain about prayer; but I mean those people who take time to pray." ~ S.D. GORDON

LESSON 14 – LIVING A LIFE OF OBEDIENCE

1 John 2:3-6; Eph. 5:1-14

OPEN IT:

What do you think delights God above everything else in your life?

DIG INTO IT:

1. *Read 1 John 2:3-6* and answer the following questions:

   a) Do the words "know him" in reference to Jesus mean more than intellectual knowledge? Explain:

   b) Which commands are we to be obedient to?

   c) Would it be better to say, "Keeping God's commands saves us," or "Keeping God's commands demonstrates we are already saved"? *(Hint – See Eph. 2:8-10).*

2. *Read Eph. 5:1-14* and answer the following questions:

   a) How does being an "imitator" of God help me to know God better?

   b) How does Christ's sacrifice prove His love? In what ways can we imitate that kind of sacrifice for each other?

   c) Look again at the list of sinful behaviors in vv. 3-5. Do the sins on this list appear to be of equal weight? Why or why not?

d) List some specific ways we can "live as children of light" (v. 8)? Should we live this way because we owe it to God, or because it is best for us, or both? Explain:

e) When you live in the light, how exactly does your life expose the "deeds of darkness"?

f) Why is it "shameful" to mention disobedient activity (v. 12)?

REFLECT ON IT:

1. What is the most difficult thing about leading a life in imitation of Christ's?

2. Does God give us the ability to actually live up to His expectations for us? If so, in what way?

3. Would you say that living in obedience to Christ makes your life run smoother or causes more difficulty?

4. In what area do you struggle the most when it comes to following Christ's commands?

5. When God looks at your life, do you think He is pleased with the way you are living? If not, why not? Can the group help?

6. How can we pray for you today?

PRAY ABOUT IT:

"Prayer is a shield to the soul, a sacrifice to God, and a scourge for Satan." ~ JOHN BUNYAN

LESSON 15 – OUR PRAYERS

1 Pet. 5:7; 2 Kings 20:1-6; Psalms 51:15:17

OPEN IT:

If you only had one more prayer request to make before your life was ended what would you ask for?

DIG INTO IT:

1. *Read 1 Peter 5:7* and answer the following questions:

   a) Is Peter's advice hard for you to follow? Why or why not?

   b) What exactly is God offering to do with our anxiety?

   c) What does God's willingness to do this reveal to you about God?

2. *Read 2 Kings 20:1-6* and answer the following questions:

   a) According to this passage, are all future events settled and cannot be changed?

   b) Can our prayers change God's mind? If so, how? If not, what does this passage mean?

   c) Fifteen years later, Hezekiah died. In other words, the end result was the same. Knowing this, why did God answer his prayer?

3. Read *Psalms 51:15-17* and answer the following questions:

---

a) Why did the Psalmist need God to open his lips? Why couldn't he do it on his own?

b) What kind of sacrifice does God desire? Can that desire be fulfilled in prayer?

c) Is there a connection between brokenness and prayer? Explain:

REFLECT ON IT:

1. What type of prayer is easiest for you to pray – request, praise, meditation, or something else? Which is hardest?

2. Do you believe that your prayer can really change your circumstances and/or the circumstances of others?

3. Why do you think God wants you to pray to Him?

4. What if we had a God that didn't want us to communicate to Him? What would we be missing?

5. What in your prayer life could be better than it is right now? Do you feel that you pray the way God wants you to?

6. How can we pray for you today?

PRAY ABOUT IT:

"The prayer power has never been tried to its full capacity...if we want to see might wonders of divine power and grace wrought in the place of weakness, failure and disappointment, let us answer God's standing challenge, "Call unto me, and I will answer thee, and show thee great and might things which thou knowest not."
~ J. HUDSON TAYLOR

LESSON 16 – COMMITMENT

Matthew 7:21-27

OPEN IT:

Other than to Christ and the Church, what is the biggest commitment you've ever made? Did you follow through on it?

DIG INTO IT:

1. *Read Matthew 7:21-23* and answer the following questions:

   a) Explain in your own words what it means to accept Jesus as "Lord"?

   b) Why will Jesus reject those referred to in this passage who address Him as "Lord, Lord"? According to this passage does everyone who addresses Him in this way get rejected? Explain:

   c) Does the ability to perform miraculous acts demonstrate an acceptance of Jesus as Lord? Why or why not?

2. *Read Matthew 7:24-27* and answer the following questions:

   a) What is the difference between the "wise man" in this passage and those who address Jesus as "Lord, Lord" in the verses prior (vv. 21-23)?

   b) How much value does Jesus place on us putting His words "into practice"?

   c) Explain the difference between addressing Jesus as "Lord, Lord" and truly living as if He is "Lord"?

d) How can we know for sure what Jesus will say to each of us on the Day of Judgment?

REFLECT ON IT:

1. Do you consider yourself a wise or a foolish builder? Why?

2. What is the hardest part of keeping a commitment to Christ as Lord? The easiest?

3. How does having Christ as your foundation keep your spiritual house from collapsing even when your life experiences are negative ones?

4. Is there anything in your life that is keeping you from being fully committed to Christ that you can share with the group?

5. If you died today and Jesus asked you, "Why should I let you into heaven?" what would you say in response?

6. How can we pray for you today?

PRAY ABOUT IT:

"Prayer is not eloquence, but earnestness; not the definition of helplessness, but the feeling of it; not figures of speech, but earnestness of soul." ~ HANNAH MORE

LESSON 17 – PERSECUTION

Revelation 2:8-11

OPEN IT:

If you could write your own epitaph, what would you have written on your tombstone?

DIG INTO IT:

1. *Read Revelation 2:8 (compare with Rev. 1:17-18)* and answer the following questions:

a) Why does Jesus describe Himself as "First and Last"? What does this description tell us about Jesus?

b) What impact would the fact that the one addressing them had risen from the dead have on the church at Smyrna? Why?

2. *Read Revelation 2:9-11* and answer the following questions:

a) How can someone be poor and rich at the same time? (v. 9)

b) Consider the phrase, "synagogue of Satan." What does this imply about this particular group of Jews? (v. 9)

c) Why would the Jewish people in Smyrna be so opposed to the Christians there?

d) How difficult would it be to follow Jesus' admonition to not fear in the face of what was to come? (v. 10) What about Jesus' identity (v. 8) could help in this area?

e) Do Jesus' words (v. 10) imply that some of those He is writing to will face death for their faith? If so, how could they remain faithful during that time?

f) What challenge is given in verse 11? What assurance?

REFLECT ON IT:

1. What picture comes into your mind when you hear the word "persecution"? (check out **www.persecution.com** for updates on those being persecuted for their faith today)

2. How does knowing about the torture Jesus endured and triumphed over impact your ability to deal with hardships due to your faith?

3. If faced with the level of persecution the church in Smyrna endured do you think you would remain "faithful...to the point of death"? Why or why not?

4. Some have said that the church would be stronger if we had to suffer persecution? Do you agree or disagree? Why?

5. If next Sunday at church you were held at gunpoint and told "renounce Christ or die" what would you do?

6. How can we pray for you today?

PRAY ABOUT IT:

"God shapes the world by prayer. The more praying there is in the world the better the world will be, the mightier the forces against evil..." ~ E.M.BOUNDS

LESSON 18 – TOLERANCE

Revelation 2:12-17

OPEN IT:

When is tolerance a good thing? When is it a bad thing? Explain:

DIG INTO IT:

1. *Read Revelation 2:12 (compare with Heb. 4:12-13 & John 1:1)* and answer the following questions:

   a) How is the Word of God like a sword? What specific things can you do with both?

   b) Why does Jesus begin with this particular description of Himself?

2. *Read Revelation 2:13* and answer the following questions:

   a) Does it comfort you to know that Jesus knows where you live? Why or why not?

   b) What does it mean to say that "Satan has his throne" in their city? Where is Satan's throne today?

   c) What does Jesus commend the Church for?

3. *Read Revelation 2:14-16* and answer the following questions:

   a) What specific sins does Jesus rebuke the Church for?

   b) Did the church actually commit sin; just tolerate sin, or both?

4. *Read Revelation 2:17* and answer the following questions:

a) What two gifts are given to the person who overcomes?

b) Based on this verse, does it appear that Jesus is confident some will repent?

REFLECT ON IT:

1. Would it be accurate to describe our town as a place where "Satan has his throne"? Why or why not?

2. How can the church be loving to those with whom we disagree, yet also take a stand on biblical principles?

3. Do you look more to the Word of God for direction, or to the culture around you? Which is more effective?

4. What impact does Jesus being a "double-edged sword" have on your life?

5. If you could pick the "new name" that Jesus will give you as an over comer, what name would you choose and why?

6. How can we pray for you today?

PRAY ABOUT IT:

"There has never been a spiritual awakening in any country or locality that did not begin in united prayer." ~ D.A.T. PIERSON

LESSON 19 – COMPROMISE

Revelation 2:18-29

OPEN IT:

Growing up, how were you taught to respond to authority figures like teachers, police officers, etc...?

DIG INTO IT:

1. *Read Revelation 2:18 (compare with Daniel 10:6)* and answer the following questions:

   a) For the first time in Revelation Jesus identifies Himself as the "Son of God." Why?

   b) When you read the description of Jesus' eyes and feet, what thoughts come to mind?

2. *Read Revelation 2:19-23* and answer the following questions:

   a) What was this church commended for?

   b) What two specific sins did Jezebel lead the church into?

   c) Are you surprised that Jesus gave her an opportunity to repent (v. 21)? Why or why not?

   d) Specific punishment is described for Jezebel and those who follower her (vv. 22-23). How will this action enlighten the other churches?

3. Read *Revelation 2:24-29* and answer the following questions:

   a) What one instruction did Jesus give to the faithful?

b) In your own words, describe the blessings promised to those who overcome.

c) What synonym could be used for "ear" in v. 29?

REFLECT ON IT:

1. If Jesus came to you tonight in a vision with flaming eyes and bronze feet how would you react?

2. Jesus commends the church for "doing more than you did at first" (v. 19). In what ways would that be true in your own life?

3. In what specific ways is the church being called on to compromise in our day and age by the culture and by other churches?

4. When have you been personally tempted to compromise your beliefs? Explain:

5. What specific ways can you defend yourself and your church from giving into compromise?

6. How can we pray for you today?

PRAY ABOUT IT:

"To desire revival...and at the same time to neglect(personal) prayer and devotion is to wish one way and walk another."
~ A.W. TOZER

LESSON 20 – DEAD OR ALIVE?

Revelation 3:1-6

OPEN IT:

What was your reputation among your peers when you were growing up? Was it accurate? Why or why not?

DIG INTO IT:

1. *Read Revelation 3:1* and answer the following questions:

a) What, if anything, is the significance of the number seven?[1]

b) What does Jesus mean by the descriptive word "dead"? Give some examples of what a "dead" church would look like.

2. *Read Revelation 3:2-3* and answer the following questions:

a) What specifically must the church in Sardis do to regain the life they once possessed? Where should they begin?

b) What will happen to the church if they don't do what Jesus says?

3. Read *Revelation 3:4-6* and answer the following questions:

a) What do "white clothes" symbolize?

---

[1] Seven stands for "completeness" and the full expression of the Spirit. The "stars" are most likely representative of the seven churches Jesus is addressing.

b) Which blessing in v. 5 do you look forward to the most and why?

c) What is the significance of Jesus acknowledging believer's names?

REFLECT ON IT:

1. Would you agree that many churches in our culture have a reputation for being alive but are in reality dead? What specific factors contribute to this?

2. Would you say that our church is dead or alive?

3. Assuming our church has a reputation for being alive, what can be done to make sure that our reputation matches reality?

4. What can you do personally to make that happen?

5. What color will your robe be when Jesus returns? Why?

6. Is your name written in the book of life?

7. How can we pray for you today?

PRAY ABOUT IT:

"The supreme thing is worship. The attitude of worship is the attitude of a subject bent before the King...the fundamental thought is that of prostration, of bowing down." ~ CAMPBELL MORGAN

LESSON 21 – HOLY AND TRUE

Revelation 3:7-13

OPEN IT:

Philadelphia (Greek – **Philía** = Love; **Adelphos** = brother) When have you experienced "brotherly love"? Tell us about it:

DIG INTO IT:

1. *Read Revelation 3:7-8* and answer the following questions:

   a) Jesus describes Himself as "holy and true." What does His description of Himself imply?

   b) What is the "key of David" (see Isa. 22:22 & Matt. 16:19)?

   c) How does the "open door that no one can shut" apply to the church of then and now?

   d) What had this church done well?

2. *Read Revelation 3:9-10* and answer the following questions:

   a) What is the purpose behind having the false Jews fall down at the feet of the church at Philadelphia?

   b) What is the "hour of trial" Jesus will spare them from?

3. Read *Revelation 3:11-13* and answer the following questions:

   a) What does Jesus mean by "soon"? What do you think the church at Philadelphia thought He meant?

b) Consider the blessings of v. 12. What is the significance of each one?

REFLECT ON IT:

1. What difference does it make to you personally that Jesus is "holy and true"?

2. What "open door" have you been walking through lately?

3. In what area do you need to have patience like the church at Philadelphia had? Why?

4. Do you really want Jesus to return soon? Why or why not?

5. What is the one thing you can do to make sure that you will overcome? How will you do it?

6. If Jesus came back today, would you be ready for Him?

7. How can we pray for you today?

PRAY ABOUT IT:

"There is a place where thou canst touch the eyes
Of blinded men to instant, perfect sight;
There is a place where thou canst say, "Arise"
To dying captives, bound in chains of night;
There is a place where thou canst reach the store
Of hoarded gold and free it for the Lord;
There is a place–upon some distant shore–
Where thou canst send the worker and the Word.
Where is that secret place–dost thou ask, "Where?"
O soul, it is the secret place of prayer!"
~ ALFRED LORD TENNYSON

LESSON 22 – HOT OR COLD?

Revelation 3:14-22

OPEN IT:

What food or drinks do you like served lukewarm?

DIG INTO IT:

1. *Read Revelation 3:14* and answer the following questions:

   a) What three titles does Jesus use for Himself?

   b) Which of these three titles stands out the most to you and why?

2. *Read Revelation 3:15-17* and answer the following questions:

   a) What does "hot and cold" refer to in this text?

   b) Why is Jesus so upset about the Laodicean's lukewarm attitude? What effect could it have?

   c) How were the Laodiceans deceived? Who caused the deception?

3. Read *Revelation 3:18-22* and answer the following questions:

   a) What exactly are the riches that Jesus is offering to the church?

   b) When Jesus disciplines us, what does it teach us about how He feels toward us?

c) Why would Jesus offer the Laodiceans the opportunity to turn back to Him after all they had done?

d) How can a person be "victorious" in God's eyes? Is it something we do, something we believe, or both?

REFLECT ON IT:

1. If Jesus addressed our church like He did the Laodicean church, how would you react?

2. Would you describe your relationship with Christ as "hot," "cold," or "lukewarm"? Why?

3. If you could give advice to a person who is "lukewarm" what would it be?

4. In what areas of your life have riches kept you from experiencing the fullness of a relationship with Christ?

5. How does it make you feel to know that Jesus knows "all the things you do" (v. 15)?

6. How can we pray for you today?

PRAY ABOUT IT:

"Learn to worship God as the God who does wonders, who wishes to prove in you that He can do something supernatural and divine."
~ ANDREW MURRAY

LESSON 23 – OUTREACH

Acts 13:1-12

OPEN IT:

When was the last time you did something new and exciting? Tell us about it.

DIG INTO IT:

1. *Read Acts 13:1-3* and answer the following questions:

a) What two types of leaders were prominent in the church? What is unique and similar about them?

b) From reading the names of these leaders would you say the church was diverse or were they all alike?

c) What was the church doing when the Holy Spirit spoke to them? What effect did it have?

d) Is there a connection between fasting and prayer and fulfilling our God-given mission?

2. *Read Acts 13:4-12* and answer the following questions:

a) Who decided where this team would travel?

b) Where was the first place they preached and why?

c) Why was Bar-Jesus so opposed to the missionaries speaking to the proconsul?

d) Describe the encounter between Paul and Bar-Jesus: Are you surprised by Paul's actions? Why or why not?

e) What was the positive result of Paul's actions?

f) What significance, if any, can be found in the Holy Spirit leading these men to both religious establishments and secular government leaders?

REFLECT ON IT:

1. What is your first thought if someone tells you that they are fasting?

2. If there is a direct correlation between worship, fasting, prayer and the Holy Spirit's guidance, why do you think most Christians don't practice these things more often?

3. Would you consider yourself to be more of a prophet, a teacher, or neither one? What is your role in the church?

4. What would you do if you ran into someone like Bar-Jesus?

5. How can our church be effective in reaching those in religions other than Christianity as well as those in secular government? What can you do personally?

6. How can we pray for you today?

PRAY ABOUT IT:

"God's way of answering the Christian's prayer for more patience, experience, hope, and love often is to put him into the furnace of affliction." ~ RICHARD CECIL

LESSON 24 – PERSONAL RENEWAL

Romans 12:1-2; Phil. 3:13-14

OPEN IT:

Give us a definition of *who you are* in seven words or less.

DIG INTO IT:

1. *Read Romans 12:1-2* and answer the following questions:

   a) Why is personal sacrifice considered an act of worship?

   b) What should be evident in the lives of those who have had their minds renewed?

2. *Read Ezekiel 36:24-27* and answer the following questions:

   a) Do these promises to Israel sound familiar to the promises God gives to the church/individuals? If so, in what ways?

   b) What specific things does God promise to remove? What does He promise to put in their place?

   c) Does God merely improve our spiritual status or completely replace it? Explain:

3. Read *Philippians 3:13-14* and answer the following questions.

   a) What happens to a person who understands their identity in Christ?

b) What benefit is derived from "forgetting what is behind"?

c) At what point do we receive the "prize" that Paul speaks of? What is it?

REFLECT ON IT:

1. Compare your Christian identity to an automobile: are you a used car with a new paint job, or a brand new model fresh off the assembly line?

2. Is it easier to experience the newness of life God offers theologically or practically? Explain:

3. What could you honestly say is different about your life now compared to your life before you knew Christ?

4. How does being a new person help you to function at a greater level spiritually? As a mother/father? As an Employee/Boss?

5. Has your concept of who you are changed since the beginning of this study? Explain:

6. How can we pray for you today?

PRAY ABOUT IT:

"I'm convinced that the man who has learned to meditate upon the Lord will be able to run on his feet and walk in his spirit. Although he may be hurried by his vocation, that's not the issue. The issue is how fast his spirit is going. To slow it down takes a period of time."
~ CHARLES STANLEY

LESSON 25 – OUR PURPOSE

Ephesians 3:7-13; 5:21-32

OPEN IT:

As a group come up with a one-sentence statement that would summarize the purpose of the church:

DIG INTO IT:

1. *Read Ephesians 3:7-13* and answer the following questions:

a) How would you describe Paul's attitude concerning his role in the spread of the Gospel?

b) What specific things did God call him to do?

c) God promised to use a certain group of people to reveal Himself to the world. Which group was it? Why did He choose to reveal Himself in this way?

d) What, in particular, did God choose to be made known? To whom should it be made known to?

2. *Read Ephesians 5:21-32* and answer the following questions:

a) How is Christ's relationship to the church similar to the relationship between husband and wife? Why does Paul use this particular analogy?

b) Explain what it means to say that Christ is the "head" of the church? If Christ is the head of the church, what part do the rest of us play?

c) What has Christ already done for the church? What will He do for the church in the future?

d) How does the "one flesh" concept apply to Jesus and the members of His church?

REFLECT ON IT:

1. Would you say that most churches have the same purpose theologically speaking? How about practically speaking?

2. Have you ever been part of a church that has lost its sense of purpose? If so, tell us about what happened (no names please):

3. How is God using our church to make His wisdom known to the "rulers and authorities in the heavenly realms"?

4. While Christ is the head of the Church, would you also say He is the head of your life? In what ways is He, or is He not?

5. Are you presently "one flesh" with Christ as well as the members of your church? In what ways?

6. How can we pray for you today?

PRAY ABOUT IT:

"Pursuing prayer is prayer on a mission. It is diligent, fervent, constant, persevering, determined, and convinced."
~ DAVID BRYANT

LESSON 26 – GOD'S WORD

Psalms 1:1-6

OPEN IT:

What experience or activity do you find the most delight in and why?

DIG INTO IT:

1. *Read Psalms 1:1-2* and answer the following questions:

   a) What three behaviors are mentioned in v.1 that a person will be blessed by if they avoid them?

   1) Walk in _____

   2) Stand in _____

   3) Sit in _____

   b) What are some specific ways a person might do these three things?

   c) Describe how can a person find delight in God's Word?

   d) What does it mean to meditate on God's Word "day and night"? How can that be accomplished?

2. *Read Psalms 1:3-6* and answer the following questions:

   a) The person who stays in God's Word is compared to a tree. What do they have in common?

b) What specific blessings come to the righteous (vv. 3b; 6a)?

c) The wicked are described as "chaff" (finely cut straw or hay). How does this compare to the righteous being like a tree?

d) What two things can the wicked not do (v.5)?

REFLECT ON IT:

1. Describe some ways that you find delight in God's Word:

2. How can God's Word keep you from giving into sinful behavior? Is it really effective?

3. Would you say that God's Word is simply a good guide for righteous behavior, or that it actually has supernatural power to change your life? Explain:

4. Are you ready to make a commitment to spend more time studying the Bible? If so, what kind of commitment are you going to make? If not, why not?

5. God promises to watch over the way of the righteous. Do you feel like He is watching over your life right now?

6. How can we pray for you today?

PRAY ABOUT IT:

"Since God knows our future, our personalities, and our capacity to listen, He isn't ever going to say more to us than we can deal with at the moment." ~ CHARLES STANLEY

LESSON 27 – GOD'S LAW

Matthew 5:17-20

OPEN IT:

When you hear the word "law," what is the first thing that comes to your mind?

DIG INTO IT:

1. *Read Matt. 5:17-18* and answer the following questions:

NOTE: The Jews used the expression "Law" in four different ways: 1) The 10 Commandments; 2) First five books of the Bible; 3) The entire Old Testament; 4) The Oral or Scribal Law.

   a) Was Jesus referring to all the specific laws of the Old Testament, the principles those laws stood for, or something else?

   b) Did Jesus ever break the law? Explain:

   c) Is there a difference between the letter of the law and the spirit of the law? Explain?

2. Read *Matt. 5:19-20* and answer the following questions:

   a) What will determine whether a person is "least" or "greatest" in the kingdom of heaven? Does this mean there are different levels of status in heaven? Explain:

   b) Compare v. 19 with *1 Corinthians 3:10-15*. Is there a connection? If so, what is it?

c) According to v. 20, what must take place for us to enter the kingdom of heaven? How is that possible?

d) How do you understand Jesus' statements in this passage in light of *Romans 10:1-4?*

REFLECT ON IT:

1. If you had been in the audience when Jesus spoke the words we've studied today, would they have inspired hope, hopelessness, or something else?

2. Have you kept the law perfectly?

3. When it is "okay" to break the law (biblically speaking)? Give some examples:

4. If telling a lie would spare someone else's life, would it be against God's law to tell that lie? Would you be following the letter of the law, the spirit of the law, or something else?

5. Does your righteousness surpass the righteousness of the Pharisees and teachers of the law? If so, how? If not, why not?

6. How can we pray for you today?

PRAY ABOUT IT:

"Men may spurn our appeals, reject our message, oppose our arguments, despise our persons, but they are helpless against our prayers." ~ J. SIDLOW BAXTER

LESSON 28 – TRUE WORSHIP

John 4:19-24; Psalms 22:22; 35:18; Rom. 12:1-2

OPEN IT:

All who are willing please give a one-sentence personal definition of "worship."

DIG INTO IT:

1. *Read John 4:19-24* and answer the following questions:

   a) What misconceptions did the Samaritan woman have about worship?

   b) In what two ways do "true worshippers" worship?

   > S_____
   > T_____

   c) What specifically does it mean to worship in these two ways? Explain:

2. *Read Psalms 22:22 and Psalms 35:18* and answer the following questions:

   a) Why is it important to worship God in a public assembly?

   b) Can worship be private? If so, give some examples:

3. *Read Romans 12:1-2* and answer the following questions:

   a) Are we to literally "offer our bodies"? If so, how?

b) How does renewing our minds become an act of worship toward God? How does a person actually do this?

c) In what was does renewal help us to know God's will?

REFLECT ON IT:

1. Do you feel that you draw closer to God in corporate or private worship? Why?

2. What practical steps, if any, do you take to make sure you are worshipping God in spirit and in truth?

3. Is there anything about worship that you find difficult? Tell us about it.

4. What do you do to make sure you are offering spiritual sacrifices to God? If you are offering spiritual sacrifices, what type of sacrifices are you making?

5. What do you believe God desires the most from you in worship?

6. How can we pray for you today?

PRAY ABOUT IT:

"Worship and intercession must go together, the one is impossible without the other. Intercession means that we rouse ourselves up to get the mind of Christ about the one for whom we pray."
~ OSWALD CHAMBERS

LESSON 29 – GIVING THANKS

Luke 17:11-19; Col. 3:15-17

OPEN IT:

What is your most memorable Thanksgiving?

DIG INTO IT:

1. Read *Luke 17:11-19* and answer the following questions:

a) The lepers requested "mercy." What did they mean by that request?

b) Only one of the healed men came back to thank Jesus. What is significant about him being Samaritan?

c) How would you describe Jesus' reaction to those who did not return to give thanks?

2. Read *Colossians 3:15-17* and answer the following questions:

a) What specifically, are we to be thankful for (v. 15)?

b) List all of the things we are admonished to do in v. 16:

1. Let _____
2. Teach _____
3. Sing _____

c) Name some specific ways we can do the above with "gratitude in our hearts to God."

d) When we do things in Jesus' name (v. 17), are we giving thanks through our actions by themselves, or is a spoken word of gratitude to God necessary also?

e) Who is the "him" we give thanks through (v. 17)?

REFLECT ON IT:

1. Would you say that most people in our culture have gratitude for God? Why or why not?

2. What is it that you are most thankful for?

3. Can you think of a time in your life when God came to your aid, yet you forgot to thank Him?

4. What practical steps can we take to remember to show gratitude to God for what He has done? List specifics:

5. How does your gratitude to God spill over into your gratitude toward others? How do you demonstrate that gratitude on a day-to-day basis?

6. How can we pray for you today?

PRAY ABOUT IT:

"All vital praying makes a drain on a man's vitality. True intercession is a sacrifice, a bleeding sacrifice." ~ J.H. JOWETT

LESSON 30 – STARTING OVER

Genesis 6:11-22

OPEN IT:

Describe the worst storm you've ever experienced.

DIG INTO IT:

1. Read *Genesis 6:11-13* and answer the following questions:

    a) Why was God so upset with humankind?

    b) What word appears three times in vv. 11-12? (Hint: it starts with a "C.")

    c) What specifically did God promise to do?

2. Read Genesis 6:14-17 and answer the following questions:

    a) As far as you know, did Noah have any boat-building experience? How would he know what to do?

    b) The ark was approximately 450' long x 75' wide x 45' feet high. Why was such a huge vessel necessary?

3. Read Genesis 6:18-22 and answer the following questions:

    a) Who would survive the flood God would send?

    b) What "covenant" would God make with Noah and his family? What is a covenant?

    c) Did Noah have to go out and round up all of these animals, or would God send them to him? (see v. 20)

d) Read v. 22 and describe for the group Noah's reaction to God's commands:

REFLECT ON IT:

1. Are you surprised at the way God reacted to humankind when they rebelled against His will?

2. If you were Noah, what would have been your first thought when God said, "Build an ark"?

3. What level of faith would a person have to have to respond in the way that Noah did, and then actually carry out the task God had given?

4. Are there any monumental tasks that God has placed on your heart? If so, do you have the faith to see them through?

5. The ark was a place of safety and refuge for Noah, his family, and the animals. What is your place of refuge and safety today?

6. In what way can we pray for you today?

PRAY ABOUT IT:

"To get nations back on their feet, we must first get down on our knees." ~ BILLY GRAHAM

LESSON 31 – GRACE

John 8:1-11

OPEN IT:

What is the most dramatic conversion story that you are aware of?

DIG INTO IT:

Read John 8:1-11 and answer the following questions:

a) How do you think the teachers of the law and Pharisees caught this woman in adultery?

b) What do you think she was feeling as she was made to stand before the crowd and receive the accusation?

c) Were the religious leaders really interested in this woman's sin, or were they more interested in putting Jesus on the spot? If the latter, what does that say about the condition of their hearts?

d) Why did Jesus initially respond by writing with His finger on the ground? Any guess as to what He was writing?

e) Jesus challenge in v. 7 had a dramatic effect on the religious leaders? Why? What would your response have been?

f) Why did everyone leave after Jesus challenged them? Why did the older ones leave first?

g) For what purpose did Jesus ask the woman the questions in v. 10? Was it for His benefit or for hers?

h) Did Jesus tell her that sin was no big deal or something else?

REFLECT ON IT:

1. Put yourself in this woman's shoes…what would you have done if made to stand before the crowd caught in your sin?

2. Have you ever met anyone who had a similar attitude to that of the teachers of the law and Pharisees? Without naming names, give some examples.

3. What does Jesus' response teach you about grace? How can a similar response be given to judgmental people today?

4. What is the most moving part of this story for you? Why?

5. Jesus told the woman to "leave your life of sin." What does that tell us about how Jesus views sin?

6. What sin do you need forgiven for?

7. In what way can we pray for you today?

PRAY ABOUT IT:

"God never gives us discernment in order that we may criticize, but that we may intercede." ~ OSWALD CHAMBERS

LESSON 32 – WILLINGNESS TO RISK

Matthew 14:22-34

OPEN IT:

What is the riskiest thing you have ever done? What made it risky?

DIG INTO IT:

1. Read *Matthew 14:22-27* and answer the following questions:

   a) Why did Jesus stay behind and send His disciples across the lake without Him?

   b) Why do you think Jesus spent time alone in prayer?

   c) What purpose was there in Jesus walking across the lake instead of around it? Did He mean for the disciples to see Him?

   d) The disciples thought they saw a ghost; how did Jesus reassure them?

2. Read *Matthew 14:28-34* and answer the following questions:

   a) Why did Peter insist Jesus invite him out onto the water?

   b) How do you think Peter felt when his feet first touched the water and he didn't sink?

   c) Why did Peter sink? What was the first thing he said when he started to go under?

d) Why did Jesus say Peter had, "little faith"?

REFLECT ON IT:

1. When you read this story, does it make you see Peter in a positive or a negative light?

2. Many have criticized Peter for becoming afraid and sinking, but do you think most of those critics would have gotten out of the boat in the first place? Would you?

3. In what areas of your life does Jesus want you to "get out of the boat"? What is holding you back?

4. If Jesus came to you today and asked, "What risks are you taking for the kingdom of God?" how would you answer?

5. Do you think the church and individual Christians should search for ways to "risk" for God? Why or why not?

6. In what way can we pray for you today?

PRAY ABOUT IT:

"All I know is that when I pray, coincidences happen; and when I don't pray, they don't happen." ~ DAN HAYES

LESSON 33 – BLOOD SACRIFICE

Heb. 9:11-15; Rom. 5:6-9

OPEN IT:

What is your first reaction when you see blood? What if it's your own?

DIG INTO IT:

1. Read *Hebrews 9:11-15* and answer the following questions:

a) Why is Jesus described as "High Priest"?

b) What made Christ's tabernacle better than the earthly one?

c) Jesus entered the Most Holy Place "once for all by His own blood." Why was it necessary to have many entrances by the blood of goats and calves?

d) What did the blood of the sacrificed animals clean (v. 13)?

e) What did Jesus cleanse through His blood and why was He able to accomplish so much more than the sacrifice of animals (v. 14)?

f) Explain how Christ's sacrifice served as a ransom (*see 1 Peter 1:18-19*)?

2. Read *Romans 5:6-9* and answer the following questions:

a) What stands out to you as the most powerful statement in these verses?

b) What does it mean to be "justified by His blood"?

REFLECT ON IT:

1. Why do you think most churches today don't spend much time preaching/teaching about the blood of Christ?

2. Before you became a Christian, did you think of yourself as one held hostage in need of ransom? Why or why not?

3. When you think of what Jesus did for us on the Cross, what stands out to you the most?

4. Why would Jesus go to such great lengths for us while "we were still sinners"? What does this tell you about how God feels toward humankind?

5. There is an old song that says, "There is power, power, wonder working power in the blood of the Lamb." Have you experienced that power in your life? Tell us about it:

6. In what way can we pray for you today?

PRAY ABOUT IT:

"Any concern too small to be turned into a prayer is too small to be made into a burden." ~ CORRIE TEN BOOM

LESSON 34 – DEATH AND RESURRECTION

Romans 6:1-18

OPEN IT:

What is the first thing that comes to your mind when you hear the word, "slave"?

DIG INTO IT:

1. Read *Romans 6:1-7* and answer the following questions:

a) What should be the Christian's attitude toward committing sin?

b) Why would someone think that an increase in sin would result in an increase in grace? Is this logical?

c) What, specifically, were we baptized into?

2. Read *Romans 6:8-14* and answer the following questions:

a) If we experience Christ's death through baptism, what other promise is made to us?

b) What does God expect us to do when we come into a relationship with Him?

c) Who is the Christian's master?

3. Read *Romans 6:15-18* and answer the following questions:

a) What are we called to be slaves to?

b) Is this type of slavery something that is forced or voluntary?

c) What changes in us when we begin to obey God?

REFLECT ON IT:

1. Is it best to work on eradicating sin from our lives before we become Christians or after? Why?

2. In what way is baptism an accurate physical description of death and resurrection?

3. Have you ever met anyone who thought the more they sinned, the more they could demonstrate grace? If so, tell us about it.

4. What are you a slave to? Is it sin, or righteousness?

5. What does God to do help you to overcome sin? What, if anything, is your part in the process?

6. In what way can we pray for you today?

PRAY ABOUT IT:

"Prayer lays hold of God's plan and becomes the link between His will and its accomplishment on earth. Amazing things happen, and we are given the privilege of being the channels of the Holy Spirit's prayer." ~ ELISABETH ELLIOT

LESSON 35 – KNOWING CHRIST

Philippians 3:1-11

OPEN IT:

If you had to make a list of the most important things in your life, what would the first three things be on your list?

DIG INTO IT:

1. Read *Philippians 3:1-6* and answer the following questions:

   a) What three designations does Paul give to the men in v. 2? Why such strong language?

   b) What does it mean to, "worship by the Spirit of God" (v. 3)?

   c) Take a moment as a group to list some ways that we tend to put confidence in the flesh (vv. 3-4).

   d) What specific examples did Paul give for why he could have confidence in the flesh? (vv. 4-6).

2. Read *Philippians 3:7-11* and answer the following questions:

   a) Consider the contrasts between Paul's former life, and his life at the time of this writing (vv. 7-9). Which can you relate to the most and why?

   b) Whose righteousness did Paul gain and how did he gain it? (v. 9)

   c) What things did Paul want to "know" in vv. 10-11?

d) Which of these things (above) seems to be the most unusual desire to you?

REFLECT ON IT:

1. How do you feel about your own religious background and upbringing?

2. Since you have begun your journey to know Christ, has your focus become clearer or more confused? Why?

3. Do you find yourself able to rely on Christ's righteousness instead of your own? Why or why not?

4. Contrast your life before Christ with your life now. Did you have a list of accomplishments you were relying on to see you through?

5. Of the things Paul wanted to know (vv. 10-11), which one applies to you the most and why?

6. In what way can we pray for you today?

PRAY ABOUT IT:

"I did not see that it is the process of being worshipped that God communicates His presence to men..." ~ C.S. LEWIS

THANK YOU FOR INVESTING IN THIS STUDY GUIDE!

We'd love to hear your feedback. Please stop by and leave a review at: **http://www.amazon.com/author/barrydavis** . You can also check out our other books there.

If you'd like to see some of our many resources for Bible Study leaders and Pastors, please go to: **http://www.pastorshelper.com**

I hope to hear from you soon! May God bless you as you continue to serve Him.

In Christ,

Barry L. Davis

Made in the USA
Monee, IL
22 September 2019

80517551R00229

Never Say

Adventures in NY Politics

By

Sen. John A. DeFrancisco

ACKNOWLEDGMENTS

I could not have written this book without the help of many people. To Lindsay Turk, Jill Arlukewicz, and Jordan Denzak, who assisted with the drafts and redrafts, and to my grandaughter, Arianna, who bailed me out when I was confounded by computer technology, thank you. To Herm Card who helped in editing the manuscript and who gave me suggestions on the structure and titling of the book, thank you. And to Benedicte Doran, for her assistance in getting me through the many technical phases of converting the manuscript into a published work, thank you.

Special thanks to my wife of 51 years, Linda, who worked tirelessly on my campaigns, gave her blessing for me to serve 41 years in elective office, and who endured the slings and arrows directed at me, but affecting her and my family. And special thanks to all the volunteers, too numerous to list here, that helped in my campaigns and who gave me the opportunity to serve, and to the members of my staff, who always made me look good.

And thank you to all of my constituents who elected me over these many years and who made it possible for me to have the experiences related in this book. Without them, there would have been no *Adventures in NY Politics*.

CONTENTS

FORWARD

Never Say Never

In April, 1968, Syracuse University baseball team captain John DeFrancisco slid into second base attempting to break up a double play. His drive to succeed caused him to slide too high, and the Naval Academy shortstop's throw to first hit him in the face, smashing his cheekbone. It was apparent that his senior season was over.

But...what followed was an illustration of what has become DeFrancisco's mantra, on and off the field for the ensuing fifty-plus years: "Never say never." Less than three weeks later, what was never supposed to happen, did. Wearing a lacrosse helmet to protect the steel pin holding his cheekbone together, he returned to second base for the Orangemen, batted .330 for the season, and led the Syracuse team to their best record in over 20 years.

While his election to the role of captain of the baseball team was not his first "official" term in office, the courage, tenacity and dedication he displayed then was an indication of the service he would render to his country, state, and community in the decades to follow.

A cum laude graduate of Syracuse's College of Engineering, he served as President of the American Institute of Industrial Engineers and combined his studies with earning a ROTC Air

1

Force commission and playing four years of NCAA baseball. He earned the Eastern College Athletic Conference and the Syracuse University Manley Scholar athlete awards his senior year and was later named a Syracuse University Letter Winner of Distinction, the university's highest athletic honor.

Following three and one-half years as a United States Air Force captain in the Judge Advocate General Corps, he embarked on a legal career that led him to serving in the Onondaga County District Attorney's office, followed by the private practice of law and 41 years in elected public office. He served as president of both the Syracuse Board of Education and the Syracuse Common Council before beginning his 26-year career in the New York State Senate, where he rose to the position of Deputy Majority Leader, the position he held at the time of his retirement at the end of 2018.

A list of his extensive achievements and contributions during his time in public service is well-documented and easy to find. That is all part of public record and the obvious results of a career dedicated to doing the right thing for his clients and constituents, regardless of their political affiliation or public prominence.

What is less obvious is the essence of the man behind the headlines, the character that propelled him to lead his esteemed career as an attorney and public servant, the character which drove him to fight the political machine, to "tell it like it is," and earn him The New York Times characterization of him as an "irascible straight shooter" during his attempt to gain the nomination as a candidate for the New York State Governor's office.

Throughout his life he has been the man who would step up to do the right thing, whether as a college baseball captain, an Air Force JAG officer or trial practitioner representing the underdog, or a state senator championing causes that made a difference in the lives of New Yorkers.

In the process, he has stepped into the ring against boxers for charity, played his saxophone in front of festival audi-

ences to help fund the arts, led the sometimes contentious floor proceedings of the state senate to productive outcomes, read to groups of elementary school students at public libraries, walked many miles in parades to support veterans, sponsored thousands of bills to enhance peoples' daily lives, sung with rock and roll groups at fundraisers, dug countless shovelfuls of dirt to open public health and safety facilities he had championed, battled political interests that were not in line with the best interests of his constituents, fought and won battles to enhance public arts funding, cut endless lengths of ribbons to open fairs and other public celebrations, and ultimately, maintained the drive and determination of the second baseman who sacrificed himself to help his team.

So...why "never say never?" Because John DeFrancisco has consistently avoided "never" as a likely outcome. He has faced his challenges, on and off the field, with the attitude that they should, and could, be overcome. Just as that 21-year-old student athlete overcame the possibility that he would never return to the playing field, he has lived his life believing that anything is possible as long as it is the right thing and as long as he is in the position to make it happen.

Herm Card

Educator, author and poet,
college athlete and friend

INTRODUCTION

S o you want to be a senator, or a member of the school board or City Council...or President of the United States? Why? I know. You want to serve the public. Or maybe it just looks like fun. Or is it that you want an easy glamorous job?

At one point during my years of elective office, I thought I had the answer. In fact, when my son ran for public office and became a city councilor, I knew I had the answer. It is a "genetic defect".

Few people who have not actually been in elective office realize the amount of work it takes, the scrutiny that you get from the media, the second guessing of each of your decisions, the back-stabbing by those who should be your political allies and the stress on your family. That's why I say with tongue in cheek, that what causes someone to run is that "genetic defect".

In my case, I ran for my first public office because I was upset with the Syracuse Board of Education, whose decisions I believed were about to have a devastating effect on my young children. That was over 41 years ago, and I have run ever since. And I would have it no other way.

Everyone should either run for public office or be in-

volved in a political campaign. It is truly an eye opener. But where do you start? That was a question I hadn't really considered when I first decided to run for the Syracuse School Board. I have learned a lot about campaigns and being in public office over four decades. Although I'm undefeated, I have been scored upon. Maybe my journey, which is set forth in the pages that follow, will help to make your journey smoother no matter what role you desire to play in the game of politics.

PART I- GETTING THERE

GETTING ENGAGED

"**Y**ou mean all of our jobs are in jeopardy?," I said to the Onondaga County Chief Assistant District Attorney, John Shannon. "That's right, our jobs are all dependent on the will of the district attorney," John replied. "And now that Jon Holcomb resigned, the governor will appoint a new district attorney who will serve until the next election," John continued. "And no doubt, since the governor is a Democrat, he will appoint a Democrat, and most of us are Republicans," John concluded.

I was appointed an Assistant District Attorney in 1975 after completing my tour of duty with the United States Air Force as a judge advocate. Having had the good fortune of participating in courts martial in the Air Force for three and one-half years, I gained substantial experience in trying cases. I was fortunate an opening occurred in the Onondaga County District Attorney's Office when one of the then assistant district attorneys ran for town judge and was elected.

I thought that I was receiving the appointment because of my experience in trial work, but I was later told that the District Attorney, Jon Holcomb, actually knew that I had been the captain of the Syracuse University baseball team and he was trying to beef up the office softball team for the next competition with other DA offices throughout the state. So much for experience.

The office was loaded with outstanding attorneys, such as Chief Assistant District Attorney John Shannon, Michael Cogswell, John Cirando, Norman Mordue, (who later became Chief Judge of the Federal District Court for the Northern District of New York), Richard Hennessey (who later became DA himself), Robert Rossi and Bryan Hedges (who later became Family Court Judges), and many others, including a young law clerk by the name of William Fitzpatrick, who later became the longest serving DA in Onondaga County.

My concern, at the time of District Attorney Holcomb's resignation, was that I had an uncertain future with the DA's office, and I had a wife and three young children to support. "I will never again allow my livelihood and the livelihood of my family to depend upon a political office," I told John Shannon.

Never say "never." That's rule number one. I stayed in the DA's office for a little over a year, and then began my own private practice of law, concentrating in litigation. To supplement my income, I took a half-time teaching position at the Syracuse University Law School teaching constitutional law, criminal law, and trial practice. But I knew that I would never, ever run for public office.

When we moved back to Syracuse, my wife found a beautiful older home in the Sedgwick Farm area of the City of Syracuse. Linda and I had lived in that area growing up and were childhood sweethearts, dating since we were juniors in high school. In fact, Linda asked me out first because I drove (illegally) at night, and she didn't like the idea of her parents driving her and her date to the Cotillion at The Convent School, the all-girl school she attended. I attended Christian Brothers Academy, the male counterpart. How romantic — I drove at night — but it did get us together and we've been together ever since.

Years later, our home was about half way between her parents' home and my parents' home, and all were within a

three block radius. It was perfect. Our children, who were then 6, 4 and 2, would be able to grow up within a couple of blocks of their grandparents, and near their aunts, uncles and cousins. They could go to Salem Hyde Elementary School, the school which I had attended, just one block from our home. It was a great neighborhood and Salem Hyde was a wonderful neighborhood school.

Not so fast. Enter the Syracuse school board. The Board of Education was embroiled in a lengthy litigation over the integration of the Syracuse City School District and it was under a court order to integrate the schools. The Board Members came up with a plan which they named the "Triangle Plan." It was the most asinine proposal to ever come out of the Board of Education, at least up to that point in time – there were many more to come.

The plan called for the elimination of neighborhood schools and for the creation of separate schools with the following grade levels: kindergarten through second grade, third grade through fifth grade, and sixth grade through eighth grade. If this plan had been implemented, it would have meant that each of my three children, so close in age, and so close to a neighborhood school, would be placed in separate schools in different areas of the city during their formative years. To put it mildly, I was mad, and when I get mad I don't stew about it, I act.

And I acted. I started by going to all the school board meetings. These meetings had to be moved to school auditoriums, since the Board of Education offices could not accommodate the hundreds of people that also were mad and who also became engaged. We all understood that the schools had to be integrated, but this plan literally disrupted most families in the City of Syracuse.

I remember one meeting in particular where the school board members, and the Superintendent, Edwin Weeks, lis-

tened to public comments. They received plenty of comments from me and others who felt the same way. Of the seven school board members, only one agreed with the parents who were against the so-called Triangle Plan, and that was Robert Cecile. After the meeting, Bob approached me and complimented me on my remarks. He then said "if you feel that strongly, you should run for the school board this November."

"No way," I replied. Little did I know that the cock would begin to crow, since I was denying a run for office again.

Quite honestly, Bob's remarks were flattering, primarily because Bob was a diehard Democrat and I was a Republican. Maybe politics, at least on a school board, could be bipartisan.

There were more public meetings and excruciatingly frustrating school board meetings, where the public could not speak, but only listen to the gibberish that was billed as debate on the issue. It was obvious that the School Board members had already made their minds up and were going to vote for, and then implement the Triangle Plan. What was most frustrating was that one of the members of the school board who advocated for and, ultimately, voted for the plan had her children in a private school!

I was so incensed that I spoke about this Triangle Plan issue to everyone who would listen. Most couldn't care less, others appeared to sympathize, but only those who were to be actually affected by the plan could understand the frustrations of the parents who protested against it.

One person who actually listened, and after listening, challenged me, was Jack Kinsella, with whom I was serving in the District Attorney's office. Jack was a political animal. He understood the system and, in fact, had run for office himself. He was as true blue a Republican, as Bob Cecile was a Democrat. Jack used almost identical words in telling me that I should run if I truly felt as strongly as I did. I respectfully de-

clined. The cock crowed again.

Individuals decide to run for public office for many many reasons – some good and some bad. My reason was simple. I was mad as hell about a decision that was about to be made by the Syracuse school board, which would have drastically and adversely affected my children. So shortly after I rejected Jack's challenge to run for office, I changed my mind and decided I would go for it.

After making that decision, and obtaining the Republican and Conservative parties' nominations to run for the Syracuse School Board, I was in the race and there was no turning back.

It's far easier to become a candidate than anyone might think, especially now, since it is difficult to get good candidates to run for office. I will explain the reasons later. However, now that I was the nominee, I had only one question: "Now what?"

THE LIFE BLOOD
OF CAMPAIGNS

Over the years I have spoken with many new candidates, too numerous to mention. Virtually all of them had no clue on how to run a campaign. They had various reasons for wanting to run for office and they knew the process to seek and obtain the nomination, but once they received the nomination, they had no idea where to start, let alone how to run a campaign. Whenever I have had these conversations, I would chuckle because I had been there.

You would think that political parties that seek good candidates and nominate candidates for important positions would provide some type of training on how to run a political race. But generally they don't. I met with a candidate once who was the nominee for a New York state Assembly seat. He had never run for public office. He wanted to meet with me about his campaign. I met with him approximately a month after he was nominated. When I asked him who his campaign manager was, he gave a name of an individual who was going to be the "volunteer coordinator." I asked him again who the campaign manager was, and he indicated that he did not have one. I then asked "who were his volunteers for the race," thinking that maybe one of the volunteers might fit the bill. He gave

me the names of three family members and a friend.

I then asked him who was in charge of raising funds. He informed me that just last night he was thinking about asking someone to be his finance manager for his campaign. When I asked him what he had been doing for the last month, he had no answer. Not surprisingly, he lost his maiden voyage by a two-to-one margin.

I was in the same position as he was during my maiden voyage, but the thought of losing anything was something totally unacceptable to me. So I met with a few family members and friends, and some who had been actively involved with campaigns, to help map out a campaign plan and strategy. Interestingly enough, that plan and strategy did not change much in the over forty years that I ran for elective office.

During my political career, I had spoken at hundreds of schools and spoken to thousands of students. One question that always came up was: "What are the qualifications to become an elected official?" It dawned on me when answering this question on one of these many occasions that the answer to the question was very simple. The qualifications needed to run for office were that you had to be 18 years of age, be a resident of the district, and get more votes than your opponent. Obviously, the voters are looking for someone with qualifications, someone who agrees with them on the issues, and someone that can relate to them and with whom they feel comfortable. But in reality, how many people actually take the time to study the qualifications of a candidate, really understand where the candidate stands on the issues, and have a face-to-face discussion with the candidate to see if the candidate can relate to him or her?

Having never run for public office, I hadn't realized that running city-wide for a Board of Education position was such a monumental task. At the time, the city had about 150,000

people and approximately 40,000 to 45,000 people that voted in each city-wide election. I also had no clue how many Republicans and how many Democrats lived in Syracuse, nor did I know the philosophical leanings of one neighborhood from the other, and there were deep philosophical differences.

However, I wasn't sophisticated enough to really be too concerned about these things and it probably was good that I wasn't. All I knew was that I had to become a member of the Board of Education to try and put a stop to this absurd busing plan. Fortunately, there were enough like-minded people that felt the same way and were motivated by a common purpose. As a result, many volunteered to be part of my campaign.

Another cardinal rule that I learned quite quickly was that there are volunteers and there are "volunteers". Many say they will volunteer, but will do absolutely nothing; others have the intention to volunteer, but in reality never make the time to do so. Still others will actually help in a very substantial way. The last category is usually just comprised of close friends and relatives, and a handful of true believers.

As I journeyed through my many campaigns, I started keeping a small notebook with me. The notebook included things that had to be done in the campaign and the dates by which they needed to be accomplished. This allowed me to be armed and ready when someone offered to help in the campaign. Once they offered, I wrote down their names and phone numbers and immediately told them when the next date was when volunteers were needed. Invariably the individual would tell me that that day was a bad day due to a conflict. I then would give him or her the next date where something had to be done by volunteers and usually he or she would have another conflict or tell me that they would get back to me. On rare occasions, an individual actually would be available on one of the days, but would show up only half of the time.

I don't intend to demean people because everyone has

a life with obligations that are much more important than stuffing envelopes, making phone calls, putting up lawn signs and the like. The point of all of this is that you must determine who really will volunteer and who will be reliable to do the job correctly so that you don't spin your wheels in getting the many necessary tasks of a campaign accomplished.

So when it came right down to it, in my first campaign, I had people I could rely on, most of whom were family and close friends. This amounted to probably forty people. I know that doesn't sound like a lot, and I know that candidates usually say that they have hundreds of volunteers on their campaigns. However, there are "volunteers" and there are volunteers.

But the volunteers in my first campaign were the best. First, there were a lot of people that were truly upset about what the Board of Education was doing. Second, it was my first campaign and my relatives and friends were excited about being involved in something that they never had been involved with before. Third, we were all young. I was 31 years old when I ran for the School Board and all my friends and relatives were young as well, and very energetic. You can imagine as I went from campaign number 2 to campaign number 17, there was less excitement for volunteers, and campaigns became work, rather than fun for them. You can only expect family and friends to be truly motivated for a few campaigns. I know I wouldn't be able to devote the time and energy year after year on someone else's campaign.

There are many talented people who help candidates on campaigns. They do so for all of the right reasons. Some people work on campaigns in the hopes of getting a job if you're successful. The media has uniformly condemned the practice of patronage hiring, but I have always defended it.

If you win an election and are in a position to hire people, you should hire those who you can rely on and who

have been there for you, provided of course, that they are capable of performing the jobs. In my first race for School Board, no one expected a job since there were no jobs to give. The position was a no pay position and the school board members did not have individual staffs. The administrators in the school district did all of the hiring. That's not to say that you couldn't put in a good word for someone to get an interview for a position, but the determination of who obtained that position was not under the control of any individual school board member. That is why I have always been grateful to those who helped me during my first campaign, since no one did so expecting anything other than better school board decisions.

However, further on in my career I was able to hire people to become part of my staff. I remember when I was elected President of the Syracuse City Council. There was one staff member that was appointed by the President---the secretary to the Common Council. When I was elected, the position went to a long-time, hardworking, campaign volunteer, Mike Sommers, who was more than capable of performing the job. It was only fair to do so, since he had worked on campaigns since he was seventeen years old. No elected official before me, who Mike helped win an election, ever gave him a decent opportunity to work.

My favorite example of patronage came after I was first elected to the New York State Senate. An individual asked for an appointment with me to discuss possible employment. Quite frankly, I didn't know the person at all, and didn't remember him being involved in my campaign or in any campaign for anyone else but I was happy to meet with him.

When he came to my office, after discussing his qualifications and what he was looking for, he told me that he was a huge supporter of mine. I told him that I appreciated that, but I didn't remember ever laying eyes on him. He told me that he voted for me. I asked him if he was involved in the campaign

at all, and he said "No." In fact, he said, "I am a Democrat, but if given the job, I will definitely change my registration to Republican." Needless to say, the interview was a very short one.

In any event, after speaking with many people who have been involved in other campaigns, it became very obvious that for my school board race I needed someone to act as campaign manager, treasurer, finance chairman, volunteer chairman, and scheduler. Someone was put in each of these positions, but throughout all of my campaigns I made sure that I was involved in the day-to-day operations to make sure that everything that had to be done, got done. It probably was not a great idea, since the candidate has enough to do just meeting his scheduled appearances. But that's the way I did it.

Although all of my campaigns had an organizational structure, as the campaigns moved forward, the lines began to blur among those with specific responsibilities since as the pace quickened from the beginning of the campaigns to the end, all bodies were needed to do the work of the day.

NITTY GRITTY OF CAMPAIGNING AND "STUFF"

We now had a campaign organization and some excellent volunteers. Now what? Well, what happens next is that you have to decide how much money you believe you can raise for the campaign, and then determine what you are going to spend the money on. Obviously in a school board race you are not going to expect to buy television commercials. Most believe that television commercials are the most effective use of money, but unless you can raise at least $100,000 in Central New York (and much more in other areas), there is no way you are going to be able to devote enough money to television to make it worthwhile. Radio is cheaper and can be used effectively on a lower budget.

Never having run before, I had no idea how much money I should raise or could raise. School board races were notoriously underfunded and, for the most part, the candidate got his or her message out by door-to-door campaigning, or meeting people one-on-one where many people congregate.

I never could understand how anyone could possibly do a door-to-door campaign throughout an entire city the size of Syracuse. It seemed to me that if you knocked on a door in May and introduced yourself and talked to that person that day, that person would forget you within the next few weeks. Moreover, at most, you could only meet maybe 50 people a night by knocking on doors and meeting them in their neighborhoods. You don't have to be a mathematician to recognize that there aren't enough days to meet every potential voter if there will be 40,000 voters on Election Day. That's why I chose for my first campaign, and all campaigns that followed, to meet people where people congregate.

My favorites were bingo games and bowling alleys. I always made a matrix of the names of bowling alleys and bingo games on the left column and the days of the week across the top of the chart. I would then put a check mark in the appropriate box when I went to each location. This enabled me to hit every bowling alley and bingo game that went on throughout the week. You would be amazed at how many people bowl and play bingo, and how many of them do so more than one day a week. As a result, I could hit at least 2,000 people in half-hour stops each week.

But you need to give them something by which they might remember you. Many candidates felt that it would be best for them to have some type of written material listing their qualifications, which is worthwhile, but, during my board of election campaign and every campaign thereafter, I bought thousands of emery boards with my name on it to hand out. In later years, I had basketball schedules printed for both the men's and women's Syracuse University basketball teams, which I always handed out at the Carrier Dome during the last Syracuse University football home game before the election. These things people kept.

Some have told me that they looked forward to the

emery boards that they got from me each campaign, and people sought out the basketball schedules due to the popularity of the Syracuse University basketball teams. Of course, my name was prominently shown on the emery boards and the schedules so that each time someone would file their nails or read the schedule, he or she would be reminded of the fact that they had met me or one of my campaign volunteers.

So you need "stuff". And what stuff you get depends on how much money you have to spend. On various occasions the campaign bought packs of playing cards with my name on them, which I handed out at senior citizen centers. Other times I handed out rulers. Other candidates handed out potholders, which became extinct in view of the cost. The important point is that you have to buy stuff that someone will keep and, hopefully, reuse or at least look at on many occasions before the election. This serves as a reminder that they met you and, hopefully, they will remember your name.

One of the most humiliating moments I ever had with respect to stuff that I handed out, happened during my race for the Board of Education. I went to undergraduate school at Syracuse University and obtained an engineering degree before I went to law school at Duke University. While at Syracuse University, I played varsity baseball and was captain of the 1968 baseball team.

As a result, we had the excellent idea of preparing a palm card, which provided all of my academic and professional qualifications and all my contacts with Syracuse University. The card was printed in orange and blue, the Syracuse University colors. I really felt the palm card would be a winner. However, I violated the cardinal rule of stuff. You must hand out something that people will want to hold on to. They didn't hold on to this card. In fact, many cards littered the outside of Archbold Stadium, where they were handed out before a Syracuse football game.

It was bad enough to loiter outside of the football stadium, but to see my face walked on by thousands of people
was a little disconcerting. However, this was mild in comparison to my horror as I entered the men's room at the stadium.
Any male who had used the facilities at Archbold remembers
that the urinal was a long trough that was attached to the wall
higher on the ends and pitched towards the middle. As I was
doing my business, I was horrified to see many of my palm
cards in this trough floating as people were urinating on my
photograph. That was the first and last time I handed out palm
cards at a sporting event. Other stuff was much better.

I've used emery boards for my "stuff" every single campaign primarily because they are so inexpensive. You could
get 20,000 imprinted emery boards for under $2,000. Simi-
larly, the basketball schedules were very inexpensive. You
could buy 20,000 basketball schedules for about $1,000. This
stuff obviously goes a very long way.

You definitely have to have lawn signs, especially during a first campaign. The lawn signs in neighborhoods show
that you have support from voters in different neighborhoods. Hopefully, the people's homes at which you put lawn
signs are people that the neighbors like, but you never really
know. Some candidates buy signs and just put them anywhere. It gets the name out, but I don't think people like seeing illegally placed signs in public places.

During the first campaign we made plywood signs. As
I look back on it, they looked horrible, but they were really
cheap. Those large signs were put on properties owned by
supporters on heavily travelled roads. In later years, when we
were able to raise more money, we had professional signs done
and put up by very close friends who were responsible for that
duty year after year after year.

Another unique thing we did in that first campaign,
that I don't think was ever done before or since by some-

one running for the Board of Education, was that we hired a plane with a large campaign streamer with "John DeFrancisco for Board of Education" attached. The plane flew over Archbold Stadium at half-time of a SU football game. Amazingly, it wasn't as expensive as you might think, but who knows whether it was effective or not.

In later years, after the Carrier Dome was built on the Syracuse University campus, I had balloons made with my name on it and the office I was seeking. I handed them out to 20 or 30 people who sat at different locations at the Dome. While seated, they blew up the balloons and, at half-time, they launched the inflated balloons throughout the stadium. A lot of people saw the name while they were hitting my balloons back up in the air. Once again, no one knows whether it was effective but it was something that was unique, and was later copied by others on occasion. In short, you have to have good stuff and new ideas so that people can see the name. The theory is the more times someone sees you and sees your name, the more likely they are going to remember it on Election Day.

We went to other places where people congregated. One such place was in front of grocery stores, at the times when there was the most traffic. We often got kicked off the grocery properties by their managers. However, we generally could get a good half hour in at a busy grocery store and meet a few hundred people in that time. It sure beat going door-to-door.

I heard hundreds of times that people remembered seeing me at some location, and they got an emery board or a basketball schedule from me. Repetition and recognition, especially during your first campaign, is obviously important. In later years we had money for television commercials. Then , when I met people face-to-face many would say that they saw my commercial on television. Once again, repetition

and recognition is essential to being elected.

Another great venue at which to hand out basketball schedules are bars. During the Syracuse University football season, we would make a circuit of sports bars during televised SU football games and hand out SU basketball schedules, since the basketball season was rapidly approaching. Similarly, Monday night football was a winner at bars. Again, since there are so many rabid Syracuse University basketball fans, people were glad to accept the schedules and in many instances actually asked for them.

Of course there are meet-the-candidate nights, debates, and the like, but the nitty gritty of campaigning is interacting with people repeatedly and giving them stuff.

RAISING MONEY

The most disagreeable task in any campaign is raising money. For a school board race, the minimum needed is about $5,000 but probably most candidates are unable to raise even that amount. We raised approximately $10,000 to $15,000 that first campaign. Half was raised at just one campaign fundraiser, where we charged $15 per person and $25 per couple. This fundraiser was at the Everson Museum in Syracuse and all the food was prepared and brought in by family members. As a result, the cost was just the rental of the room at the museum. Thereafter, there were direct solicitations from people who had donated to other candidates in prior campaigns. We got the names and addresses from campaign financial records filed by candidates at the Board of Elections in previous elections.

My fundraising was not very sophisticated during this first campaign because, fortunately, not that much money was really needed. With that $10,000 to $15,000 we were able to pay for the signs, the "stuff", and some radio ads. This turned out to be enough to win. As I continued to run over the years, the cost of campaigns became substantially greater. When running the city-wide campaign for president of the City Council, I had to spend some money on television, and television is expensive.

For that race we raised about $70,000, which was sub-

stantially more than I had to raise for the two city-wide councilor-at-large races, which were after the school board race. For the councilor-at-large races we raised approximately $30,000 to $40,000.

When we got to the senate races the numbers escalated. Rather than having to reach 140,000 City residents, we had to reach 300,000 people in the senate district. Obviously, substantially more television was necessary to do that, especially if you were not well known in the district.

When I first ran for the Senate in 1991, a poll was taken by the Senate Republican campaign committee. I was absolutely floored when I found out that only 20% of the people in the Senate District recognized my name. This seemed unbelievable to me considering that I had run in four prior city-wide races. However, if I had analyzed the population more closely and considered that only half of the City of Syracuse was in the senate district, I had only represented 75,000 people out of the 300,000 that I would be representing in the Senate if I won. This fact also made it extremely difficult to even get the nomination for New York state Senate, as will be discussed in a subsequent chapter.

As you run more and more races, it's much easier to raise money and, if you are as fortunate as I was to win with large margins, I was able to raise more money than I spent in every race that I was involved in. As a result, after each campaign, my post-election campaign fund balance increased.

There is much talk about the unfairness to those who are running against long-term incumbents because of their inability to raise money. However, this depends upon the race and the candidate, and other circumstances. For example, in 2008 there was a battle to take control of the New York state Senate. In that year, President Barack Obama won in a landslide and the State Senate was taken over by the Democrat Party for the first time in years, even though Republicans out-

spent Democrats.

In the next New York Senate election in 2010, the state-wide Democrat Party raised plenty of money to finance strong candidates running against incumbents, as did the Republicans. There were races where contenders were not able to raise a substantial amount of money against incumbents. That was simply a matter of economics, namely, that neither the Democrat or Republican Senate Campaign Committee wanted to invest in candidates that weren't likely to win. In any event, the results of these campaigns were that six Democrat incumbents lost and one Republican incumbent lost. Also, one new Democrat was elected to an open seat, resulting in a Senate consisting of 32 Republicans and 30 Democrats. Similarly, six Democrat incumbents lost Assembly seats and one Republican won an open Assembly seat in 2010.

The point is that if there is a good candidate, and if it is an important race, the individual candidate can raise money and also the party will raise funds. So, incumbents can be and are beaten.

Some have called for public financing of elections. I am opposed to it. I don't believe the taxpayers should be paying for campaigns, especially when they would be paying for campaigns of individuals that may be running with philosophies contrary to theirs, or running against their preferred candidate for a specific position. If a candidate is a good one, he or she can raise the money necessary to have a competitive race.

As you get into races that are more costly, you really need a very strong finance committee who can reach out to the money people in the community to raise large sums of campaign contributions. And, quite frankly, the only way that money comes in is if the candidate has made personal contacts with the individuals who usually donate substantial sums to candidates.

Obviously, some people invest large sums of money in

campaigns because they think they are going to get something from the candidates. Hopefully, most are just looking for good government. However, I always got a kick out of the fact that business people would donate to both sides in a campaign to hedge their bets and give them access to the winning candidate. I never could quite understand why people believe that they had to contribute to get access. My door was always open to virtually anyone who wanted to meet with me on issues. This also is true for most elected officials.

It's also interesting to see how the money flows to the candidate, whether Republican or Democrat, who is likely to win the race. The political philosophy of one party or another appears to be less important, especially to large donors. They definitely believe it's to their advantage to back the winners, especially for higher offices.

What has always been annoying to me is when someone contributed, for example, $100 to my campaign and later was hired by me or was helped by me to try to get a job, the newspapers would report the reason the person was hired was because of his or her $100 contribution. That is ridiculous, but it was repeated so many times that it is worth mentioning.

In fact, one of my close friends, Dom Episcopo, who did the hardest campaign work by putting up large signs, obtained a job with the state for which he was qualified. He would also drive me in parades, on his own time. He forever became known in the newspaper as my "driver" who contributed to my campaigns.

Similarly, I recommended an outstanding attorney, John Brunetti, to be appointed to a judgeship. His family had made contributions to me in the past, and the newspapers often implied that these campaign contributions were the reason I made the recommendation. That was unadulterated nonsense. Not only was John qualified, he was the most quali-

fied person that I could have ever recommended. But it makes good news – actually bad news, but it might sell a paper or two.

The most fertile source of campaign donors is the financial records on file with the Board of Elections. Each candidate must file a complete list of the donors, their addresses, and the amounts donated to all campaigns. It was always interesting to see who donated to my opponent, or to other candidates who ran for other offices. Many times when reviewing these lists, I would find people I knew very well that donated to a lot of campaigns, that I never asked to contribute. The main rule in campaign financing is that "there is no harm in asking." More often than not, if you ask the right people and you are respected by them, you will get a donation.

In fact, at times we just sent out general mailings to Republicans and Conservatives to get out a message and asked them to donate, whether it be $25 or $50 or even less. In most cases we would only get back enough donations to pay the cost of the mailing. Though we netted no additional campaign dollars, the mailing got a specific message out, a message that maybe we couldn't have otherwise afforded.

As I progressed through my various New York state Senate campaigns, I got into a pattern. I would have a fundraiser in a nice restaurant in Syracuse in February of each year, a fundraiser in Albany in March, and a golf tournament in Syracuse in September. I would hold these same fundraisers every year. In other words, I wouldn't only do this during election years, but also non-election years. No one seemed to be offended. Money was raised and kept for when that money was needed. Remember, there is no harm in asking.

I would like to think that I did a good job in each of the elective offices I held, and that people were investing in a good candidate. No arms were ever twisted, nor did I try to put any pressure on anyone to donate anything.

Of course, the media, especially the local newspapers, would also try to connect a political donation with a bill or a grant that I was instrumental in either passing or obtaining. It was the other way around. If I did the right things, people would be willing to donate. There never was an occasion where anyone could possibly have felt that if they donated money to me I would do something special for them. This is one of the reasons why I never had a problem sleeping during my many years of public service.

There were many reported cases of individuals being charged with crimes for abusing their public office. Those that were convicted deserved everything they got. My problem was that when this happened, all public officials were painted with the same broad brush. There are some good and bad in every occupation and profession. It was very difficult to take it when that broad brush was applied to me. So another rule for running for public office is that your skin has to be thick to start with and get thicker as you go on.

I never got used to unfounded allegations and implications made in the media, but I was able to deal with them. It was a much greater problem knowing that my family was reading or hearing these things. I always wondered how it truly affected my wife and children. However, I don't think it affected them much in that they always had full confidence in me and my integrity.

Another key player in a campaign organization is the treasurer. Certain reports have to be filed on specific dates throughout the campaign. These reports must be filed on time and be accurate, in accordance with the many requirements of state law. The exact requirements and the timing are too numerous to list, and they change periodically. As a result, it's good to be able to have an accountant as treasurer and, if not, someone who is, or can become, familiar with the state election law requirements.

Whomever you choose as treasurer, that person's first stop must be at the Board of Elections to get copies of all of the rules and the filing requirements, so that the campaign disclosure forms are filed properly and timely. There are penalties imposed by the State of New York if these forms are not filed correctly, but as importantly, if the campaign does not comply with all of the rules and regulations, it could become a campaign issue and a media event that will hurt the candidate's campaign.

So, you need to raise money to at least buy signs and other "stuff," and eventually buy media time. Raising money is a necessary evil, but as long as you follow the rules and are able to ignore the baseless accusations that may be leveled against you, it can be accomplished.

ISSUES

O h, I almost forgot that the reason I decided to run for office was that the Syracuse School Board was about to make an absolutely ridiculous decision to implement a "Triangle Plan" that would have put each of my three children at different elementary schools, even though we had a neighborhood school one street over.

Well you know something? Before the campaign was over, everyone else forgot about it too. The campaign started in the summer, but by the time we got into the Fall campaign season, a new superintendent was appointed by the school board, namely, Sid Johnson. He was a retired Air Force Major who happened to be African American which, in fact, was relevant since he had to deal with the racially charged integration issue.

Voila! The issue was taken care of shortly after he became superintendent. He had a wise and simple solution—close a couple of underutilized elementary schools and redraw the neighborhood school boundaries. He also provided the option to parents that if they wanted their child to change schools, as long as there was room at the school they chose, the child could transfer. It was a brilliant solution, which totally defused the issue. Parents, including my wife and I, were very relieved with this practical solution to a difficult problem.

When I began my run for office there were meetings at which hundreds of parents were clamoring for a change in the plan. A few months later, there were meet the candidates nights with seven candidates running for the three school board positions in attendance, and an audience of all of twenty people, at least half of whom were affiliated with one candidate or another.

This was a powerful lesson in how one person can make a difference and provide a solution to a serious problem rather than create chaos. It also was a great lesson in practical politics. The school board members that were making a horrible decision were still running for office, but now that the issue was resolved, people didn't care anymore. Never mind that the same people, if re-elected, would likely make other bad decisions. So what started out as a campaign before a passionate electorate, turned out to be a campaign that lacked very little, if any, voter interest.

Many candidates prepare position papers outlining their beliefs about certain issues and their solutions to the problems of the day. I don't believe that very many people read these position papers, and still fewer make them the basis of how they are going to vote. Obviously, this isn't always the case, as was true at the beginning of my first campaign. It also sometimes does not apply in races for higher office since there are often stark differences between the positions of the candidates, and it helps each candidate to have a written summary to show that contrast. However, there is so much spin in campaigns, especially in television commercials, that it's almost impossible for the average voter to determine who truly stands for what, and which assertions are true and which are not.

Many congressional races are perfect examples. There are so many charges and countercharges in television commercials that it is difficult for anyone, even those who were aware of the issues, to determine who is telling the truth. The

spin doctors of campaigns totally confuse the average voter.

As I was campaigning for my tenth two-year Senate term, I spoke to hundreds of voters, many of whom were so disgusted with the charges and countercharges in commercials that they were either going to vote against the incumbent simply because the person was an incumbent, or against the person with the most negative ads.

This is truly unfortunate because, once again, candidates are often painted with the same negative broad brush. The incumbent may be the person who advocates and votes in accordance with the voter's desires. By voting against the incumbent in this case, the voter is voting against someone who supports his or her positions. Similarly, to vote against someone because they have the most negative ads makes little sense, since negative ads are not always bad. There is nothing wrong with being negative about a candidate's voting record, if that voting record is accurately reflected in the commercials.

A case in point was the 2010 campaign for New York state Senate in the district adjoining mine between incumbent Democrat David Valesky and challenger, Republican Andy Russo. Russo's commercials correctly were pointing out David Valesky's voting record, which included voting for 14 billion dollars in new taxes, and 14 billion dollars in increased spending over a two year period, at a time when the state was in a serious recession. These commercials were negative, but they accurately reflected the incumbent's record.

Valesky raised the issue in his commercials that Russo did not vote for many years when he was out of the country. Well, that was true, but Andy Russo was a concert pianist, who was a finalist in the world-wide Van Cliburn piano competition. One could argue that being out of the country might be a legitimate reason not to vote under these circumstances. Once again, that commercial was negative but it was also true.

The weight that the voter gives to that commercial is up to the voter.

A voting record of a public official is clearly fair game. If it wasn't, then the elected official's voting pattern would be meaningless. However, when the truth is stretched to the point of it being misleading, there should be some real remedies available to the candidate who is aggrieved by those commercials. Otherwise, the noise of the electronic media will shut out a true, constructive and meaningful discussion of legitimate issues.

There are some commercials that are really over the top. We've all seen these truly negative ads where a candidate calls another a name and makes broad attacks on his opponent's character. I find it quite amusing when the media is appalled at the negative campaign ads, but eagerly accepts payments to place these ads.

I also get a kick out of people who lament that there's no longer any civility in politics and yearn for the good old days. When were these good old days of civility? Our founding fathers weren't as civil as you might think.

In his 1800 presidential campaign against John Adams, Thomas Jefferson called Adams "a blind, bald, crippled, toothless man who wanted to start a war with France." Jefferson further charged that when Adams "isn't busy importing mistresses from Europe, he was trying to marry his son to a daughter of King George." Jefferson went on to argue "haven't we had enough monarchy in America?"

Not to be outdone, Adams hurled some vicious shots at Jefferson. Adams claimed that: "If Thomas Jefferson wins, murder, robbery, rape, adultery and incest, will be openly taught and practiced." Adams went on to ask "are you prepared to see your houses in flames, female chastity violated and children writhing on a pike?" After all, he charged "Jefferson is the son of a half-breed Indian squaw." Civility? The good

old days? Maybe things now aren't as bad as we think. The problem is that in the present day and age, the public is inundated with repetitious TV commercials, rather than having to simply try to make sense out of outrageous and scandalous charges in weekly newspapers.

But getting back to my first political race for school board, my one and only issue, the rejection of the "triangle plan" became moot. As a result, there was no longer an issue of interest to the voters to run on. Again---Now what?

CAMPAIGN

O nce the Triangle Plan was history, the media had absolutely no interest in the board of education races, which was usually the case. Moreover, the angry citizens were no longer angry. On the contrary, they were grateful for the practical solution implemented by the new superintendent, Sid Johnson.

After the issue was resolved, there were more candidates and people affiliated with the candidates at meet the candidates nights than other voters. So the only thing that we could do was go back to the basics. In fact, we chose "Back to the Basics" as our campaign slogan. Children needed to learn how to read, write and do arithmetic, rather than spending valuable school time on other matters. Interestingly, over the next thirty years, many of the candidates for the City of Syracuse School Board chose that same slogan.

The campaign went back to basics too. Since we weren't going to get any free media by discussing issues, and since we weren't going to have an audience before whom to debate issues, we hit the bingo games, the bowling alleys, the bars, the grocery stores, the farmers' market, and banks (on paydays). We hit the plant gates, since at that time we had Carrier Corporation, New Venture Gear, Syracuse China, General Electric, Pass & Seymour, and other manufacturers who had employees working on more than one shift. We would meet

and greet them as they were going on or off their shifts with donuts or cookies or basketball schedules, or whatever else we could hand out.

The lawn signs were placed. Senior citizens centers and senior residences were visited. Generally where there were more than a few people, I was there handing out *stuff*. That campaign and all of my subsequent campaigns were time consuming and, at times, tedious and exhausting. However, believe it or not, for the most part, the campaigns were fun.

It is fun meeting people and running into people who you haven't seen in a long time. Fortunately, I had a close family, the members of which were well respected. My parents' acquaintances that I met during the campaign would fondly tell me stories about my parents and other family members. As I moved to my later races, my children were all married with children. I would meet their friends and acquaintances, and hear stories from them about my children – all good ones.

There would always be some unpleasant people, and some outright jerks, but the vast majority of people that I met were friendly and willing to talk. Some would stop me on the street and want to talk forever and to have in-depth discussions on an obscure issue, when the issue had nothing to do with the office for which I was running. But it still was an interesting experience and an education in human nature.

Campaigning is fun, and it's like any other competition. Having played high school baseball and basketball and college baseball, I didn't like to lose. When you are a competitor, you don't want to leave any stone unturned. So even when I was at the point of exhaustion, since I was also practicing law full time while I was campaigning, I just kept pushing myself to make one more event, or make one more stop where people gathered.

And just like any competition, there are hills and valleys as you go through the campaign. When I ran for president

of the Syracuse City Council, which was my fourth campaign for office, I wanted to capture those highs and lows. To do so, each night after campaigning, I would dictate in a hand-held dictating machine about what had happened that day, and how I was feeling about it. There were many days when I was on a high, believing that I would win by 20 percent. Other days I would feel like there was no way that I could win. Just like any other competition, you can't take the highs too high and the lows too low – you've got to keep an even temperament and your eye on the goal.

The lowest of lows came on my birthday, October 16, 1989, during the campaign for president of the Syracuse City Council. My opponent was the incumbent, Theresa McCarthy, a wonderful woman who was very well-liked and respected. Democrats outnumbered Republicans in the city and Theresa had a good campaign organization. It was truly a difficult race. On my birthday we had an inexpensive fundraiser at a bar in Hanover Square in Syracuse. We had beer and pizza and we were having a great time charging up the volunteers and supporters for the final push to the November election.

I was feeling really good until Channel 9 News anchor woman, Cheryl Nathans, came in to interview me. At that time she told me that the station had a poll done by a well-respected pollster, John Zogby, and the results were going to be released the following day. I asked her what it showed and she refused to tell me, since it was suppose to be news on October 17th. After a lot of whining and cajoling, Cheryl finally told me the results. I was 10 percent behind in the campaign! Needless to say, I was devastated since we were only three weeks away from the election.

I remember that after the fundraiser I was with one of the volunteers and we hit some of our normal spots to meet some more people, but my heart wasn't in it. I kept wondering how I could possibly be behind by 10 points when I was doing

everything humanly possible to win this election.

The poll motivated me to work even harder, which I did, but I was very nervous up to and including election day. On election day, another well respected pollster, Jeff Stonecash, was doing exit polls on the races for one of the local television stations. Exit pollsters ask voters who they voted for, as they leave the polling place. They then take a representative sample of the data and somehow, magically, come up with predicted results.

Knowing that Stonecash was doing this, I called him about an hour before the polls closed, and asked him if he would please tell me what his exit polls were showing. He, of course, started by saying that he could not do that and that I would have to wait until the report was on television. Again, whining and cajoling sometimes goes a long way. He finally told me that it looked pretty close, but my opponent was up by a couple of points. Again, I was on pins and needles for the next few hours until the results came in. Amazingly, despite all these scientific polls done by well-respected pollsters, I won the president of the Common Council race by over 5,000 votes or by about 10 percent.

Oh, by the way, I did win the Board of Education race. Remember there were seven candidates for three positions, so that the three highest vote-getters would become members of the School Board. I came in third and slipped past the fourth candidate by only 200 votes. If it wasn't for good planning, frenetic campaigning, and the help of my friends and relatives, there would have been no way that I would have won that race for School Board. I often wondered what would have happened if I would have lost that race. Would I have run again? I am not so sure I would have.

There are parts of a campaign that you never forget. One of my favorites was when there was a debate between Clyde Ohl, of Camillus, and me in my first race for New York

state Senate. The debate was hosted by the Greater Syracuse Chamber of Commerce. Each of us was asked questions by a panel of three. Clyde was asked what he felt was the key issue that he would want to address if he got elected to the New York state Senate. He answered that he was big on consumer protection and that he wanted businesses to be more customer friendly and stand by their products. He then proceeded to give an example of how his wife, who was five foot one inch tall, bought a new motor vehicle and when she got home she realized she was having difficulty reaching the gas and brake pedals.

Clyde explained that he was mortified when the dealer would not take the car back. He felt that the dealer had an obligation to take the car back, since it would be dangerous for Clyde's wife to drive that vehicle. A panelist asked me to respond. My response was that my wife was five foot one inch tall as well, but she test drove the vehicle before she bought it. The audience erupted into laughter, but if you think about it, it wasn't really funny. There are elected officials who believe exactly the way Clyde Ohl did. I believe that people have to be responsible for themselves before they demand others to be responsible for them.

In any event, there are many other stories, but campaigning was always fun, or usually fun – well sometimes.

POLLING

There is little question that polling is now big business. Polling isn't just done by big companies to determine consumer buying preferences, but also by all types of organizations so that they can attempt to predict how an individual is going to act, and what motivates people to do what the organizations want them to do. In my mind this use of polling makes good economic sense. Why spend millions of dollars in developing a product or start a marketing campaign, without knowing whether the product is likely to sell and how to motivate people to buy it?

Polling is used in many ways in politics. The first use is in determining who the candidate should be in a political race. Just like businesses don't want to invest a lot of money in a product that won't be purchased, political organizations don't want to invest in a candidate, if that candidate can't win.

As a result, when several candidates step forward and express an interest in running for the same political office, a poll is often taken to see which candidate has the greater identification with the voters. The higher the name identification and the greater the favorability rating, the greater the likelihood the candidate will be selected to run. In my mind this type of polling is useless when you have relatively unknown candidates among those that are being polled. However, this polling is done quite frequently.

You may be surprised to learn that in the majority of races, including those where the political parties are attempting to find the best candidate to run against an incumbent, the pool of candidates consists of those who ask to run, rather than those that should be asked to run. Unfortunately, it is becoming increasingly more difficult to find good candidates who are willing to step forward and subject themselves and their families to the ever-increasing critical eye of the media, at a time when nothing about a person is off limits.

In actuality, the poll that is used to help determine which candidate is more suited to run for a specific office is more often a tool for the candidate who wants to convince the party regulars that he or she should be selected. Since a candidate who wants to run for office has to convince the party's committee members that he or she should be the one chosen to run, in many instances a poll commissioned by that candidate, which shows that that candidate would be the most attractive one, helps to convince undecided committee members. However, since a change in one word in a poll question can alter the results so significantly, I have little faith in these types of advocacy polls.

But polls are very useful in helping campaign organizations to determine how they should spend their money. Obviously, if campaign dollars have to be allocated to their best use, it is foolhardy to spend a lot of money on a campaign where a poll shows that a candidate has absolutely no chance of winning. This is why you see the Republican and Democrat state and federal campaign committees doing polling on various races during the course of campaigns. A candidate that seemed to be an excellent candidate might not sell, and rather than continuing to throw good money after bad, the committee will often pull the plug on contributions to a floundering candidate. Conversely, if a candidate didn't at first seem to be a likely winner, but proves otherwise during the course of his or her campaign, more money is directed to that candidate.

A third type of poll is often done by the candidates themselves during the campaign. All candidates want to know how they are doing, either to see if their strategy is working, or simply for peace of mind. What many candidates forget, however, is that the poll is just a snapshot at that point in time, and things can and do change rapidly.

In 1984 there was a New York state Senate race be-tweeen Democrat Nancy Lorraine Hoffman, a Syracuse Com-mon Councilor, and the long-term Republican incumbent, Martin Auer. About three weeks before the end of the cam-paign a poll was taken showing Auer was up by about 25 per-cent. As a result, he didn't spend a lot of money during the last weeks of the campaign, resulting in him having funds still on hand at the end of the campaign. On the other hand, Hoffman put in a substantial television buy over the last three weeks of the campaign with very effective commercials. She ended up winning by less than 200 votes in a race where approximately 80,000 votes were cast. The campaign funds that Auer had left on hand didn't do him much good since he never ran again.

The questions asked on candidate driven polls don't vary much. There is always a question which lists candidates for different offices and elected officials who may not even be running that year, and the person being polled is asked how he or she feels about each of the people named – "favorable," "unfavorable," "undecided," or "never heard of." Obviously, if you are in a campaign and people never heard of you, you're in trouble. You are in even more trouble if the polls show that the people who have heard of you, don't like you.

There is always a question as to whether or not the per-son being polled believes that the city, state or federal govern-ment is moving in the right direction or the wrong direction. An individual is usually asked what that person believes to be the most important issue facing the city, state or country. The person being called would have to verbalize that issue,

whether it be jobs, taxes, the economy, or whatever, and that response is recorded to give the candidate an idea of what issues that candidate should concentrate on for the rest of the campaign.

Finally, there is almost always a head-to-head question, such as, "If the election was held today, would you vote for Democrat John Jones or Republican Sheila Smith?" That question would not only be asked about the candidate for whom the poll was being taken, but also on other races that are going on at the same time. This helps a candidate gauge not only how he is doing in his race, but also how he is doing in comparison to other candidates running during the same election cycle.

Again, this is simply a snapshot in time. If you are doing well, you should keep doing whatever you are doing in the campaign. If you are not doing well, you might consider a change in strategy or try to raise additional funds to obtain more identification and more favorable ratings from the voters.

Presently, many candidates still rely on polls. However, I wonder how valuable they are when you consider that usually the only people polled are those who have land-lines, since mobile phone numbers are not as easily accessible. With the increase in use of mobile phones and answering machines, with which people screen their calls, how valuable are the phone polls?

The other problem with polling is that you can get whatever result you want depending on who you decide to call. Your results are going to be much more reliable if you call likely voters than voters who rarely, if ever, vote. You can get lists from the Board of Elections of registered voters, with their phone numbers, who have voted, for example, in two of the last four elections, in one of the last four elections, or in any other combination.

Why would anyone want to skew the sample? Well, as one pollster once told me, "You do what you've got to do." In 1993 there was a race for Mayor of Syracuse between Republican Roy Bernardi and Democrat Joe Nicoletti. My campaign group was helping Bernardi, and part of that help included doing our own polls at virtually no cost to him. We wrote the questions for the poll (which is not rocket science), got the likely voter lists from the Board of Elections, and got volunteers to make the phone calls. We also had a computer program that compiled the answers and printed out a campaign report. It is not unheard of for people to pay $8,000 to $10,000 for a poll, just like this poll that we did at no cost, except volunteer time.

Prior to the general election, there was a primary between Nicoletti and Joe Fahey for the Democrat nomination for Mayor. Our polling for Bernardi showed that he was far behind, and that the favorite was either Fahey or Nicoletti. The Democrat enrollment, at the time, was substantially greater than the Republican enrollment in Syracuse.

However, after a bitter primary between Nicoletti and Fahey, the poll numbers started moving, and Bernardi's numbers kept increasing against Nicoletti's. It became obvious that the Fahey people were not going to support Nicoletti, who had beaten Fahey in the primary. Moreover, not so coincidentally, campaign contributions started flowing in for Bernardi.

Two weeks before the election, our polls showed Bernardi up by almost two to one, which was truly remarkable. However, at about the same time, a poll commissioned by Joe Nicoletti reported the race as a dead heat. This really shocked me in view of our poll results. I thought that maybe we were doing something wrong, since the poll results shouldn't be that different. Two weeks later Bernardi won the election by almost two to one, as our polls had predicted.

Sometime thereafter, I ran into Nicoletti's pollster, Jeff Stonecash, at a high school function where students, including one of his children, were being honored. I was there as a state Senator to help recognize the students. When the event was over, I approached Jeff and explained what our polls were showing prior to the election, and how shocked I was when his poll showed the race to be a dead heat. That is when he told me "You do what you've got to do." So much for the science of polling.

There is another type of polling that has developed over the years, namely, "push polling." Push polling is polling where people are being pushed to change their opinion about a candidate. A typical question might be, "Did you know John Jones worked for a large corporation that laid off hundreds of workers while he received a huge bonus?" This type of question is usually followed by the question "Now that you know this, are you more likely or less likely to vote for John Jones?"

The purpose of this type of poll is to try to get out negative information about a candidate, in many cases either misleading or untrue, to try to change the voter's opinion about the candidate. This, in my mind, is despicable.

This type of campaigning is sometimes done in another way, which is very annoying to the recipients of these calls, named "robo calling". Robo calling is simply recording a message from the candidate or from someone on behalf of a candidate providing a negative message about the opposing candidate. For example, "Did you know that John Jones hasn't paid his taxes in the last ten years?" No questions are being asked, just information planted, whether that information is true or not.

A milder version of robo calling is to have some famous political figure or celebrity call on behalf of a candidate voicing his or her support. In the 2010 election, I even received an email from a company in California that actually dealt in

celebrity voices (who knows whether they were the real celebrity or not), who recorded messages on behalf of the candidate. For example, "Hi, this is Paul Newman, and I support John DeFrancisco." That one would have been tough to sell, since Paul Newman was not alive at the time.

I can't imagine that anyone truly believes these types of calls, but I do know that most find them extremely annoying. I don't know how people believe these calls help their cause. But it is still done.

SELECTING CANDIDATES

E ach political party has a process to select candidates. Both the Republican and Democrat parties have a committee system whereby committee members actually select candidates. To become a committee member, you have to circulate petitions and gather the number of signatures required. If more than one candidate obtains a sufficient number of signatures to become a committee member, then whomever receives the most votes at the next election, becomes a committee person, just like candidates for other offices.

In Onondaga County, there are Republican and Democrat committees for each of the towns, and within the City of Syracuse for each of the 19 wards. Each town and ward committee should have a chairman and vice-chairman and committee members for each individual district. Due to a lack of interest or, in some cases, lack of leadership, some political committees have numerous vacancies. With or without vacancies, the committee members select the candidates. The town and village committee members select the town and village candidates, and the city committee members select the city candidates. For seats, such as State Senate and Assembly, which district lines overlap city and county boundaries,

the candidates are selected by committee people within the legislative districts.

Oftentimes you hear an individual who is not selected as the candidate to run for a specific office cry "foul." This always amused me since each candidate has the opportunity to appear before the committee members of the district and they determine who will be the candidate. It's similar to a general election, in that a potential candidate must convince a sufficient number of committee people to support him or her to become the candidate.

In any event, if an individual doesn't get selected, he or she has the ability to circulate petitions and be placed on the ballot to run a primary against the party-designated candidate. Not only has that happened, but some individuals who were not selected by the party, became the party nominees after winning a primary, and then won their general elections.

In 2008, Joanie Mahoney did not get the Republican party nomination to run for Onondaga County Executive. However, she circulated petitions, ran a primary and beat the party's designated candidate, Dale Sweetland. Joanie then ran in the general election and handily beat the Democrat candidate, Assemblyman Bill Magnarelli.

Similarly, when the Republican party was unfortunate enough to have Bob Smith as its Chairman, he decided that he wanted to be rid of Nancy Lorraine Hoffmann, the former Democrat, turned Republican State Senator for the 49th State Senate District. As a result, he backed Tom Dadey for the nomination to run for that State Senate position. Dadey got the nomination, and also the third party backing of the Conservative Party.

Hoffmann beat Dadey in the Republican primary, but Dadey still had the Conservative line. Dadey siphoned off a sufficient number of votes on the Conservative line at the general election resulting in David Valesky becoming the New

York state Senator for the 49th District. That was the beginning of the erosion of the state Senate Republican Majority, which eventually led to the Republicans losing control of the New York state Senate in 2009.

Amazingly, six years later, in 2010, Tom Dadey was elected Chairman of the Onondaga County Republican party, having the strong backing of Joanie Mahoney. Another cardinal rule of politics - never burn any bridges.

GETTING THE NOMINATION

Generally speaking, in order to run for public office you have to obtain the designation of a party, and that party in New York state could be the Republican, the Democrat, the Independence, the Conservative, the Working Families Party, the Green Party, or others. Lacking a party nomination, you can circulate petitions and run under your own named party. In the early 2000s several candidates ran on the "Tea Party" line, even though there was never really a formal party, but it was comprised of a group of people circulating petitions under that name.

When I ran for the Syracuse City Council for the first time. I received the Republican endorsement, but did not receive the endorsement of the Conservative Party. As a result, I ran a Conservative Party primary, which will be discussed in more detail later. However, I also circulated petitions under the name of the "Independence Party" and used the letter "I" with a circle around it as its symbol. This was before there was a formal party known as the Independence Party.

The theory of doing this was to match my opponent who was likely to have the Democratic and Conservative lines, by having two lines myself on the ballot. But back then

you really needed a major party endorsement to have any chance of winning a general election, simply based upon the number of people enrolled in the major political parties. A third party designation, and its ballot line, is also helpful so that Democrats, for example, who may want to vote for you but don't want to vote for someone on the Republican line, have an alternative line upon which to vote for you.

The classic example of how you usually can't win without a major party line is the mayoral race in the City of Syracuse in 1981. When Sidney Johnson decided to retire as superintendent of the Syracuse City School District, many people, including myself, encouraged him to run for Mayor. Sidney was a registered Republican. Based upon a lot of encouragement, he decided to seek the nomination of the Republican Party. The other Republican candidate was the City auditor, Roy Bernardi. Roy had run for Mayor before and lost. He later won on his third try. Hey – you never know.

I thought that Sid had an excellent chance, not only to get the nomination, but to win the general election. Some said that Sidney Johnson could not win the mayoral race since it was impossible for a Black man to win a mayor's race in the City of Syracuse in 1981. I strongly disagreed. My rational was as follows.

The year before the mayoral campaign year we encouraged Sidney Johnson to run for city-wide Councilor-at-Large. One of the councilors resigned from office, which left a one year unexpired term. By running for Councilor-at-Large, Sid could prove his vote-getting ability, serve for a year, and then run for Mayor.

Sid was extremely popular in the City of Syracuse. As was mentioned before, he got rid of the Triangle Plan by coming up with a practical common sense solution that made him a hero among City parents. Moreover, he was an outstanding administrator. He got parents involved in just about every

major decision. Obviously, even though they were involved, he would make the ultimate decision, but parents really supported him based upon the inclusive process that he had established.

I was sure that Sid Johnson could win a city-wide race since he won the Councilor-at-Large race by 17,000 votes, garnering more than 65 percent of the total. Although his opponent was not the strongest of candidates, it was still unheard of back in 1980 for someone to win a city-wide race by 65 percent to 35 percent. This was especially true for a Republican, since at the time there were more Democrats than Republicans enrolled to vote in the City.

I was Sid's campaign manager and was astounded at the volunteers that he had working on his campaign. And I mean real volunteers, not those in name only. Each section of the City was divided into groups of volunteers who had specific duties and who actually fulfilled those duties, exactly as planned. It would be a very simple transition to run for Mayor, with that body of devoted people who had helped in the Councilor-at-Large campaign.

The problem was that Sid Johnson had never really been involved in party politics before this. Roy Bernardi had a long history of being involved in party politics and that long history meant that he knew a lot more committee people than Sidney Johnson did.

Sidney was not the type of guy that would go door-to-door or make calls to committee people to try to encourage them to vote for him to run for Mayor. He believed that people should look at an individual's record and make the decision on who was the best qualified candidate. Well, that's not always the case in politics. And it wasn't the case with respect to this nomination, since Roy Bernardi got the nomination to run for Mayor, even though he lost in a mayoral race against Mayor Lee Alexander four years earlier.

I had predicted that Sid would not get the nomination from the Republican committee people, and told him that on many occasions. However, I strongly believed, with the vote that he received the prior year in the Councilor-at-Large race and with his army of rabid volunteers, he would easily beat Bernardi in a primary. Sid was not a happy camper when he didn't get the nomination and indicated that he would circulate petitions and run on a third-party line. Well, he wasn't going to get the nomination for the then existing third parties---the Conservative Party or the Liberal Party. As a result, to do this he would have to circulate petitions and name a new independent third party of his own.

That certainly was his prerogative, but it would never be successful and I, and others, advised him of that. He seemed to agree and said that he would run a primary for the Republican nomination. We started to gear up for such a primary, and get ready to circulate Republican petitions. Getting the required number of petitions would be a piece of cake with the number and quality of volunteers we had.

Just when I thought everything was moving in the right direction, I read a headline in the newspaper that Sid Johnson decided he was going to circulate petitions and run on his own line for Mayor of the City of Syracuse. Needless to say, I was not happy. He had told us that he would run a Republican primary, and it was one heck of a way to learn about his change of heart by reading the newspaper. More importantly, there was no way he could win at that time without a major party endorsement.

That was the end of it for me, until one day I received a call from my law office secretary, Joan Guinto, who was a devoted Sid Johnson fan and volunteer. She and others were trying to resurrect the concept of a primary in the Republican party and they thought they had him convinced to do so. They asked me to please come to a meeting of volunteers to discuss

it with Sid. I reluctantly did.

After the meeting, I once again thought that Sid was convinced to run a Republican primary but, as it turns out, he was so upset with the Republican party for having nominated a person he believed to be the less qualified candidate, that he decided to go it on his own. I was really done at that point, and so was Sid Johnson. He did not obtain the necessary signatures to run as an independent candidate and was not on the ballot in November. Sidney Johnson's political career ended quicker than his meteoric rise the year before.

Getting a nomination is sometimes very easy. In my school board race, there were three openings and there were three candidates wanting to run. That made it pretty easy to pick the candidates. Similarly, once I was well established in the New York state Senate, I never had opposition in getting the Republican nomination, and rarely did I have opposition in getting nominations from the Conservative and Independence parties.

On the other hand, the first time I sought the nomination for New York state Senate, there was plenty of competition and a nomination was decided by the narrowest of margins. My predecessor, Senator Tarky Lombardi, had served in the Senate for twenty-eight years, and everyone anticipated that he would continue to run. The people in his district were shocked when he announced that he would not seek re-election at the last minute, in June of 1991.

I hadn't even thought of running for state senate, but when there was an opening, I received calls from many people indicating that I should consider running. At the time, I was president of the City Council and had run and won city-wide four times – once for the City School Board, twice for Councilor-at-Large, and once for President of the City Council.

Having been in those positions for that period of time, my name had been mentioned in the media on many many

occasions and I thought I had good voter identification. However, the part of the City of Syracuse that was in Tarky Lombardi's senate district only amounted to twenty percent of the entire senate district. I had never run outside of the City, and I hadn't had much contact with any of the Republican committee people outside of the City of Syracuse.

To compound my problem, one of my opponents, Bernie Kraft, was a long serving County Legislator from the biggest town in the district, the Town of Clay. In fact, the Town of Clay had many more voters in the senate district than the portion of the City of Syracuse that was in the senate district. Moreover, Bernie was supported by his colleagues on the County Legislature that represented all areas in the Senate district outside of the City of Syracuse.

That's not all. Jerry Mingolelli was one of those county legislators, who happened to have a legislative district which included part of the City of Syracuse. Jerry had absolutely no chance of getting the nomination, but he put his name in the mix as a third candidate. Needless to say, since part of his district was in the City, some of the committee people that likely would have voted for me would be be peeled off to vote for Jerry Mingolelli, the net effect of which was to help Kraft.

Michael Sommers, who helped me in each of my City Council races, and who I appointed as my sole employee in the City Council, encouraged me to go after it. Others did as well. The difference was that Mike got everything in motion. He suggested that we march in the annual County volunteer firemen's parade, which by the way, I had never heard of before. That parade was going to be held less than a week from the date that Tarky Lombardi announced he wasn't going to run.

In less than a week, Mike had obtained a campaign van, decorated the van with "DeFrancisco for Senate" signs, ordered lawn signs and obtained pencils with my name on them to hand out in the parade. He also organized volunteers to

walk in the parade with me to try to create some excitement.

I will never forget that many people thought that Tarky Lombardi had given us a heads up that he wasn't going to run, since that had to be the explanation of how we could have been ready so quickly. That was definitely not the case. It was just a very efficient group of people, headed by Mike Sommers, who got everything together in virtually no time.

In fact, after the committee votes were in for the nomination, it was obvious that Senator Tarky Lombardi not only didn't give me a heads up, but also was actively supporting Bernie Kraft. First, Jerry Mingolelli, the spoiler candidate, was on the New York state Senate payroll, and his spoiler role was not a coincidence. Second, a very active and influential member of the Town of Clay Republican Committee, the biggest town in the district, Naomi Bray, was a Lombardi staff member. The entire Town of Clay, except for one lawyer friend of mine, Jeff Gosch, voted for Kraft.

However, I caught a major break. One of the other potential candidates, who would have been much stronger than Bernie Kraft, was out of the country. Bill Sanford, a County Legislator at the time, was the crew coach at Syracuse University and his crew was rowing in London, England the week that I was preparing to launch a campaign. That really put Bill out of the picture. When he returned, late in the process, he gave his support to Bernie Kraft, as did virtually every County Legislator.

It gets even more interesting. The Republican Party rules, at the time, did not call for a run-off if a candidate did not get the majority. Simply stated, whichever candidate got the most votes was going to be the nominee. This obviously was an advantage to Kraft since the town in which he lived vastly outnumbered the portion of the City of Syracuse that I represented in the Senate district. Moreover, the spoiler, Jerry Mingolelli, would be taking votes away from me and, as a re-

sult, Kraft wouldn't have to worry about a run-off if he could just get more votes than me on the first ballot.

The County Republican Chairman at the time was the legendary Bob Giarrusso. Bob proposed a change in the rules that would require the winner to receive fifty percent of the vote, and if no one received a majority vote, then the candidate getting the fewest votes would be dropped, and there would be a run-off between the remaining two.

As a result, on the night of the vote, there was also to be a vote on a by-laws change to require a majority to win the nomination. The vote on this by-law change was to take place just before the vote for the nomination for the state Senate seat. This did not help me since it energized the Bernie Kraft people to argue to committee people that the chairman was trying to fix the election against their candidate.

Immediately before the meeting there was a short get-together among the three candidates and the party Chairman. At that meeting I told Bob Giarrusso that changing the rules was something that was not right, and I asked him to take it off the agenda. I didn't want there to be any question as to whether the selection of the state Senate candidate was influenced in any way by a change in the voting procedure. Obviously, the other two candidates were more than happy to agree with me, and Bob took the rules change off the agenda.

At the general meeting with all committee people for the Senate District in attendance, each candidate was given an opportunity to speak. Thereafter, a vote was taken and it turned out to be one of the closest votes ever for a nomination for an elected position in Onondaga County. I won by the weighted votes by the equivalent of three people out of approximately three hundred voters in the room. How was it done? A lot of hard work, and I would like to think that I convinced the committee members that I would be the better candidate. But specifically, how did I get the votes?

Immediately after I completed my military service with the Air Force, I was appointed an Assistant District Attorney for Onondaga County. The office included outstanding lawyers who lived in different towns in the county. All were very well respected. As a result, I contacted each of them for help. They talked me up to each of their committee people in their towns, and arranged for me to be invited to meet the committee people one-on-one.

These face-to-face meetings were outstanding, especially when the introductions were made by people like John Shannon, Mike Cogswell, Norm Mordue, and others. Based upon their recommendations and me not doing or saying anything that would have persuaded them not to vote for me, I gained a lot of support.

I also got on the phone and talked to as many committee people as I could, and met others at their homes. I simply tried to convince each of the committee people that I was the stronger candidate because of my name identification, and my qualifications. My pitch was basically asking them who they would hire, me or Bernie Kraft, if they had to hire one of us? I felt that framing the question in that way made it into a question of qualifications. Many years later when I was running for my tenth term in the New York state Senate, my television commercials had the tag line "I would like to continue to work for you", which slogan focused on one of the most important factors in an election – qualifications.

I knew only a few on the Town of Camillus committee. Mike Sommers knew a lot of people on that committee and helped arrange for me to speak with each of them individually, and collectively at their town committee meetings.

Fortunately there were several influential members of the committee, including Dave and Ruth Elleman. Dave was the County Comptroller at the time and Ruth was one of the hardest workers that I ever met. Also, committee members

Maureen and Ken Osborne strongly advocated for me. This resulted in almost all of the Town of Camillus committee members voting for me for the nomination. In short, it was an awful lot of hard work to overcome the obstacles that I was facing to win the nomination.

I have always been grateful for the committee people in the Town of Camillus and all of the committee people who voted for me. I also was extremely grateful to Mike Sommers for the role he played in the process in encouraging me to run, getting me off the dime faster than anyone else could have, and helping me secure enough votes.

When I won the general election, I hired Mike as one of my staff members. This was unadulterated political patronage. But so what? Who else should I hire other than someone who was instrumental in me obtaining the opportunity to become a state Senator and someone who was capable of performing the duties that he had to perform for constituents in my office?

Moreover, when I first became a state Senator, one of my 1992 Senate classmates was George Pataki. We became friends. Two years later, he was elected governor. At that time I recommended Sommers to become Deputy Director of the New York state fair. Political patronage? Absolutely, and I won't deny it. As long as the individual can perform the duties of the position, he should be given the same opportunity as anyone else. Put another way, why would I recommend someone who I don't even know, when I know of someone who is a hard worker, capable of performing the job, and who was instrumental in me having the opportunity that I got.

Mike was interested in becoming the Director of the New York state fair. However, there was a line to be drawn. I did not believe he was qualified to be the number one person at the state fair and, as a result, I recommended Peter Cappuccilli, who did an absolutely outstanding job (notwithstanding

the political witch hunt later launched against him).

Some people become a candidate for a party even if they do not obtain the endorsement of a party's committee people. That is the avenue I was trying to convince Sidney Johnson to take. That is also the avenue that County Executive Joanie Mahoney took. She did not get the nomination to run for County Executive, but rather Dale Sweetland, the Chairman of the County Legislature, was the one that was selected by the Republican committee people to run for the office.

To her credit, Mahoney circulated Republican petitions, got an organization together, and won the primary for the Republican nomination. She deserved to become County Executive, because she did the work to become the party's nominee. The Republican enrolled voters chose her at the polls as the party's nominee and the voters chose her in the general election to become the County Executive.

Sometimes the voters don't do such a great job in a primary election. A good example of this was seen in the 2010 gubernatorial race. Andrew Cuomo was selected by the Democrats. The Republicans chose Rick Lazio. Unfortunately, for the Republicans, there was another candidate who wanted to be governor, Carl Paladino. Paladino ran and won a Republican primary and got the Republican nomination to run against Andrew Cuomo. Paladino was a very successful businessman, who had many good ideas about how the state's financial house could be put back in order. However, he was a horrible candidate. He was constantly putting his foot in his mouth by making comments that were jumped on by the press.

It was bad enough that he would make verbal gaffs, but Paladino would also be apologizing every week for the prior week's gaffs. He was hardly a candidate that inspired much confidence. But to become the Republican candidate for Governor, he organized a petition drive, and got enough

signatures on the petitions to be put on the ballot and, in a shocker, beat the Republican party's candidate Rick Lazio, by a substantial margin in the primary. The final vote total in the general election was Andrew Cuomo 2,911,721, and Carl Paladino 1,290,082. This disaster at the top of the ticket also kept the vote total down and hurt other Republican candidates in other races.

Fast forward to 2016. Paladino was one of the most ardent supporters in New York state for Donald Trump when no one thought he had a chance to get the Republican nomination, let alone become President. Well Carl was right and Trump won. From humiliated gubernatorial candidate to friend of the President. Hey, you never know. Unfortunately, Paladino couldn't behave himself after attaining his "friend of the President" status. Shortly after the election he made racist comments about President Obama and his wife which earned denunciations from virtually all elected officials and from members of the President's team.

As an interesting side note, a man named Jimmy McMillan circulated petitions and got on an independent line in the Cuomo/Paladino race for Governor. He named his party the "Rent Is Too Damn High" party. He got substantial national attention after his appearances at the debates and actually got 41,131 people to vote for him! I guess there were a lot of people in New York state that had rent that was "Too Damn High."

The moral of the story about obtaining a nomination is that if you have the fire in your belly and you are able to get more people on your side than your opponents, you can get the nomination either by a vote from the party's committee members, or in a primary.

MINOR PARTIES

Even though it's usually impossible for a candidate to win an election with the endorsement of a minor party alone, whether it be Conservative, Independence, Green or Working Families, third party endorsements are crucial in some elections. Each year you will find examples of successful candidates who would not have won with only the votes on the major party's line. This is why candidates work hard to get the endorsements of minor parties and, ultimately, the additional votes on that minor party's line.

Some believe that being on a third party line gives the voter an opportunity to vote for a candidate when that voter would never vote, for example, for a candidate on the Republican line, but would vote for that candidate on a minor party line. My guess, however, is that if there were no minor parties, and the voters had to choose between one candidate or the other on major party lines only, they would chose the same person. But we'll never know.

To become a recognized minor party and have the party's name on the ballot for the next four years, the party must garner 50,000 votes in a gubernatorial election year. For example, in the 2018, the last gubernatorial election year, six minor parties received at least 50,000 votes, and will have lines on the ballot, at least for the four years until the 2022 gu-

bernatorial election year. Those parties are the Conservative Party, Working Families Party, Green Party, Libertarian Party, Independence Party, and SAM (Serve America Movement) Party.

The ballot position is also important. The party whose candidate wins the gubernatorial election, in the case of 2018, the Democrat Party, will be on line A, and the party whose candidate with the second most votes, in 2018, the Republican Party, will be on line B for the next four years. The rest of the lineup, on ballots for the four years following the 2018 election, as a result of a vote totals in the 2018 election, will be as follows: Conservative Party, line C; Working Families' Party, line D; Green Party, line E; Libertarian Party, line F; Independence Party , line G ; and SAM Party, line H.

An interesting example of the importance of a third party line is the 2010 Florida race for the United States Senate. In 2008, Governor Charlie Crist was a much talked about Republican candidate for Vice President of the United States. Since that time, he didn't act much like a Republican and, as a result, didn't get his party's nomination in 2010, when he next ran for office. After losing a Republican primary, he was relegated to a minor party line - the Independence line. Once again, despite his notoriety and his one time great popularity, a third party line alone didn't do it for him. He lost to the Republican candidate, Marco Rubio. Rubio had 2,645,743 votes, Crist had 1,607,549 votes on an Independence line, and Democrat Kendrick Meek had 1,092,936 votes.

From time-to-time, a minor party selects a candidate within its own party ranks to run on its line alone. These candidates don't win, with rare exceptions. Moreover, if that candidate was put on the line in a race for governor, it is very unlikely that this candidate would garner the 50,000 votes and, therefore, it would result in the minor party losing its ballot status for the next four years. So, minor parties usually back

major party candidates, especially in bigger races.

It is also obvious that if a minor party's endorsement is a significant reason why a candidate wins an election, that minor party will have some influence in government by having backed that major party candidate rather than its own who lost.

It being in the mutual interests of the minor party and the candidate to connect, how is that accomplished? Well, with some minor parties, such as the Conservative Party, the party actually has a philosophy. The Conservative Party is, in fact, conservative philosophically and wants less government and more personal responsibility. Presumably, if a candidate has been in office for a while and has voted on various pieces of legislation, those votes will either pass or fail the litmus test of the Conservative Party.

In my case, I got the Conservative endorsement when I ran for the Board of Education and the Conservative endorsement every single year thereafter in all of my seventeen elections, except for one. That one was when I ran for Councilor-at-Large after my four year term on the School Board. That year there were two seats that were contested. The Republicans fielded two candidates, one of which was me, and the Democrats fielded two candidates. At that point the minor parties stepped in.

The only important minor party at the time was the Conservative Party and that party endorsed Charlie Borgognoni, the nephew of a very popular Catholic Monsignor, with the same name. Borgognoni had attempted to get the Democrat nomination, but was not designated by the committee members as the Democrat candidate. Instead, Constance Timberlake and Bob Cecile were nominated by the Democrat Party.

The way the election works for a councilor-at-large election is that you pick any two out of the four candidates.

As a result, two Republicans could win, two Democrats could win, or one of each could win. In this case, Borgognoni could technically win on the Conservative line, though very unlikely. But even if he didn't win, he would most likely take votes away from me or my main opponent, since he would have been in the same column as Bob Cecile and me on the ballot.

By the way, do you remember Bob Cecile? He was the Democrat who encouraged me to run for the Board of Education. Now, as it turns out, we ended up running against each other for a City Council seat. Moreover, the ballot positions were such that I was directly under Bob Cecile on the ballot, which meant that voters would likely choose either me or Cecile, even though the ballot stated that you could pick any two of the candidates running for an at-large seat.

The complication for me was that in that column listed with Bob and me was the Conservative party endorsed candidate, Charlie Borgognoni. I was extremely concerned that Charlie would take enough votes off that line so that it would be more difficult for me to beat both Cecile and Constance Timberlake, both of whom had been in office more years than I had in a Democrat dominated city.

Why didn't I get the Conservative nomination in the first place? I think I knew the reason. Borgognoni was a staff member of Mel Zimmer, an Assemblyman who was running for Mayor in a primary against, at that time, a very popular Democrat, Mayor Lee Alexander. Why he lost the primary is another story, which I will discuss later.

Mel Zimmer was extremely popular with the Conservative Party and he carried Borgognoni along with him as far as the nomination for councilor-at-large was concerned. As a result, it wasn't really philosophy that determined the Conservative candidate in this race, but rather an effort by the Conservative party to help Mel Zimmer in his attempt to be-

come Mayor.

So, what could I do? Well, my best option was to run a primary. However, there is a substantial problem in running primaries when you are not a member of the party whose nomination you seek. That major problem is that even if you obtain enough signatures to force a primary, your name cannot be on the ballot, and you have to win by write-in votes only. There is an exception, and that is if the primary you are running in is for a judicial position. I am not quite sure what the logic is behind that, but that is still the rule in the New York.

Although I should have thought long and hard about running a write-in primary, I didn't. I felt very strongly that Charlie Borgognoni was going to split up the vote in the column that listed Bob Cecile, me, and him, and the other two candidates in the other column would win, since there were only two candidates in that column.

To win the write-in primary, you not only had to get more votes than your opponent, but you had to educate voters on how to cast a write-in vote, which at the time was not an easy task. To do so, I first had to identify the voters that were likely to vote and convince them that since I was the better candidate, they should go through the exercise of writing my name in.

But, even before that exercise, I had to get on the ballot by having Conservative party members circulate petitions and get Conservative party members to sign the petitions to qualify for the write-in. Fortunately, I had enough Conservative party members who were willing to circulate petitions for me and get enough signatures. Winning the primary was a lot more difficult.

Not having done it before and not knowing anyone who had, I embarked on a city-wide write-in campaign. The first step was to contact every Conservative voter by mail. Just as I

thought, there were many registered Conservatives that were no longer living in the city, or were no longer registered Conservative. These people were easily eliminated.

The next step was to contact the properly registered Conservatives, first by telephone and then face-to-face. It was interesting to me that there were probably ten to fifteen percent of the people that I contacted that argued with me saying that they were not registered as Conservatives. So much for an informed electorate. When I finally showed them proof that they were registered as Conservatives, they believed me, but they were not too enthralled about getting involved in a Conservative primary.

Prior to contacting everyone, I checked their voting records, which you can do at the Board of Elections, to see if they voted regularly, not how they voted. To eliminate some of the people that I had to contact, I limited my contacts to those people who voted in the last races for these City Council seats.

In addition to contacting people myself, I got a copy of the list of city Conservative voters from the Board of Elections, which any candidate can do. I then made many copies of those lists and handed out copies to as many friends and relatives, as were willing to go through them and pick out the people they knew. Once that was done, I had those volunteers contact the people first and give me an introduction to them so that I didn't have to make a cold call to try to get in their doors.

By the process of elimination, I was able to identify the people that were likely to vote, and those that I thought would be willing to write in my name, as opposed to pulling the lever of the Conservative party endorsed candidate, Charlie Borgognoni. Although, at that time, the candidate who had the Conservative line usually received around 2,000 votes in the general election, the vast majority of those votes were

from individuals who were not registered as Conservatives. When it got down to it, there were probably no more than 300 to 400 hundred registered Conservatives that were likely to vote in the city Conservative primary for councilor-at-large.

To get to these 300 to 400 hundred voters it took many phone calls and face-to-face meetings, but the numbers were actually manageable. Of these 300 to 400 voters, I knew I was not likely to get the party officers and the regular Conservative Party volunteers to vote for me, since they endorsed Charlie Borgognoni.

As a result, I concentrated on the rest, but did not ignore the party officers and regulars. I'm convinced that some of them did vote for me after they got to know the two candidates, and after they learned that Borgognoni did not get the endorsement of the Democratic Party, and would not likely win the general election on a minor party line alone.

Once I had voters that I thought would vote for me identified, I then prepared a short written document, giving instructions as to how to cast a write-in vote. Prior to running this write-in primary, I had no clue how to cast a write-in vote myself and I was sure none of the people that I was writing to did either. I sent these instructions only to the voters I thought I would have a chance with.

That wasn't the end of it. I spoke to many of the individuals and described to them the write-in vote process and again encouraged them to vote for me. Some of them were so impressed with the efforts that I was making to obtain their vote, that they actually began helping me by talking to some of their friends who were registered Conservatives.

The week before the primary election, and again on Election Day, I made calls to each of the voters we had identified, reminding them to vote for me, and reminding them how to do it.

The night of the primary election I had great anticipation because of the amount of work that we had put in to attempt to win this write-in primary. The excitement quickly dissipated as the vote totals were being reported on television. It was reported that Borgognoni got 118 votes and John DeFrancisco got none. Although I knew it would be difficult to win this primary, something had to be wrong since some of the people assured me that they would write in my name.

When it came time to canvas the voting machines, which every candidate is allowed to do to check the accuracy of the vote, my wife, Linda, took on the responsibility of accompanying the election inspectors to each of the polling booths to look for votes. This took place two days after the primary. As it turned out, at nearly every polling place, the election inspectors didn't bother to open up the back of the machines to see if there were any write-in votes. This was understandable. There were so few write-in campaigns that this procedure was not normally done.

When the machines were finally opened and the write-ins tallied, I was getting close to the 118 votes. If it wasn't for my wife's insistence on opening some of the machines that the inspectors claimed had no write-ins on them, I would never have known that I actually got more votes. As it turned out, the final tally was Borgognoni with 118 votes (by people pulling his lever), and me with 121 write-ins. This was incredible. In fact, this write-in primary was more difficult than every general election I've had. I was sure that after having done this once, I would never attempt it again, and I didn't.

The other interesting thing about opening the backs of the machines and finding write-in votes, was learning who else got votes. We found Mickey Mouse and Donald Duck were favored by some voters over Borgononi and me.

The general election was actually anti-climactic. I won one of the two seats by a large margin, and the votes cast on

the Conservative line didnt turn out to be even a factor. However, I didn't know that would be the case at the time that I had to make the decision on running the write-in primary campaign. Interestingly, I received the Conservative endorsement every election thereafter.

More amazingly, in the 2010 U.S. Senate race in Alaska, Lisa Murkowski, the incumbent Republican Senator, did not receive the Republican party endorsement. That endorsement instead went to Joe Miller, who was favored by individuals who were part of the movement of the day, that of the Tea Party. Although the Tea Party was not a formally recognized party, this movement was big in the elections of 2010.

Senator Murkowski did not give up and, in fact, continued the race as a write-in candidate. Needless to say, this was quite an undertaking, especially since Miller was also supported by former Alaskan governor and former vice presidential candidate, Sarah Palin.

Despite the odds, Senator Murkowski won the general election for U.S. Senate by having more people write in her name than those who pulled the lever for Joe Miller. The final write-in vote for Senator Murkowski was 102,091, and lever vote for Miller was 90,839. The Democratic candidate, Scott McAdams came last with 60,045 votes. Needless to say, this was an incredible victory, being a successful write-in campaign in a state-wide general election for the U.S. Senate. Write-in victories are few and far between.

There are discussions year after year as to whether legislation should be drafted to either eliminate the third parties or increase the number of votes necessary for the third party to get on the ballot from 50,000 to a greater number, which would effectively block most, if not all, third parties from the ballot. However, despite the discussions, there aren't enough legislators bold enough to support the legislation. If unsuccessful in passing the legislation, the chances of

these representatives ever getting third party endorsements again would be slim to none.

FREEDOM OF
THE PRESS

The first amendment of the United States Constitution protects free speech and the freedom of the press. The concept of free speech is pretty straight forward. Of course there are some limits, such as the protection against libel and slander for malicious and untruthful statements.

The explosion of the internet and such easily abused creations such as political blogs, sponsored by virtually every media outlet, increases the chances of a person being libeled by an anonymous poster. I believe that if someone wants to blog negatively about people, they should at least be identifiable. There is little more frustrating than reading an anonymous untrue malicious comment about you on a political blog. Why should the writer be shielded from a remedy for anonymously untruthfully maligning someone else? Hopefully, at some point there will be a real remedy.

Freedom of the press is also a very clear concept to most. The press is so free, except in rare occasions, that the reporter and the newspaper need not disclose sources of information. But once again, what if the information is untrue? What remedy does the target of the article have against the

individual who libels him or her? If you are a public figure the standard that must be met to obtain redress is virtually impossible to meet, namely proof of actual malice.

But does freedom of press mean that the press can advocate for and promote a specific point of view, a political party, or a favored candidate? That answer is clearly "yes" and it may come as a surprise to some, but it happens all of the time, not only on the editorial page where opinion is expected, but in news articles as well. More people became aware of this during the Trump/Clinton 2016 Presidential race and thereafter. I saw it many years before.

The first time that I really noticed it during my time in elected office was in 1981, and it occurred during a primary race for mayor. I had no personal involvement in the race, nor any horse in it. It was the Democrat primary for Mayor of the City of Syracuse. Mel Zimmer, a well-liked and well-respected state Assemblyman, was running a primary against the incumbent Mayor Lee Alexander. Needless to say, it was an uphill battle for Zimmer and would have been an uphill battle for anyone else against the then popular mayor. A few years later, however, he was indicted, found guilty, and sentenced to ten years in prison for corruption,which included receiving kick-backs. He spent six years in jail and then died three years after his release at age 69.

At the time of the primary, however, Lee Alexander was at the top of his game. But Zimmer thought he could do better and had a lot of support in that primary campaign. Most thought that the race was going to be close. Apparently, so did the Syracuse newspapers, since they weighed in on it, subtlety, but effectively.

On the Saturday before the Tuesday primary, the newspaper ran an article with the headline something like "Mel Zimmer's insurance company refuses to pay claim." Well, there are three occupations that the public hates the most,

and I am not quite sure which is on the top of the list, but they include politicians, lawyers and insurance companies.

The headline was a pretty powerful one, but with little relevance in the campaign other than to turn people against Zimmer. The subtle message was "How could anyone vote for someone who works for an insurance company that fails to pay a claim?"

Well, the story went on to explain that a woman lost an expensive ring when it fell into a garbage disposal. She made a claim against the insurance company that issued her policy. The insurance company denied the claim. No doubt, those reading the article up to this point, and after seeing the headline, would have come to the conclusion that Zimmer and his company were simply no good.

The first problem with that conclusion is that Zimmer had his own insurance agency and was not an employee of the company that issued the policy and denied the claim. Mel was a selling agent for many insurance companies and sold different policies issued by various insurance companies. He didn't deny the claim. The insurance company that issued the policy did ! This, in and of itself, should have made this a non-story. However, that didn't stop the Syracuse newspapers from this damaging headline, less than three days before the primary election.

So what did the newspaper have against Mel Zimmer? Absolutely nothing. However, I don't believe it was a coincidence that, in the past, Mel's father helped in a movement to unionize newspaper workers. So you don't have to do anything wrong to raise the ire of the print media, the sins of your father are more than enough.

It gets better. For those people that actually got around to reading the whole article they would have learned in the last paragraph, that the insurance company had a reason to deny the claim—the woman had not paid her insurance pre-

mium. That seemed like a pretty good defense for the insurance company, but it wasn't a good enough reason for the newspaper not to publish the story. But there *was* a reason to publish it, namely, to create a negative headline in order to hurt the newspaper's disfavored candidate, and help the the paper's choice.

Also the media loves to come out for reform of government, the reform that they want, not necessarily reform that is needed. When I was first sworn in as a Syracuse Common Councilor, there was a provision in the Charter of the City of Syracuse that created a Board of Estimate. The Board of Estimate's responsibility was to make virtually all financial decisions for the City of Syracuse, including what consultants and professionals the City hired.

In reviewing the composition of the Board of Estimate, it was obvious that it was not only redundant, but it was simply a cover for the Mayor of the City of Syracuse, whomever he or she might be, to make all these financial decisions under the cloak of a truly fictitious Board. This was clear since the membership of the Board included the Mayor, his appointed Commissioner of Finance, and the president of the Syracuse City Council. Obviously, even if the president of the City Council was independent, the Mayor, with the ability to hire and fire the Commissioner of Finance, would always control the Board of Estimate's decisions.

As a result, I thought it would be a good idea to get rid of this fictitious board that simply provided cover for the Mayor on financial decisions. I asked the corporation counsel, David Garber, to prepare a proposed ordinance that would eliminate the Board of Estimate. That ordinance would have to be passed by the Common Council, and then put to the voters at the next election in November. I thought it was a reasonable request to ask the corporation counsel to do this since he had the obligation to represent both the Mayor and the Common

Council. He chose to back the Mayor, who hired him, and refused to prepare the ordinance.

Fortunately, I was a lawyer so I prepared the ordinance myself and got it passed by the Common Council. It was then put on the ballot in November. Of course, the Syracuse newspapers weighed in on the issue. Its editorial board's argument was that we should keep the Board of Estimate because "if it's not broke, don't fix it." With the help of the Syracuse newspapers and their deep insight on this issue, the proposal was soundly defeated.

A couple of years thereafter, Lee Alexander was indicted and a good part of the indictment was about taking kick-backs from consultants and professionals, who, by the way, were approved by the Board of Estimate (i.e. the Mayor). Well, apparently something was broken and, as a result, I prepared the same ordinance, which was again passed by the Common Council, and put to the voters the following November. Well, the Syracuse newspaper apparently saw the light, since they editorialized in favor of the change in the Charter this time, which would eliminate the Board of Estimate, and the proposal passed overwhelmingly. Apparently, reform was needed.

Fast forward to the 2010 elections. These elections were one of the most important ever in New York state. As a Republican member of the State Senate, I experienced two years when state government was under the total control of New York City democrats. The governor was David Paterson (New York City), his appointed lieutenant governor was Richard Ravitch (New York City), the leader of the Assembly was Sheldon Silver (New York City), the leaders of the Senate were Malcom Smith (New York City), and later, John Sampson (New York City), and the Attorney General, was Andrew Cuomo (New York City), all democrats.

During 2009 and 2010, virtually every decision of im-

portance was made to benefit New York City. For example, when the Metropolitan Transportation Authority, which runs the subways and trains in the New York City metropolitan area, was in trouble financially, it was bailed out, but there was little corresponding road and bridge money for upstate New York. When monies were doled out for home care of the elderly and infirm, 2.8 billion dollars was spent, 2.1 billion dollars of which went to New York City which had half of the population of the state. There are many other examples but suffice it to say that the 2010 election was an important one to attempt to at least wrestle the Senate from New York City and provide some semblance of regional balance, since Republicans in the Senate were mostly from upstate and Long Island.

With this backdrop, I spoke to the Syracuse newspaper's editorial board, spending virtually all of my time explaining how important this election was to upstate. However, this was never reported and certainly not advocated for by the newspaper, in my opinion, to the detriment of the region.

In any event, during the course of the 2010 elections, the Inspector General of the State of New York, a democrat, completed an investigation which concluded that a contract for running the Aqueduct Race Track in New York City was corrupted by information that had been leaked during a sealed bid process by Senate leaders John Sampson and Malcom Smith. The Inspector General also referred the matter for a criminal investigation, the allegation being that they attempted to steer the contract to a political crony. It seemed like a pretty important story but not to the Syracuse newspaper. Even though the downstate papers had extensive articles about this Inspector General's report, the incident was buried in a column with general state news.

At the same time, there was an important Senate race

going on between a republican candidate, Andrew Russo, and the incumbent democrat candidate, David Valesky. I received a call from a reporter asking me whether I received a $150 political contribution from a music organization run by Andrew Russo some five years earlier. I told him that I had no idea, but that all the reporter had to do was to go online and check on the Board of Election's website, since all campaign contributions were on file and available on the site. He said he had already done that, but he wanted my confirmation. I told him I don't remember, and thought no more about it.

Within a couple of weeks there was a headline at the top of the front page of the Syracuse Post Standard that Andrew Russo's organization had given John DeFrancisco $150. The article reported that this was an illegal contribution because the check came from an organization which received a state grant for young musicians. Andrew Russo's comment was that he did not remember the actual check, but that if it was from the organization and if it was improper, then he would rectify it. By the way, the Aqueduct contract that the Inspector General concluded was being illegally steered to a political friend by New York City Senate leaders Sampson and Smith was a $500 million contract.

Disproportionate coverage? Do you think? Russo ended up losing that election, but fortunately the senate republicans gained two other seats and took back control of the state Senate, so that at least there was a chance for some geographic balance and fairness in state government.

Another example. In the 2010 election cycle, the Attorney General, Andrew Cuomo, did not run for re-election since he ran for governor, and he was successful in doing so. This left an open seat for state Attorney General. There were five candidates for the position on the democrat side and one on the republican side. One of the democrat candidates was Eric Schneiderman. Schneiderman was a long time state Sen-

ator against who I debated on many many occasions. He was much too liberal for me, but that's not the story.

Remember, Eric Schneiderman was running for Attorney General, which is the top law enforcement officer in the state. During the primary campaign against his democrat opponents, Eric was a passenger in a car driven by one of his interns. When the intern side-swiped a parked New York 1 news vehicle they left the scene of the accident.

Fortunately, someone saw the accident, got the license plate number, and the car was tracked down. When asked why they left the scene of the accident, the police were told that they didn't realize that they had struck another vehicle, even though there was substantial damage to each vehicle.

The downstate papers fully reported the incident. It was never reported in the Syracuse newspapers. I would think that if someone who was running for the top law enforcement officer of the state had left the scene of a property damage accident, it would have relevance to some voters. However, the voters in central New York never heard about it, unless they surfed the internet or read papers from other areas of the state.

I called the Editor-in-Chief of the newspaper, Maria Morelli, and asked her why there was such little coverage on the Aqueduct investigation, and no mention whatsoever of the Eric Schneiderman story in the Syracuse newspapers. She responded that there was something about Aqueduct in the paper (buried in a general article). As to Schneiderman, she said that he was going to be meeting with the paper's editorial board the following week, and that she would ask him about the incident. Whether she did or didn't is unknown, but the incident was never reported in the Syracuse paper. And guess what? The newspaper endorsed Eric Schneiderman for state Attorney General and he won the election. He eventually resigned in 2018 on the heels of the #MeToo movement, when it

was revealed that he had abused several women. Go figure---he was a strong supporter of the movement.

The most outrageous example of the media's use of its constitutional protection of the freedom of the press, that I personally experienced, occurred during the 2016 legislative session. The month of March is the busiest of the legislative session because hearings are being held on the budget proposed by the governor. Not only are hearings being held but an inordinate amount of meetings with constituents, legislative staff and fellow Senators are held in order to determine the priorities for the budget.

During that busy time, I was stopped by a reporter, Ken Lovett, of the *NY Daily News* who asked me if I would be willing to answer a question that was totally unrelated to the budget. I delayed going into one of the budget meetings to answer his question. He asked me what I thought of a bill proposed by Assemblywoman Margaret Markey, which would eliminate criminal and civil statutes of limitations for child sex abuse cases.

I responded that I believed there was a legitimate purpose for statutes of limitations. I explained that justice required that trials be determined based on reliable evidence. The further away the trial is from the alleged incidents of wrongdoing, the less reliable the proof; witnesses die or are unavailable; and witness recollections fade over time. I explained that to allow for an unlimited period of time for an individual to bring a criminal or civil proceeding could result in a false verdict.

Unbeknownst to me the *NY Daily News* had been repeatedly reporting on this bill and trying to generate support to have it passed in the Assembly and the Senate. The reporter, apparently, also spoke to one of the other leaders in the Senate who indicated to him that we were in budget negotiations and that he did not then have time to really deal with that issue.

The following day, photographs of the other senator and me appeared on the front page of the *NY Daily News* with the caption "Predator Enablers." Towards the bottom on the page there was a line to the effect that DeFrancisco is more concerned about "pervs" than victims.

The next day before I saw the headlines, the reporter came up to me and apologized for the photograph and the headline, claiming that he had nothing to do with it, other than to report my answer of the previous day to his superiors. Quite frankly, I believed him since my quotes were accurate in the body of the article that extended over a couple of pages in the paper.

When I saw the front page and the article, I was absolutely furious. I considered writing a letter to the editor, expressing my opinion. After I cooled down, however, I realized that responding would only extend the story and extend the attacks on me.

Once the budget was done in mid-April, I went to Florida, as I did at that time on many Senate breaks, and spent time playing tennis and golf. On the tennis court, one of my fellow players, from Boston, Massachusetts, commented on the article. It didn't dawn on me until then that this article, on the front page of the *NY Daily News,* was read by so many, even those who are not involved in New York state politics. Fortunately, he was a lawyer and understood my answer, but I can't imagine how many people read it and didn't understand. This was truly embarrassing.

When I got back to Albany, and session reconvened, as always, my schedule was jammed with meetings, hearings, conferences, legislative sessions and the like. On one of those days, I had invited the Syracuse University Women's Basketball team to Albany to honor them in the Senate for earning runner up in the National Championship. The women were very proud of their success, as was I, when we honored them

with a Resolution on the Senate floor.

Before presenting the Resolution, the women, coaches and Syracuse University officials were all in my office, at my invitation, having pizza and soda, and celebrating their success. As was normally the case, I was moving from one meeting to another. One such meeting was on whether New York City Mayor Bill de Blasio should be given mayoral control of the New York City schools. I attended that education hearing and questioned Mayor de Blasio on the issue.

When I rushed back to my office, the Syracuse University Women's Basketball team and the others had already begun lunch. Before I could get into the conference room, there was a group of about six people who demanded to see me at that moment to discuss Markey's bill and my opposition to it. I learned later that, prior to my arrival, they had given my staff a very hard time when staff explained that there wasn't any time for me to see them that day.

When they demanded an immediate meeting, I politely told them that I just could not do it and that I was actually late and behind schedule. I offered to have them make an appointment to come back and see me on another day, but they continued to demand to see me right then and there. I told them again, I just couldn't do it.

I didn't know at the time but one of the individuals with this group was a photographer from the *NY Daily News*. Since there were many people in the conference room, some taking photographs, I didn't realize that the *NY Daily News* photographer came into the conference room unannounced and started taking photographs of the girls eating pizza and me talking to them.

You guessed it. These photos were on the front page of the *NY Daily News* the next day and the headline was "Pie in the Face." The main thrust of the article was that I had time to have pizza with people in my office but I didn't have time to

speak with the victims of child sex abuse and their advocates.

When I saw the article I immediately called the Syracuse University officials to alert them about the article and apologize, although there was nothing I could have possibly done about it. Unfortunately, it soured a very important day for these young ladies. On the other hand maybe they got a little education on the meaning of "freedom of the press."

Well it wasn't over yet. The following day another reporter approached me in session and asked me what I thought about the article in the paper. I didn't realize the reporter also worked for the *NY Daily News*. When he told me that he was referring to the article in the *NY Daily News,* I immediately said, "No comment." He continued to press by repeating the question "You have no comment about the article?"

Finally I said, "Yes I have a comment. I thought that the picture on the front page and the article were absolutely outrageous." I went on to say, that the group had no appointment and shouldn't have expected to come in at any time to talk to me or anyone else for that matter. I also told him "It was obviously a 'gotcha' moment, which was planned by the *NY Daily News*, having sent its photographer."

Needless to say, the next day there was another front page article with repeat photographs that their photographer had taken. The body of the article basically said that I had time to whine to their reporter about the ill treatment I received, but I didn't have time to meet with the victims and their advocates. Amazing, simply amazing! I had told the reporter, that the group didn't have an appointment but they were welcome to come another time, but that was not mentioned at all.

The group did make an appointment for the following week. Before meeting with them I thought it would be a good idea to make certain that what happened was recorded in some way. As a result, I had a videographer come to the meet-

ing to videotape everything that happened. Well, the group came in, together with a reporter, as well as the *NY Daily News* photographer. Again, this clearly was not a meeting to discuss the issues, it was a meeting to continue the *NY Daily News* attacks.

When we started the meeting, I learned that the members of the group were not even New York state residents, but rather, they came from Massachusetts. The first thing I asked them was whether they would mind if a videographer was in the room to record exactly what would transpire in the meeting. They said they had no problem, and thanked me for letting them know it was being videotaped. I couldn't help myself, so I responded, "Which is unlike the prior time you came to my office, when you brought the *NY Daily News* photographer with you, without informing me."

As it turned out, the 45-minute meeting was uneventful. I explained my position, they explained theirs, and everyone was cordial, with one exception. The photographer could not just take a few pictures of me, he needed to take at least fifty. At one point I stopped him and asked if he had enough photos. He replied "Not the right one." I then asked him if he wanted me to make a menacing face and put up my fists for a better photo for the next front page of his newspaper. He didn't answer, but he stopped taking photos.

There were more stories but the stories were beginning to be aimed at other individuals. It wasn't too long before the Syracuse *Post Standard*, picked up on the issue and reported about my position. In fact someone, who claimed he was abused as a child was reported to be ready to put up $100,000 to help candidates run against me and others in the Senate who were opposed to Markey's bill.

Another person, who was allegedly abused as a child, wrote a blistering letter to the editor alleging I was blocking legislation for the removal of the statute of limitations

for child sex abuse cases, and that it was "unconscionable, unethical, and immoral" to do so. That needed a response and I did so within 48 hours. First I explained my position and then I went into the fact that I was not blocking anything but expressing my opinion as to the merits of the bill, and that I would not support it. I concluded that as a legislator, I weighed all sides of an issue before taking a position. The fact that some may disagree with me is understandable and expected. However, no matter how many would disagree with my analysis and decision, I would continue to make the best decisions I could for my constituents and explain my reasons. I have no idea if my response did any good but it sure felt good to answer.

I rarely had a problem with newspapers reporting my position in a fair way, but the manner in which this issue was dealt with by the *NY Daily News*, including the vicious headlines and front page coverage, in my opinion, was way out of line. I even toyed with the idea of suing the paper, but as a public official, in addition to proving defamation, inaccuracies, and untruths in the reporting, you also had to prove that it was published with "actual malice." This standard is almost impossible to meet in a lawsuit. And no doubt, the bar was made so high because there is a constitutional protection of "freedom of the press."

Freedom of the press, in real life, means that the press is free to report and advocate for whatever it wants, with whatever information it has, and with whatever emphasis it chooses. After all, the Constitution guarantees it.

PR

In order to run for public office, and if elected, to properly perform your duties, you need to have good public relations. Good public relations starts at the top – with the candidate or the elected official. No matter how difficult the issue, one has to address it honestly and in a straight forward manner. The end of many candidates and public officials comes as soon as people realize that the person is telling them what they want to hear, not what the person truly believes. If you are honest with the people that you seek to represent or ultimately do represent, you won't win them over on every issue but, over time, the people will come to respect you.

I have seen so many public officials put their finger to the wind and once the wind was tested, make the decision of least resistance. That may get that official off the hook on that one issue, but soon there will be another issue. You can't always tell people what they want to hear or else you will be digging a deeper and deeper hole and putting yourself in a position you don't want to be in or shouldn't be in.

While in elective office, I disagreed with some people. Quite frankly, you can't agree with everyone all of the time. I often said to those who who disagreed with me on issues that I had been married for many years and my wife and I don't agree on everything, but we still loved each other. Whether they

think that was a cornball comment or not, I truly meant it. And I concluded by asking them to please look at all of my positions on all the issues that are of concern to them and, hopefully, we will agree more than we disagree. You simply can't be all things to all people, and you have to be true to yourself. If anything, it avoids trying to remember what you last said, and it avoids many sleepless nights.

With that principle in mind, you have to communicate to the public, whether you are a candidate or a public official. How do you do that? Well, it is pretty obvious that there are many different opportunities to get a message out. One is by paid commercials, through the electronic or print media. The main benefit of paid PR is that you can frame the message any way you want to frame it, and it's not going to be changed or colored by the media. The problem is that it's expensive.

In central New York it could cost anywhere from $3,000 to $10,000 to have a 30 second commercial produced, and anywhere from $100 to $10,000 to have that commercial aired on television for 30 seconds depending on what program it is aired on. It could cost $6,000 to $9,000 for a one page ad in the newspaper, and substantially more for a similar ad in newspapers in major cities.

Most candidates, especially for local office, simply cannot raise that kind of money and, therefore, cannot afford to spend it. During my first three races, I did one radio commercial for the school board campaign and two radio commercials for the city's councilor-at-large races, each airing for about two weeks. This was all I could afford.

It wasn't until I ran for president of the city council, my fourth race, that we had some television commercials. However, we were very careful in choosing the placement of those ads. Each television station and radio station, for that matter, will provide you with a list of programming and the corresponding costs for placement of the ads for each of those

programs. Clearly the most expensive programs are the ones that are those most watched. Many feel that it's best to hit these programs, even though it is an infrequent hit, because you are reaching more people. However, as a practical matter, sometimes you simply can't; so rather than debate the philosophical arguments you have to make do with what money you have.

If a professional places your ads, generally 15 percent of the cost is kept by the agency for its services. In later campaigns for the Senate, we did our own ad placements, and were able to save the 15 percent so our budget went a lot further.

What I found out about television ads when I first used them during my campaign for president for city council, was that more people recognized me when I was out campaigning on the streets. I mentioned earlier that I am big on going to bingos, bowling alleys, and wherever else many people congregate. It was amazing to me to hear people say "Oh, yes, I recognize you from TV."

Needless to say, this repetition of seeing you and hearing from you gets the voter's attention and, hopefully, convinces him or her that you are the person to vote for. Some were impressed at meeting a "celebrity" who was on television, and openly expressed their excitement in seeing me. This was in stark contrast to those who previously angrily walked by me, not wanting to take my campaign stuff.

There is a danger, however, in television advertisements, and that is the negative ad. I could always tell who was behind in a political race by who went negative first. There is no doubt that negative campaigning is effective if you are the candidate that's behind. For example, if the polls show that you are losing by 60 percent to 40 percent, and that your opponent has a favorability rating of 60 percent, the only way you are going to have a chance to win is to get people to understand that your opponent is not who they think he or she is

and not someone for whom they want to vote.

When I say negative ads work, especially when you are behind in the race, I must clarify that, since there are negative ads and "negative ads." What I believe works is getting out the voting record of the individual who you are running against and trying to convince voters that that person is not someone who has beliefs consistent with theirs. Some call these negative ads because your opponent is being criticized. This criticism is not "negative", if the ads are true, and the ads are tastefully done.

The negative ads that don't work and that people have become fed up with, are those ads that just take cheap shots and make wild untrue or misleading negative claims about the opponent. In the 2010 Senate race, I received more compliments on my television ads than ever before, since they were positive. In fact, the commercials featured well-known people that praised my work in the Senate. For the production of these ads a cameraman simply asked a few questions of the constituents to get them to speak in their own words and from the heart about my work and how it affected them. Those remarks were then edited into several concise 30 second commercials. People thought that this was wonderful, especially in view of the attack ads that were used in several other legislative and congressional races that were aired at the same time.

Another very effective ad was done at the end of an especially negative campaign. It was a year when the congressional candidates on both sides were throwing the most mud ever, which adversely affected all candidates that were running. People just wanted the campaign season to end, since they were tired of all politicians. The ad we played the last two weeks of that campaign showed me with an American flag in the background, simply asking people to exercise their right and duty to vote on Election Day, no matter for whom

they voted. Because of the excessive mudslinging that year, this ad was very well received.

But there are other effective ways to promote the candidate or the public official. Free media is one of the best. By free media I mean when the candidate or the elected official calls a news conference or sends out a press release. You would be surprised the number of times that press releases were picked up by the print media, usually weekly newspapers, and became the basis of a news story. Similarly, as a member of the Senate, on virtually every occasion when I sent a release to the media announcing my availability to discuss various topics, either the print or the electronic media, or both, would show up to hear what I had to say on the topic and ask questions. It also gave the media the opportunity to ask unrelated questions that they wanted to ask.

I would like to think that this phenomenon occurred because of my expertise in selecting issues and my eloquence in explaining my positions. However, more often than not, there was some space to fill on the evening news or there were some pages to fill in the newspaper. The reason why a story was picked up was totally immaterial to me, as long as the information I wanted to get out actually got out accurately to the public.

One of the greatest things that ever happened in New York state for public officials, at least those who wanted to explain what was happening in their office, was , a 24-hour tv news program ---"Your News Now" (YNN). Its name has changed over the years. If you sat down and thought how difficult it is to put on news for 24 hours, then you would realize why there was such interest in my media availabilities by this station. An added benefit was when there weren't a lot of news stories to report on, your story would be broadcast over and over again.

This opportunity was essential to me in communicating

on issues that were important to me. And, despite my concern for some editorial writers and newspaper publishers, almost every electronic media reporter was someone I was able to easily work with because they were honest and unbiased in my dealings with them. One of my favorites was the late Bill Carey from YNN. I think there was a mutual respect between us, since he knew I was always being straight with him, and he always knew I would answer whatever question he wanted to ask me. It was very sad when Bill passed away in 2015 after a long fight with cancer. He was a true professional.

Actually, this was true for most reporters in electronic media. Dan Cummings, of News Channel 9, was knowledgeable, professional and fair, as was Christie Casciano of the same station, and Laura Hand of WSTM. Many newspaper reporters were knowledgable, and professional as well. Occasionally, some would have an agenda, usually set by the publisher, but the writers who I dealt with over the years, with some notable exceptions, truly wanted to provide fair, accurate and unbiased reporting.

The candidate or public official can also get excellent PR by simply seeking out speaking opportunities and speaking before large groups. My first large speaking engagements were when I was a member of the Syracuse school board. I spoke at a couple of high school graduations. At first it was very intimidating, but as I did more and more public speaking, the more comfortable I felt and the better it seemed to work out. I knew many public officials that simply did not want to be bothered. I don't know how a candidate or an elected official can pass up these opportunities. Not only should they be accepting these speaking engagements, but they should be actively seeking them out.

Over my more than 40 years in elective office, I have had many many candidates ask me for advice. Invariably, I would explain to them that they wouldn't always be able

to afford paid media so they would have to get as much free media as they possibly could. I explained to them about news releases, notices of news conferences, and media availabilities, but the candidates seemed rarely to follow my advice. I am sure that some tried to get some free media and maybe they weren't successful because they were new candidates, but the important thing is that you have to keep trying to get as much free media as you possibly can.

One of the most important advantages that an incumbents have is that they can communicate by mail with constituents. They can also communicate by email or twitter with their constituents, which is virtually free. In any event, if you are an incumbent and do not use these opportunities effectively, you probably shouldn't be in public office.

Many are going to complain that you shouldn't be spending taxpayers' money for mailings. However, I believe that you have an obligation to continue to inform your constituents of what is happening and what your positions are on issues. Obviously, there are a lot of useless things that elected officials send out, which communicates nothing other than photographs and stories about themselves. However, if there are important issues, and you have things that your constituents should be informed of, these opportunities should not be ignored.

At some point while a member of the Senate I began sending congratulatory letters to people when we learned that they did something special. For the most part, these letters were going to students who had done something exceptional. I refined that, as time went on, by purchasing a laminating machine for my office. Once I had the laminating machine, I would laminate the article, or I should say my staff would laminate the article, and send it with a congratulatory letter. However, I would always review and sign every letter.

What I learned, over time, was that no matter what

your positions were on various issues, the thing that people remembered most were congratulatory letters. During my campaigns and while I was out in public in non-election years, I would be stopped frequently and thanked for sending these communications.

I know that many elected officials simply send out form letters on various inquiries that come to their office and don't actually communicate. I think that this is a huge mistake. All officials have to use form letters from time-to-time when the official gets large groups sending identical letters. However, there is no excuse for not answering each other letter or responding to each email individually.

Every letter that came to my office came across my desk. If it was a form letter I would be told that by my staff. I would then prepare a form letter that the staff could use to respond to the form letter that came in. As to the individual letters, I would read every one of them, and jot notes in the margins as to how I wanted to respond to them. This was true also for emails. Every piece of correspondence deserved and got an answer from me. Obviously, I didn't write every letter, but I gave clear directions in the margins of each letter as to how it should be responded to and then I reviewed each letter for content, and made certain that it was expressed in the way I wanted to express it.

I didn't always agree with people. If I didn't agree with someone, I would say so and I would explain to them why. I don't think there is anything more annoying to an individual who has a genuine concern than receiving a response from an elected official that gives the impression that official agrees with them, and then they later find out that the official votes in another way. That person will never trust that official again. However, even though the official doesn't agree with the person, at least if the official is upfront with the constituent, the constituent eventually, when they agree on other

issues, will respect that official.

Of course you can't have good PR if you don't do anything worth doing. And you can't have good PR if you are on the wrong side of issues. You simply have to work hard to understand the issues and make good decisions. Also, you have to work hard to introduce and pass bills that you think are needed and push this legislation until it becomes law. And you should do everything you can to stop bad legislation. In short, good PR is not possible unless you have accomplished something and have something worthwhile to say.

GETTING MORE VOTES THAN THE OTHER GUY

Other than being a resident of the jurisdiction that includes the position you are running for, and being over 18 years of age, the only other qualification to become an elected official is to get more votes than your opponent. Much has been mentioned above as to how to do just that. However, there are a couple of very important parts of a campaign that are often overlooked, or not given enough emphasis – absentee voting and getting the vote out.

Candidates try to meet as many people as possible in order to try to convince those people to vote for him or her. There are some people you may never meet during the course of a campaign, including those who vote by absentee ballot. Absentee voters are people who are out of the voting district temporarily. They include military personnel, and others, who are unable to vote in the district on election day. Sick or infirm residents who cannot personally go to their election location can also vote by absentee ballot.

Unfortunately, many campaigns ignore these people

when they are relatively easy to reach. What I have done in every campaign since I started in 1981, when I had an opponent, was to write to all absentee voters. It's really not that difficult to do.

The content of the letter is very simple. On some occasions it was a letter introducing myself with my qualifications and asking the absentee voter for their vote. On occasion I would also include a sample section of the ballot that included my name as it appeared on the ballot circled for emphasis.

The beauty of the absentee contact is that you can prepare the letter and any inserts early in the campaign. You can also seal and stamp the letters and have them ready to go, except for the addresses. The addresses are the easiest part since you can get a set of labels from the Board of Elections consisting of the people to whom the Board is sending absentee ballots.

The key is to send the letter out slightly before or at least no later than the date that the Board of Elections sends out the official absentee ballots. This way the individual gets your correspondence at the same time he or she is actually going to open up the ballot to fill it out.

The first batch of absentee ballots is the largest – for a Senate district it runs in the thousands. We would get the labels just before the Board of Elections was going to send out the absentee ballots. Then we would put the labels on the already stuffed and stamped envelopes, and take them directly to the post office. As I said, the timing of this mailing is essential. It doesn't do much good for the absentee voter to get your letter after he or she has already filled out the absentee ballot.

But that's not the end of it. People apply for absentee ballots after the first batch of ballots are sent out all the way up to the day before the election. We had a system worked out, which got refined as computers became an essential part in

campaigns. In my earlier campaigns, each morning we would have someone, usually a good friend, Paul Geiss, go to the Board of Elections with the fully stamped and stuffed envelopes, get the labels for those voters whose absentee ballots were going to be sent out that day, affix the labels and take them right to the post office. This was a daily occurrence, since absentee ballots went out every day of the week from right after the first large group was sent out to the day before the election.

In the more recent elections, the Board of Elections would electronically send us the addresses the day those absentee ballots were going to go out, and we would print those addresses onto labels at the campaign office or at someone's home, affix the labels to the letters, and take them to the post office. Fortunately, none of my elections were close enough for the absentee ballots to make a difference, but "Hey, you never know."

Many close elections for state Senate weren't officially decided until months after the election. As a result, absentee ballots that had to be opened and counted were essential to the final outcomes. Of the 62 Senate races, in 2010, three were too close to call and the final winner in one race was not declared until December 21st. But this wasn't the record. In the November 2004 election, Nick Spano was declared the winner on February 8, 2005 – some three months after the election. Absentee votes did make a difference.

Another extremely important part of the election process is the "get out the vote" efforts. It's very difficult for any single campaign committee to coordinate an entire "get out the vote" campaign. It requires many people and requires an awful lot of coordination. The best "get out the vote" campaigns happen when a group of candidates, for example, city council candidates from all over the city, band together and get their vote out through a joint "get out the vote" effort. The

ideal situation would be if the political party actually had a strong joint effort so that everyone participated in a coordinated way. In my experience this rarely happened.

However, when I was a member of the city council and was running for president of the Common Council, all the republican city council candidates got together in a very coordinated campaign, not only on issues, but also in getting out the vote. This effort was so successful in 1989 that the republicans took over the majority of the city council from the democrats, in a democrat dominated city. Unfortunately, this was the last time that the republicans got control of the Syracuse Common Council. How was this successful effort accomplished?   The concept was quite simple. The execution was a lot tougher. The first step was to have a meeting with all polling inspectors and other individuals who would volunteer to be at the polls that day. Each of the individuals who was assigned to a specific election district was given a list of voters, in triplicate, just like the list the inspectors received to check in voters.

The first step was for these volunteers at the polling locations to cross off the names of individuals as they came in to vote. We then had drivers who would go to each of the election districts on three separate occasions to pick up the lists. The first run was usually around 1:00 or 2:00 o'clock in the afternoon on election day. One of the triplicate set of voter sheets was given to these drivers to bring back to the central headquarters. Then phone calls were made to registered republicans and conservatives who had not voted as yet, and whose names had not been crossed out.

The logic behind this approach was to avoid having to call people that had already voted and avoid annoying those people. It also provided for a smaller list of potential calls. No matter how many volunteers you may have, it's never enough. The most important run by the drivers was the one around

5:00 pm. The second copy of the list of voters, with the people who already voted crossed off , was picked up and brought to the central headquarters for a continuation of the calls. Fortunately, as the day wore on and as you picked up each list, there were fewer and fewer calls to make. The final list was picked up at approximately 7:00 pm, after which the final calls were made.

Now there are more sophisticated get out the vote efforts with more steps to them, but this one worked extremely well on that occasion. Other methods have developed since then, which I don't believe are very helpful. For example, many people simply do robo calls. Robo calls are calls that are pre-recorded calls to each voter asking them to vote for a specific candidate. With these calls being so inexpensive, many candidates use the calls, but by election day just about every voter is tired of them, leaving the call to his or her answering machine. A live voice is much more acceptable to a voter than robo calls, but live calls can also be very annoying especially in years with many races.

In 2010, I actually received an email offering the services of several actors who were willing to record a call advocating that people vote for me. I was fascinated by this, but I guess I shouldn't have been. I guess if you are willing to pay, you can get a famous actor to speak on your behalf. Many former elected officials recorded calls for candidates as well. I have my doubts whether this technique works.

There is another component of the "get out the vote" campaign that is very important. If a caller contacted someone who simply couldn't get to the polls, for whatever reason, we would offer that person a ride to his or her polling location. As a result, we needed a group of drivers that would pick up the voter and bring them to vote. I often wondered how many of the people that we drove to the polls actually didn't vote for our candidate, but rather voted for the opposition

and then had a good chuckle about it. Hopefully, not many.

There's really little downside in doing a get out the vote campaign since even when the efforts don't go very well, you at least kill some time on election day, keeping your nerves in check until the votes are counted.

ELECTION DAY

Election day is clearly the longest of all days in a political campaign. Obviously, the tension is at its highest, and the day never seems to end. The reason is simple--- your motor is still running to the maximum and there isn't really a lot left that can be done to change the outcome of the election.

Presumably, the get out the vote efforts are in place with volunteers at each of the polls, callers at the various headquarters to contact voters to make sure that they got to the polls, and drivers lined up to provide rides to voters who need transportation. This process got more sophisticated as time went on with the use of cell phones; and ultimately, iPhones and iPads resulting in much faster and better communications.

But the candidate cannot do much on election day other than to try to make sure that the "get out the vote" procedures are being followed. What the candidate really does is to try to stay busy and be seen as much as possible.

A tradition of many candidates is to purchase donuts or cupcakes or pastries or something to deliver to the polling inspectors at as many polling locations as possible during election day morning. It's a wonderful gesture to say thanks to the poll watchers and polling inspectors for an otherwise

thankless job. However, what is really happening is that the candidate is in the polling place and seen by those in line waiting to vote. This, not-so-subtle reminder, does help; at least candidates believe that it does. If it doesn't work, at least it burns some time and nervous energy.

During my early campaigns, I used to make these rounds with Mike Sommers and later with a childhood friend, Dom Episcopo, who later became a town councilor in the town of Geddes. There are certain rules about campaigning in or about polling places. The rules are simple – you can't campaign within 100 feet of a polling place. Candidates bearing gifts for polling inspectors is technically not campaigning, but it really is, though seldom enforced.

The other practice, which really gets close to the line, is when candidates visit polling places after the cookies and donuts run out. When Mike Sommers was accompanying me to these polling places during my early years of campaigning, he devised another technique. Technically, candidates, if properly designated as poll watchers, can go into the polling places and check to see the voter turnout, and whether there were more democrats or republicans turning out. Actually, this is part of the get out the vote process where voter's names are crossed off of lists when they come to vote. Those lists, appropriately eliminating those who voted, are then brought to the phone banks so that the phoners have only to call those voters that have not turned out.

But Mike had another twist. So that I could be seen, we would go to the polling places and he would promptly announce that he is here with John DeFrancisco, and we just want to find out how many republicans and how many democrats turned out. He would tell them that he wanted to put the results in his computer so that we could update the get out the vote. His computer happened to be a simple calculator in which he would enter the various numbers but the numbers

were never added.

It didn't help get the vote out, but it certainly reminded a few of the people that were standing in line to vote that John DeFrancisco was working hard, even on election day. This was done generally in the afternoon and early evening hours when polling inspectors were sick of cookies, donuts and the other sweets.

During the early afternoon and evening visits, I would cringe because Mike was not very shy about announcing my name and my presence. However, by that time, with the adrenaline still pumping, you want to try and get every vote that you possibly can, and it sure gave us something to do while the minute hand on the clock didn't seem to move.

But the best way to make time pass each election day was to eat a spaghetti lunch and dinner at the Our Lady of Pompei Catholic School. Yes, I did say lunch and dinner, since on election day I would have spaghetti for both meals at Our Lady of Pompei.

Every candidate that was running for office would go to either the lunch or the dinner. I may have been the only one who went to both. The food was great and you got to commiserate with other candidates. Well, you actually commiserate and blow a little smoke at the same time.

I wished good luck to numerous candidates over the years that I had already voted against. It doesn't hurt to be nice to everyone. The other candidates reciprocated and told me what they thought I wanted to hear.

Also, everyone made predictions as to who was going to win the various races. When my good friend, Tony Aloi, ran for County Court Judge for the first time, I saw him at the Our Lady of Pompei spaghetti luncheon. He was literally a nervous wreck. I told him not to worry, since he was going to win. I also told him the percentage that he was going to win by. It

turned out that I was right on the money, as far as his ultimate victory margin. To this day he believes I'm a sensational political genius. But you learn in politics that if you make enough predictions some will turn out to be correct.

Since Our Lady of Pompei was my parish, I knew just about everyone that attended the luncheon or dinner and it was great seeing everyone. They all wished me luck and, as it turned out probably the majority of them really meant it, since I won all of my races over the years. However, if all of the people who told me that they voted for me actually did, I would have won every race unanimously. My favorite was when people told me that they voted for me, and I asked them where they lived, and found out that they didn't even live in my district. However, I'm sure that they were just trying to be nice.

The other benefit of attending the Our Lady of Pompei luncheon or dinner or both is that all of the television stations and radio stations sent reporters. A last minute interview certainly doesn't hurt, especially since the polls didn't close until 9:00 pm, and those who hadn't voted as yet may see a last minute interview. What was particularly amusing is when the camera would show two candidates that were running against each other laughing and joking in the same television spot, when days earlier it took all that they had not to grab each other by the throat.

Between lunch and dinner and after dinner at Our Lady of Pompei there were numerous stops at campaign headquarters where the "get out the vote" operations were taking place. The key was to make sure the runners that were picking up the various cross-off sheets at the polls did their jobs, and that the callers got the annotated lists so that they didn't bother people who had already voted. Also, the candidates always wanted to make sure that there were enough drivers to pick up people who had called headquarters for a ride.

Usually in the years that I wasn't running, I would help at the campaign headquarters to organize the get out the vote and to make sure it got executed properly. There were a couple of situations that I recall vividly.

The first one was when Nick Pirro had a primary against Jim Walsh to determine the republican candidate for County Executive. There were hundreds of people in and out of the campaign headquarters claiming to be doing something. Most were just sitting around having coffee and donuts.

I was asked by Nick to help organize and execute the get out the vote, along with his close friend, Jim Albanese. At one point during the day, I got totally upset when so many people were just sitting around. I remember getting on a chair or maybe a table and announcing that if you had nothing to do, you should grab some phone sheets for people in their neighborhoods and go home and start calling their neighbors to make sure that they got out to vote. I started getting on the drivers to make sure that they left to pick up people who had called much earlier. At one point, when there was little movement, I got on a chair or table and yelled out "just do it."

Joanie Antonacci, who co-owned a sporting good shop with her husband, went to her shop and made a hat with the words "just do it" on it. To the present day, Joanie and I commiserate over the fact that we should have gotten a copyright on that phrase before NIKE made the slogan the underpinnings of much of its advertising. Parenthetically, Joanie's son Bob got the political bug and began running for office, ultimately, becoming the comptroller of the County of Onondaga and serving well. He also ran, unsuccessfully, for state comptroller. And in 2018, he successfully ran to replace me in the senate. At his first fundraiser I presented him with the actual "Just do it" hat that his parents gave to me some 30 years earlier.

As it turned out, these last minute efforts probably

helped since Nick Pirro ended up beating Jim Walsh for the republican nomination for Onondaga County Executive by less than 100 votes. However, Walsh didn't do too badly either in that he later was elected and served many years as our area Congressman.

Another election day remembrance happened during a campaign for Mayor by democrat, turned republican, Roy Bernardi. Roy and his brain trust separated themselves in back room offices of his headquarters to manage the election day activities, apart from the normal human beings. I went to this hallowed ground to see what they were doing and learned that they were getting the election results from various districts and coming up with statistics to help determine where the voter turnout was too low for republicans and where it was too high for democrats.

What I remember most was that the television had projected Bernardi a loser before the brain trust on the Bernardi hallowed ground came up with their own prediction. But the group looked very important, and no doubt they all would have claimed credit for his victory had he won.

As election day moved slowly on and you got closer to the 9:00 pm witching hour when the polls closed, candidates got more and more nervous, and in some cases, paranoid. This showed the most when all people gather at the designated location for the election night party. Often many candidates have parties separate from the one put on by the county political party, especially those who are running for the first time. It wasn't until my last couple of elections that I actually had a separate room. Before then, I just would go to the party held by the republican Party to view the results as they came in.

What I used to get a great kick out of was when the republican party had their event at a hotel, many of the upper level candidates had separate meeting rooms reserved in the hotel so that they could make a grand entrance once they

won. I'm proud to say that even for the two occasions when I had a separate room, I never did that. I mingled with the committee people and volunteers on election night each time I ran. I never made a grand entrance.

Members of the media attended either the republican or democrat election night party so that they could broadcast live the reactions of the various candidates. I was told that the reporters would jockey for what party they would attend, based on where the likely winners would be so they'd be at happy party and where they would likely have the better food and drink.

The psychology of an election night gathering is something that social scientists should truly study. Before the returns come in everyone is happy, complimentary of all of the candidates, and friendly with each other. It truly is a lot of fun and it's a great time to really thank people who helped over the many months of the campaign. There are really wonderful people that helped for no reason other than they think you would do a good job. That's politics at its best. Others are merely hangers-on hoping to get some benefit after doing absolutely nothing. What is most interesting about these evenings is what happens after the election results come in. It's really wonderful when you win, and not so much if you lose. Obviously, everyone gravitates towards the winners and ignores the losers.

Some of those who had helped candidates that lost would start bad-mouthing those candidates. Usually to save face, these fair weather friends would explain how the candidate refused to do all the brilliant things that they suggested, and had they been done, he or she would have won. This happened whether the candidate lost by 10 votes or 10,000 votes.

But what is the most enjoyable part of these evenings is when a candidate who wasn't expected to win, wins because of hard work by the volunteers and the candidate. This excite-

ment by volunteers is really wonderful to watch. It usually cements their interest in politics and their willingness to participate again. Unfortunately, as years have gone by since the start of my political career, fewer and fewer people are interested in participating. Hopefully, that will change. Whether it's at the local, state or federal level, good people have to get involved and true leaders must be elected.

PHOTOS

The Syracuse University baseball team (1968).

Onondaga County Republican elected officials. I'm in the front row, third from the right (1980).

Photo at the Executive Mansion with governor Mario Cuomo, future governor, George Pataki, former Senator John Sheffer and me (1992).

With a member of the International Boxing Hall of Fame, Floyd Patterson, upon his confirmation by my Senate Committee to become the head of the New York State Athletic Commission (1995).

With the greatest running back of all time, Jim Brown, at the unveiling of a sculpture of him at our alma mater, Syracuse University (1996).

With Special Olympian, governor George Pataki, and other elected officials at the New York State Fair (1998).

Sharing a hug with Sandy Scaccia at an event recognizing her as a New York State Senate Women of Distinction honoree (1999).

Fishing with then governors Jesse Ventura and George Pataki, on Onondaga Lake in payment of a wager by the governors on the New York Giants/Minnesota Vikings NFC Championship (2000).

At the scene of the 9/11 disaster, less than two months after
the attack (2001).

With Bo Diddley at the Blues Fest in Syracuse (2005).

With Dave Brubeck when he visited the state senate (2006).

Wishing Senator John Marchi farewell on his retirement from the NYS Senate after decades of outstanding service (2006).

Playing saxophone with Central New York music legend Joe
Whiting (2007).

With the Dalai Lama at his visit to the state Capitol (2009).

With Richard Gere at the North Syracuse Meals on Wheels, where his parents volunteered for years. (2009).

Governor David Patterson's State of the State message (2010). Where's Waldo ?

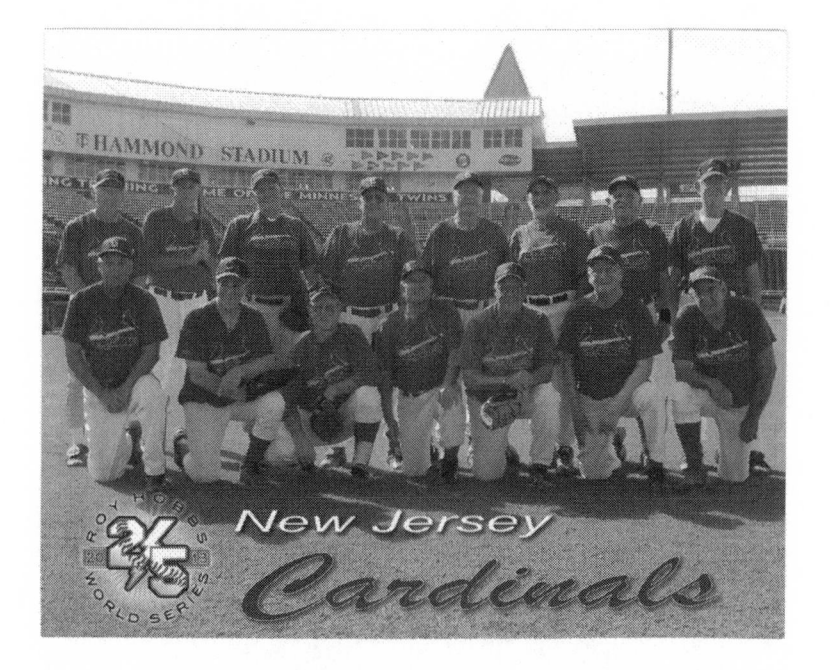

The New Jersey Cardinals team of the Roy Hobbs League, Ft. Myers, Florida. Again in the front row center some 45 years later (2013).

With Don Fida, decorated World War II veteran, upon his induction into the New York State Veterans' Hall of Fame (2015).

With the Tuskegee Airmen when they were honored by the New York State Senate (2016).

With Cardinal Timothy Dolan in Albany (2016).

Reform run amok! Sign at the NY State Library Association's lobby day breakfast with legislators (2012).

PART II- BEING THERE

NOW WHAT?

I f you are fortunate enough to win an election, your first question is: "Now What"? That was Robert Redford's first question in the 1972 movie by Warner Brothers, *The Candidate*. In this movie, Redford was recruited to run for office having no prior political experience. Those who ran his campaign reshaped his image and his political philosophy in such a way that he surprisingly won. Once the election was over and the election night hoopla was winding down, Redford sat by himself and asked that question: "Now What?"

I didn't ask the question, but I certainly thought about that question after winning my first race for the school board. The reason I ran was to change a policy of the school board that was tearing the community apart. As mentioned before, prior to the election, a new superintendent, Sid Johnson, resolved the issue. As a result, the issue that caused me to run no longer needed to be resolved.

However, I soon learned that there were plenty of issues facing all elected officials during their terms of office. It also quickly became obvious that members of boards and legislative bodies had to reach a consensus before a decision is made and consensus is not easy. This is especially true when a majority of individuals of all political philosophies from far left to far right, had to agree.

The best advice I think I got from anyone in my early years in elected office was from a former high school teacher of mine, Walt Ludovico. Walt was a mild mannered gentlemen who taught me biology at Christian Brothers Academy in Syracuse. He also was the coach of very successful CBA football teams, and was loved by all. Walt was the only politician I knew as a child. The only reason I knew him was because he was 1st District councilor in Syracuse, the district where I lived. I first saw him at the opening ceremonies of the Lincoln Little league seasons. Walt would appear each year and make a brief speech, which I did on many, many occasions much later in my life.

When Walt met you, and couldn't remember your name, he would always address you as "Sonny Boy." I can still hear him saying that today, even though he passed away many years ago.

When I became a Syracuse councilor-at-large Walt was still the 1st District councilor. Having taught me in high school, we knew each other well. I vividly remembered that I am probably the only person that Walt Ludovico ever threw out of a class in his entire career. Most people I told this to didn't believe me because Walt was the kindest, most loving person you could have ever known.

In any event, Walt's advice to me when I first became a member of the city council was for me to not get up front on controversial issues until I got my sea legs and knew what I was doing. I followed that advice for a short time and probably should have followed it longer, in view of the many controversial issues that I often jumped right into.

What follows are my recollections of what came next after being elected.

LOBBYISTS

After winning a campaign, you get to deal with lobbyists. And that is not necessarily a bad thing.

If you ask one hundred people on the street about whether lobbyists are good or bad, I would bet at least ninety of them would say that lobbyists are part of the problem in government. Well, that depends upon what is meant by a lobbyist. In any representative government, people have the right to advocate for a bill or for a policy with their elected officials. That is what representative government is all about.

Because of the greater diversity of issues and the broader scope of responsibility of a state senator in comparison to a local elected official, I was truly surprised at the number of people that wanted to speak with me once I was elected to the Senate. That is not to say that there weren't advocates for various ordinances and for various projects knocking on my door when I was a member of the Syracuse school board and the Syracuse city council, but the number of people wanting to speak with me once I got to the Senate increased exponentially.

At first it was extremely difficult because many of the issues were new issues to me and I had to learn all sides of the issues before I could take a definitive position on them. More-

over, when first confronted with an issue, on many occasions, those advocating for the proposition and those advocating against the proposition seemed to raise arguments of equal weight. So it was absolutely essential to hear from both sides of every issue and ask questions as well as do independent research before making a decision. It was on rare occasions that I waited to hear the debate on the floor of the Senate before making a decision, since I had done my research before the bill came to the floor.

Over time, after you study the information that is given to you by the various advocates, and do your own research, you get to know who to trust and who not to trust. I remember one lobbyist, representing the nurse anesthetists who told me that the bill for which they were advocating would simply put into law what was already part of the New York state health department regulations. I asked him on several occasions, if that was the case, why they would even need the bill. He gave a plausible argument, namely, that if the administration changes and the department head changes, the regulations could change, and that a law would be more permanent.

Fortunately, before agreeing with him, I met with representatives of anesthesiologists, doctors who were opposed to the legislation. They showed me that the current regulations did not go as far as the bill did, and the bill would allow nurse anesthetists to perform more functions than they were allowed to by regulation, and that those additional functions should be left to doctors as opposed to nurses. I met again with the nurse anesthetists' lobbyist and confronted him with the specific regulations, and after he waffled for some time, he practically admitted that I was right. It was obvious that he had previously misrepresented what current regulations provided. Needless to say, I didn't trust that lobbyist again.

But lobbying does have an important function. It provides the official with information so that he or she can make a much more informed decision. And if you don't have enough information and you can't get it from your own sources, lobbyists are more than willing to provide you with the information you are looking for. And, most lobbyists are honest and, quite frankly, it's in their best interest to be honest, since they will be dealing with a legislator on many different issues over that legislator's tenure.

The lobbyists like the ones I just mentioned are what most people think of as lobbyists, namely, individuals who are paid to advocate for a specific group or a specific project or on a specific issue. However, the greatest number of lobbyists are ordinary citizens. My office got inundated with senior citizen members of the American Association of Retired Persons, AARP. AARP set the agenda and card carrying AARP members descended en masse to remind you that they were all voters and that they believed that certain legislation was necessary. I always had great meetings with members of AARP, especially the older I got. When I agreed with them, I told them, and when I disagreed, I told them that as well.

In fact, I was very blunt and clear on my positions with everyone. Since the issues tended to come back over and over again, once you took positions on most issues, the job became much easier. As time passed, there was less need for additional research.

People rarely left my office after meeting with me without knowing where I stood. In fact, many complimented me for my clarity, often adding that after meetings with other legislators, they either had no clue where those legislators stood or that the other legislators always agreed with them, which they knew was too good to be true.

I remember when a group from Planned Parenthood came to see me one time advocating for a bill that would elim-

inate the requirement of parental consent for a child to receive an abortion. As in many other meetings, there was a lot of give and take and I asked numerous questions of the people that came to see me about the issue. Again, at the end of the meeting, there was no doubt in anyone's mind where I stood.

The group that came in on that occasion included individuals who were paid by or volunteered for the Planned Parenthood organization, a couple of parents, one of whom a clergyman, and three high school students. Their argument was that there are many children that come from dysfunctional families and the parents from those dysfunctional families might not give consent to a child seeking an abortion, and then the child would suffer. They argued that it should be the child's choice, as to not only whether an abortion should be performed, but also whether or not to tell his or her parents.

The volunteers from Planned Parenthood asked the students to speak. I remember two of them vividly. One had yellow (not blonde) hair. She also had a dog collar around her neck. I am not sure, but I think her makeup must have been applied by someone from the Barnum & Bailey circus. The boy had blue hair, with a similar dog collar and various piercings that were clearly visible in his exposed skin.

After listening to all of them, I asked the clergyman how he would feel if he learned that his daughter had had an abortion and he didn't know about it. His answer was that he had such a wonderful relationship with his daughter that there was no way that she would not discuss her pregnancy with him. I asked him but what if she didn't, but he wouldn't concede that that was even a possibility.

I then asked the volunteers whether a parent should at least be consulted, since the parent had the responsibility for raising his or her child. If notified, the parent could at least give input on the important decision that his or her child was about to make. They indicated that was not necessary,

since they had trained people at various organizations such as Planned Parenthood, to explain things to the children making these decisions. I then turned to the two high school students that clearly caught my eye. I asked them what they thought. They parroted what the adults said almost word for word.

After listening to them, I looked directly at the two students and asked them whether their parents knew that they came to Albany to meet with a state representative with blue hair, yellow hair, piercings, and dog collars. They said that their parents were aware of this.

I then asked them whether or not they came to try and convince me of their point of view, and they both said "yes." I then told them, in no uncertain terms, that there was no way that anybody presenting themselves in the way they did would ever convince me of anything and, if we did agree on something, it would be despite their advocacy. I then took about ten minutes to explain to them that in life each of them would have to be selling themselves before they could sell whatever their point of view was or whatever they were seeking to accomplish, and that because of their appearances it would almost be impossible for me and many others to take them seriously.

I then looked at the volunteers from the Planned Parenthood organization and asked them whether they truly came to convince me of their point of view, and whether they believed that bringing these students, looking the way they did, would help them make their case. They said "yes" to both questions. I then told them that they had extremely poor judgment and that they were doing these students a disservice.

I concluded by telling them that I believed that parents should be notified before a child makes a decision on whether to have an abortion, and that the parents should have the ability to discuss this important issue with their children

who they are responsible for by law. Quite frankly, that was my position when they walked in the room anyway. I always wondered whether or not I got through to these two high school students and whether they ever changed their style of advocacy.

The other thing I remember about this meeting is that my young intern attended the meeting and as I was speaking his mouth was open in disbelief that I would be as blunt as I was with these constituents.

I would, as often as possible, try to use these meetings with students as teaching experiences. Every class that visited Albany for my many years of service in the state Senate heard me talk about the importance of reading. It was always so gratifying when I'd run in to some of these kids back in my district and they would proudly tell me how many books they had read. That's why I always participated in summer reading programs at schools and libraries, where children would get certificates for reading a specific number of books over the summer, as well as during the school year.

In 2009, I hired a young woman who was, I believe, 24 years old at the time. After I gave my reading pitch to a group of students at a library, she informed me that when she visited Albany as an elementary student, she got the same speech. I was shocked, since I hadn't realized that I was that old. Thereafter, a second employee of mine told me the same thing, and as proof, showed me my photo with his grammar school class.

Issues advocated for by lobbyists can be trivial or they can be serious, and in some cases dead serious. Once such issue dealt with parole eligibility for violent felony offenders. On November 7, 1997, Jenna Grieshaber was killed in Albany. As it turned out, her parents, Janice and Bruce Grieshaber, were constituents of mine. As the details of the killing emerged, it was learned that the killer was a parolee who was released from jail on parole after having served five years of a seven

year sentence for stabbing a prior victim.

Soon after the murder, I heard from Jenna's parents who wanted to meet with me to discuss drafting a bill that would eliminate parole for violent felony offenders. I remember distinctly how strong and determined Jenna's parents were to make something positive out of the most tragic experience parents could ever possibly go through. Interestingly, there were already bills in the Senate that called for the end of parole for violent felony offenders. In fact, such a bill passed in the Senate prior to Jenna's murder. Unfortunately, the New York state Assembly, controlled by New York City democrats, refused to pass the bill.

The governor at the time of Jenna's death was George Pataki. I contacted the governor and he agreed to and did, in fact, meet with me and Jenna's parents in Syracuse. He committed to putting the power of his office behind the enactment of the law. Consistent with prior history, the Senate passed the bill overwhelmingly a few weeks after our meeting with the governor. Again, consistent with history, the Assembly refused to even take up the bill prior to the end of the legislative session in June of 1998.

Jenna's parents were absolutely incensed, as they should have been, since Sheldon Silver, the Speaker of the Assembly, committed to them that he would put the bill up for a vote before the end of session, but didn't. This wasn't the first, nor would it be the last time, that Speaker Silver went back on his word. However, this did not stop the Grieshabers. In fact, they redoubled their efforts to try to get the Assembly back into session to pass the bill.

Fortunately, it was an election year and substantial pressure was being put on members of the Assembly to demand that Silver call them back to session to pass the bill. Incredibly, and I don't remember another instance when this occurred, Silver finally called the Assembly back to session in

August of 1998, and the bill was overwhelmingly approved by the Assembly. Governor Pataki then immediately signed the bill into law resulting in ending parole for those serving sentences for violent felonies.

I often wondered how many people would have been saved by the earlier passage of this bill by the Assembly, which precluded violent felony offenders from being returned to the streets before their entire sentences were completed. The saddest part of all of this is that if the Assembly had passed this bill as the Senate had done in June of 1997, Jenna would probably still be alive today, since her killer was released on parole on November 6, 1997, the day before killing her.

Another example of citizen-lobbyists that made things happen is the efforts of Diane Nappa, Jasmin Paglia, Patty Herrmann, and Kathy Spicer, who came to Albany in 2001 with a dream and a very compelling case to have government help make that dream become a reality.

These very strong and determined women, who founded an organization called Familycapped, had something in common – they each had a child with multiple handicaps that required, literally, around the clock care. Diane scheduled the meeting with me to enlighten me about what it was like for a child to live with such disabilities, and what it was like to care for such a child.

They explained that not only was the child isolated from other children and unable to have meaningful interaction with his or her peers, but also the caregiver rarely had a respite from his or her caretaking responsibilities. None of them complained about the burdens they all endured. In fact, they all gracefully took on those responsibilities as acts of love of their special children.

What the women were looking for was a place that their children could go from time-to-time to socialize with other children with multiple disabilities, at which time they

could have a short respite from their daily responsibilities. Who could be against that?

Timing is everything. And fortunately, at the time, the state government had funds available for worthwhile capital projects. I was able to secure $200,000 of these funds toward building such a respite center, later named "Casey's Place" after Casey Crichton, one of these special children who died in 1996.

More funds were needed. Diane and her band of mothers relentlessly sought other funds and in-kind services from members of the Syracuse community. The donating of in-kind services was led by Doug Klepper, owner of Klepper Construction, and other tradesmen. Funds were raised from many people, including Bill Allyn and the Welch-Allyn Foundation, Jim and Julie Boeheim and Bob and Sue Crichton, Casey's parents.

But just building Casey's Place wasn't enough, since operating funds had to be secured so that there was enough money to operate the facility on a daily basis. Nurses, administrators, and other health care providers were needed to run Casey's Place.

Getting through the state bureaucracy was not easy. There were so many rules and regulations that I couldn't keep track of them all. Fortunately, I had Colleen Hassett- Mastine on my staff, who, with Diane Nappa, somehow got all the necessary approvals for money, that the state and federal governments already were providing for the care of disabled children, to be used for the operation of Casey's Place.

Diane Nappa and the other members of Familycapped were lobbyists in the purist sense of the word. They exercised their constitutional right to petition the government, and were successful in creating a jewel in our community that has helped so many children with multiple handicapping conditions, as well as their parents.

There's no doubt that mothers are the best advocates. Like the Familycapped parents who made Casey's Place happen, Mary Ellen Clausen made Ophelia's Place happen. Mary Ellen had two daughters who suffered from eating disorders, one of whom almost died from the condition. Virtually on her own, she set out to spread the word about eating disorders and their potentially deadly consequences.

Most people, including parents, in the 1990s, when faced with a loved one with an eating disorder thought the cure was just to get the person to eat. The theory was that if you are underweight, you eat and gain weight and the problem is solved. Few knew the deep psychological problems that those with eating disorders had, and still fewer knew what to do about it.

From firsthand experience with her daughters, Mary Ellen Clausen fully understood the condition and the best ways to treat those afflicted. More importantly, she knew that the ignorance about eating disorders resulted in the worsening of the condition and, in all too many cases, death, which could have been avoided.

I sponsored health fairs for constituents living in Central New York. People were given the opportunity to go to such an event and get diagnostic screening, as well as obtain information that educated constituents about various health conditions. As fate would have it, I met Mary Ellen Clausen at her booth at the New York state fair which she paid for with her own money, to help educate people about eating disorders. As a result of this chance meeting, she was invited to one of my health fairs, where she disseminated the same information.

From that point forward, I was able to get her some small state grants so she could spread the word. At the time, she was renting a building in Liverpool, New York, which she called Ophelia's Place. People would go there to obtain infor-

mation about eating disorders and information on where to get help. Most importantly, those with an eating disorder had a place to go to discuss their struggles with others who were experiencing the same problems.

Mary Ellen funded Ophelia's Place with her own money, some grants, and a lot of donations. Members of her staff were all volunteers. A crisis developed when the landlord decided to use the building for another purpose. Within months of learning that Ophelia's Place's lease was not going to be renewed, the program had nowhere to go.

Mary Ellen and some of her volunteers came to see me. I suggested that she look for a place to buy. One small problem – they had no money. Fortunately, at the time, the state did have funds for capital grants for non-profits who had worthwhile projects. Ophelia's Place definitely fit that category. It filled a desperate need in the community, and was run extremely well by Mary Ellen and her volunteers.

I was able to get a large grant to help them make the purchase and, shortly thereafter, another grant to make necessary repairs and renovations. Ophelia's Place is still alive and well in Liverpool, New York, and so are many young people who might not have been if it wasn't for Ophelia's Place.

Another example of an incredibly strong citizen lobbyist, who made something positive happen out of a deadly serious situation is Sandy Scaccia. Sandy is the mother of Lee Anne Cruz, who was murdered by her husband in the presence of Lee Anne's children, at the time aged 11 and 6. Lee Anne's husband was convicted, sentenced and incarcerated. The children were placed in the custody of their grandparents, Sandy and her husband, Frank.

While incarcerated, Mr. Cruz decided that he wanted to have visitation rights with his children while in jail, since he was not going to be released anytime soon. So he petitioned Family Court asking for visitation rights. In view of

the circumstances surrounding the murder and the fact that the children were witnesses, it was extremely unlikely that a Family Court Judge would ever have granted him visitation rights in jail with these very young children who went through such terrible trauma. However, there was nothing in law that would protect the children from having to appear in Court and go through the Court proceedings multiple times. Sandy felt, as did I, that this was wrong.

As a result, I drafted a bill that would protect children from having to appear in Court on petitions for visitation under the circumstances of the Cruz case and obtained a sponsor in the Assembly, Michael Bragman. The bill was passed in the Senate shortly after it was introduced. Unfortunately, a procedural shenanigan was pulled by Bragman that put Sandy and her family through needless agony before the bill was passed in the Assembly.

When a bill is passed in both houses and signed by the Governor, it is "chaptered," and it becomes law. The legislator who introduced the bill and whose house passed it first, is the legislator in whose name the bill is chaptered. Well, the fact that the Senate worked much more efficiently than the Assembly didn't stop Bragman from trying to get the bill chaptered in his name. To that end, he changed a couple of insignificant words in his bill so that the Assembly bill was different than the Senate bill.

When I learned this I met with Assemblyman Bragman and with a members of our staffs, and argued with Mike about the nonsensical changes in the wording of the bill and tried to plead with him that since the session would be over in a few days he should back off of his changes. With a straight face he insisted that the language was necessary, so I told him that I couldn't care less who get credit for the chapter, and that if it was so important for him to change a few words, then I would be more than happy to change them in the Senate bill. He de-

nied that his motive was to get the law chaptered in his name but wouldn't back off the changes. He then told me that when he introduced the changes in the Assembly, he would also submit the changes for the Senate bill so that the bill could pass both houses expeditiously.

Well, Assemblyman Bragman put his changes in but did not submit the amendments to the Senate bill. A bill had to be filed and on the legislators' desks at least three days before it could be considered. The bill had to age, or, in other words, legislators and the public had to be given the opportunity to read the bill, and review it before it was voted on. We were within a day or two from the session being over. Therefore, if I put in the new bill with the Bragman changes, the bill would not have had time to age, and could not have been voted on in the Senate that session.

I explained all this to Sandy Scaccia, who was upset, but not as upset as I was. Fortunately, there is an exception to the requirement of a bill aging. If the Governor is willing to submit a "message of necessity" to the legislature, the bill can be taken up by the legislative body without having to age. I contacted Governor Pataki's office and he agreed to send a "message of necessity" which waived the time requirement. He did so and the bill was passed in both houses and became law.

So when you hear the term "lobbyist" there are lobbyists in all shapes and forms. I have dealt with some of the most wonderful people that I ever met who helped make the state better by lobbying for a law, or for a project, and I have met some people who were not so nice and would provide misinformation in order to get a bill passed for a special interest group for whom he or she was working. As with elected officials, painting any individual or group, including lobbyists, with a broad brush never works.

DESTINY USA

I n my over four decades of elective office, I have never seen a con job perpetrated on the people of the state of New York like that of the Pyramid Companies in the form of Destiny USA. However, for something of this magnitude to be successful, many accomplices were needed. Some were knowing and willing accomplices; some were accomplices by simply looking the other way; some were accomplices by refusing to do due diligence to find the true nature of the deal; and some were simply too gullible or incapable of understanding the hustle.

To understand what occurred, you have go back to around 1988, when Robert Congel, Bruce Kenan and the other driving forces behind the Pyramid Companies, approached the City of Syracuse to build the Carousel Mall. At that time I was a member of the Syracuse city council.

Basically, the concept proposed by Pyramid was that it would build a 900,000 square foot mall near Onondaga Lake in Onondaga County, New York. However, Pyramid claimed that it could not get conventional financing for a project of this magnitude and that it needed assistance from Syracuse. Pyramid's founder and CEO, Robert Congel proposed that in order to help finance the project, that Pyramid be given a payment in lieu of a tax agreement by the city. This is known as a PILOT.

At that time a PILOT was somewhat unusual, but it was gaining in popularity with many cities throughout the state. The argument raised in favor of a PILOT was that, at the time of the proposal, there was no development in the area sought to be developed, and the municipality was receiving no taxes or very few taxes in the area of the proposed development. If a contractor developed the area, the property taxes would be substantially greater than what was currently being realized by the municipality. So, in short, the municipality would be giving up a portion of property taxes for a period of time, but in the long run the development would generate substantially more taxes, including sales taxes, than the municipality was realizing on the property before the development was completed.

The Pyramid Companies proposed that the City enter into a fifteen-year PILOT agreement. This meant that while the mall was being built, Pyramid Companies would pay substantially less taxes on the property, and once the mall was completed, Pyramid would pay a reduced negotiated pilot tax rate. After fifteen years, the City would begin to receive full taxes on the full assessed value of the mall property.

At that time, I took everything the owners of the Pyramid Companies said with a grain of salt. The reason was simple. In addition to being a member of the city council, I practiced law and in that law practice I represented many people in different types of litigation.

My first major piece of legislation against Pyramid was in the mid-1980's wherein I represented Malcon Developers, Inc., a company owned by my brothers-in-law. This company did site work at various developments and was unfortunate enough to do site work for the Pyramid Companies at the Salmon Run Mall near Watertown, New York.

After doing millions of dollars worth of work, Malcon was stiffed by the Pyramid Companies, which was not un-

common. The litigation lasted for years and eventually, after a thirty-day trial, Malcon got a verdict against Pyramid Companies in excess of four million dollars.

Unfortunately, Malcon couldn't hang on during the course of the litigation and had to file for bankruptcy. In view of the litigation costs and the inability to pay its bills while the litigation was in progress, even with the substantial verdict, it could not survive. During the course of the litigation, I had the opportunity to question, under oath, in depositions and at trial, many officers and employees of Pyramid. From this experience, I learned of questionable business practices and, to put it mildly, credibility issues.

As a result of the outcome in this Pyramid case, I was contacted by other companies and individuals who also weren't paid by Pyramid Companies, where Pyramid's modus operandi was exactly the same as it was in dealing with Malcon Developers, Inc. Over the years this resulted in additional verdicts against and settlements with Pyramid.

At the time of the discussions concerning the Carousel Mall project, the Malcon litigation was in progress, but was nowhere near over. However, I had enough information to be extremely wary when dealing with Pyramid, its officers and employees.

During the proceedings before the city council, I asked many questions and was very careful in trying to make sure that Syracuse was protected. What sold me on the project was that, at the time, the city was realizing virtually no property tax dollars from the property that was proposed to be developed. After many discussions and various hearings, I reasoned that, if the PILOT was granted, during its fifteen year life, the city would be realizing more taxes than it would have earned with no development, and eventually substantial sales taxes would be generated. More importantly, at the end of fifteen years, the City of Syracuse would be realizing property taxes

on the full value of a major mall. As a result, I, and all of the other city councilors, supported the fifteen-year PILOT.

Ironically, the verdict in favor of Malcon and against Pyramid came a couple of weeks before the grand opening of the Carousel Mall. On the date of the opening there was a multi-page article, beginning on the front page of the Syracuse papers lauding the new development. In the first few paragraphs of that article was a mention that I was there and was talking to Robert Congel. More than a few people asked me what we were talking about in view of the recent verdict. It wasn't about the verdict.

In all fairness, the Carousel Mall became a wonderful addition to the City of Syracuse and, I believe, that the fifteen-year PILOT agreement and other City of Syracuse concessions were wise investments for the value that the City and residents received. This was especially true in view of the fact that after fifteen years the City would be receiving full taxes on a very valuable development. Not so fast!

In about the thirteenth year of the PILOT agreement, Pyramid Companies started talking about building an 800,000 square foot big box shopping center. A big box shopping center is comprised of various large stores with separate entrances, in contrast to the indoor Carousel Mall. This big box development was well received and got favorable publicity.

A short time thereafter, this big box development morphed into what Pyramid called Destiny USA. Before the concept of Destiny USA was known to the public, there were meetings between Pyramid officials with representatives of the electronic and print media, as well as then Syracuse Mayor Roy Bernardi and then Onondaga County Executive Nick Pirro, and their staffs. When the proposal was made public, Destiny USA was billed as the greatest thing ever to hit the City of Syracuse, and would rival such destinations as the Mall

of Americas in Minnesota and even Las Vegas itself. Pyramid claimed, and studies that it commissioned showed, that the economic impact on the area of this mega mall would more than justify the benefits that Destiny USA was then seeking from government.

Over time, the attractions of Destiny USA that Pyramid promised, in addition to an expanded shopping mall, would be a world class golf course, a Tuscan village, a replication of the Erie Canal, and a New York state Tourism Center, among other things.

To prove that these features were part of Destiny USA, Pyramid made magnificent renderings of the facility. The Tuscan village had such detail that it even showed goats on hills. Pyramid claimed it would build a three thousand room hotel, and to prove it, provided renderings of a hotel that resembled Emerald City in the *Wizard of Oz*. These renderings were eagerly displayed in the Syracuse newspapers. The more outrageous the claims, the more publicity Pyramid got in order to prove to the world that it deserved the benefits it was seeking from government, and much much more.

The benefits that Pyramid were seeking and eventually received included another PILOT agreement. This PILOT agreement, for new construction, was for thirty years, not fifteen years! Never before had any developer receive a thirty-year PILOT in New York state or anywhere else for that matter. In addition, and read this carefully, Pyramid requested, and received, an additional thirty year PILOT on the existing Carousel Mall!

That wasn't all. At the time, the State of New York had a program known as the Empire Zone Program, which gave certain benefits to developers who created jobs. One of the benefits was that the state would pay the property taxes of a developer that created jobs in certain Empire Zone areas in the tate. The City of Syracuse granted Pyramid, Empire Zone

status not only for the area on which it intended to construct the expansion they called Destiny USA but also for the area on which the existing Carousel Mall was built. This meant that Pyramid, would be able to collect tax payments from tenants of the Carousel Mall under their tenant leases, and also be reimbursed by the state of New York for the payments Pyramid made to the City of Syracuse instead of taxes under the PILOT agreement. That's not all! The Empire Zone program also allowed Pyramid to get tax credits for employees it hired.

The point is that there were already existing incentives created by the State of New York to make it worthwhile for developers to build and invest in Empire Zone areas in the state. To add on a thirty-year PILOT to an existing mall and give a thirty year PILOT for the additional construction, in my mind, was way over the top. This was especially true since, despite the hype, Pyramid had signed on no tenants for the expansion.

Pyramid proposed to do Destiny USA in three phases, and claimed that in order to get the financing for these phases, it needed these additional tax incentives. However, even though Pyramid said it would build 3.2 million square feet in this Destiny USA development, the only commitment that was made, and reduced to writing in the agreement between the developer and the City and County, was an 800 to 900 hundred thousand square-foot expansion, which was billed as phase one. Does this number ring a bell? It should, because it's the exact amount of square footage that Pyramid originally claimed it was going to develop as its big box shopping center. In other words, in billing this project as Destiny USA and making incredible claims of economic development and prosperity, Pyramid obligated itself to doing nothing more than it had planned to do in a separate development for a big box shopping center, which would have been fully taxed.

By packaging Destiny USA into a project that included

the Carousel Mall, Pyramid was able to get government officials to give it an additional thirty-year PILOT after the original fifteen year Carousel Mall PILOT expired!

As I began learning of the details of this Destiny USA project, I truly went ballistic. I couldn't believe that anyone could be so naive and so gullible to provide these benefits to a developer who only obligated himself to build an 800 to 900 thousand square foot addition to an existing mall.

If the city and county wanted to provide a PILOT agreement for new construction, I couldn't argue with that, as long as the time period was reasonable. By this time PILOT agreements were becoming common with new developments. However, to provide an additional thirty year PILOT on an existing mall was unconscionable.

The main selling point for the original Carousel Mall project and its 15-year PILOT, when approved, was that after fifteen years of reduced taxes, Pyramid would be paying taxes on the full value of the Carousel Mall development. Once the Destiny USA project was approved, that would not happen for another thirty years, even if Pyramid only built 800 thousand square feet and not the full promised build-out of 3.2 million square feet. In short, the City and County gave up the benefit of their bargain made when Carousel was built by postponing receiving full property taxes on the original Carousel agreement for another 30 years.

The electronic and print media were clearly complicit. Every day, in the newspaper, on television and on radio stations, Destiny USA was shilled as the greatest thing ever to happen to mankind. When I voiced my opposition, I was vilified by the media. When I wrote letters to the editor explaining my position, I was criticized for having a conflict of interest.

By this time, I had sued the Pyramid Companies on many occasions on behalf of companies and individuals who

were not paid for services performed. There is no doubt that I had a negative opinion about Pyramid and its officers but I had a good basis for it. The cases that I handled against Pyramid on behalf of unpaid contractors were all successful, either by jury verdict or settlement. When criticized for having a conflict of interest, I reminded people of the first rule of banking, that is, to "know thy customer." I knew this customer and I did every-thing within my power to try to convince the elected officials and the general public that the deal was a bad one.

What was frustrating was that I did not have a vote on this project. I was no longer a member of the city council and would not vote on the PILOT. Even though I did not have a vote, I was a resident of Syracuse, and as a state Senator, I at least had a forum from which I could make the public aware. Many family members and friends disagreed with me and those that agreed with me thought I was engaging in a futile fight. Many advised me to back off since the negative publicity could adversely affect my political career. Despite all of this I kept fighting. What was happening was simply wrong.

I went to many public forums voicing my opinion and was soundly criticized for it. One such meeting was a meeting of the city council at Henninger High school in Syracuse. The whole room was packed with individuals supporting the pro-ject. When my name was called to speak and as I walked up to the microphone and even while I was speaking, I was soundly booed. Most of the boos came from a group of union members who thought that Destiny USA was going to be a great boon for union workers. They bought into the verbal promises of the developer. At the end, most were sorely disappointed.

I met with county legislators and city councilors and tried to explain how bad the deal was for residents of On-ondaga County. They listened, but they listened more to the drum beat of the media. They were well aware of how I was being vilified, and they didn't want to run the risk of the same

treatment.

There were exceptions, the most notable of which was Kate O'Connell, then a city councilor. She was a liberal democrat, I was a moderate republican, but we saw eye-to-eye on this issue. She tried to make the same points, but was overwhelmed and out-voted by the city council.

I met with Mayor Roy Bernardi, in whose campaign for Mayor, I was intimately involved. Roy had run for Mayor twice and lost. The third time was the charm, in large part, because of the bitter democrat primary between Joe Nicoletti and Joe Fahey. Roy seemed not to have a clue what the project was about and what the details of the deal were, and frankly didn't seem to care.

One meeting I had with Roy included Vito Sciscioli. Vito was a long-serving city employee, who, at the time, I greatly respected. I thought he was bright and also dedicated to the well-being of the citizens of the City of Syracuse. But Vito became the pied piper of this project.

During a private meeting with Bernardi and Sciscioli at City Hall, I raised separately each of the objections that I had to the project. It was amazing to me, for example, when I asked Roy how he could agree to an additional thirty-year PILOT on the existing mall when the only obligation that Pyramid had in the agreement was to build an 800 to 900 thousand square foot addition. Bernardi looked at Vito and asked him, "Vito, is that in there?" Vito said "yes." This went on for each of the points that I made. At the end of the meeting it was obvious that Bernardi was riding with the flow of the media and truly did not know the details of the agreement, or if he did, he was ignoring them.

Another interesting meeting was with Nick Pirro, the then County Executive. Interestingly, his finance commissioner was Joe Mareane. Mareane was the chief financial officer for Syracuse Mayor Tom Young when the Carousel Mall deal

was put in place. After he stopped working for Syracuse, he joined the Pyramid Companies and was involved in a mall development in the Hudson Valley region of the state. Interestingly, that mall was completed with NO PILOT agreements ! When I started to raise the various issues about the project, Nick told me that Joe Mareane said that it was a good deal. I raised Mareane's prior connections to Pyramid, and that while he was with Pyramid they had built another mall without any PILOT. This didn't move Pirro at all.

I then tried to convince Nick that he should try to get a better deal. He said that the deal that was on the table was the best deal he could get. I countered by telling him that there had been few negotiations and that Pyramid was getting everything it wanted. Nick repeated that it was the best deal that he could get, and then said that he really had to leave.

As he was leaving he told me that he had to leave since he was putting an offer in on some property on a vacation home and that he had to meet his wife at the realtor's office. I asked him if when he made the offer, did he offer the asking price? He just looked at me , shook his head and left.

As I continued my crusade against the deal, I was continually criticized as being against new development in our community. This criticism came from the newspapers, and television and radio stations. I couldn't quite get why people could not understand that Pyramid already got their 15-year PILOT on the existing Carousel Mall, and that they were supposed to pay taxes at the full market value after fifteen years, and that granting an additional thirty-year PILOT on the existing mall was unconscionable. I couldn't understand it then and I can't understand it now.

Pyramid flooded the airways with commercials which featured well known people in central New York including union officials and sports stars like Tim Green. Tim was a former Syracuse University and pro football player, who became

a successful author after his playing days. He also had his own television show for a short time, and was a football analyst for one of the networks for pro football games. The thrust of the commercials was that Pyramid should be applauded for this magnificent proposed development, especially since there was "no cost to the taxpayers."

That claim was so obviously false that I found it hard to believe that anyone would buy it. The 15-year PILOT agreement that was given to the Carousel Mall was a benefit to Pyramid since during those fifteen years, Pyramid did not have to pay the full tax rate. If the fifteen years were to be extended by an additional thirty years to make it a forty-five year PILOT at a tax rate lower than the fair market rate, there obviously would be lower property taxes being realized by the City of Syracuse. Pyramid countered by saying that the 15-year PILOT that they agreed to for the original mall really resulted in Pyramid paying too many taxes. That was ridiculous, especially since they fought for the PILOT in return for building the Carousel Mall project.

Pyramid also countered by saying the amount of sales taxes to be generated by Destiny USA would far surpass the loss in property taxes. That could possibly have been true, but only if Pyramid built all of Destiny USA, which was promised to be 3.2 million square feet. However, Pyramid was only obligated to build an 800 to 900 thousand square foot addition, not the entire project billed as Destiny USA.

In addition to all of this, the federal government, courtesy of Senators Hillary Clinton and Charles Schumer, provided Pyramid millions of dollars in energy tax credits on the promise that Pyramid was going to have an epiphany and actually have a "green development." The only thing green at the structure were green walls that were painted while Pyramid was lobbying for the tax credits, and a few small structures on the roof of the mall.

In addition to the newspaper, Clear Channels radio acted as if the company was on Pyramid's payroll. Jim Reith, a popular talk show host on WSYR radio turned his program into a Destiny USA telethon. For months someone from Destiny USA or someone from the community that was in favor of the project, was a guest on the Jim Reith show. For years I was the bad guy who didn't know what I was talking about. On one show they actually invited me to appear along with Bruce Kenan, Robert Congel's right hand man, and then city councilor Joanie Mahoney. Obviously, there were three people on the program, including Jim Reith, in favor of the deal, and me, opposed to it.

I was given ample time to state my points of view and the others were given time to rebut what I was saying. My favorite part of the program was when I raised the point that if Pyramid truly was going to build a 3.2 million square feet for the Destiny project, in return for the incredible benefits, it should be obligated to do so in writing. Joanie Mahoney responded that Pyramid had promised to do so. I countered that there was nothing in writing obligating them to do so. Then I asked Joanie whether she agreed that there was nothing in writing, and she said that was correct.

I then stated that if it's not in the agreement, then it's not enforceable and no one should be given these astronomical benefits when there is no corresponding enforceable obligation. Her answer was that she trusted Pyramid. I made the point on this live radio program, that she was a practicing attorney and that I would never go to her for legal advice. She was literally willing to give a substantial benefit from the City of Syracuse as a member of the city council in return for an unenforceable verbal representation from Pyramid.

Steve Kimatian was a high level executive with the Clear Channels television station, Channel 9, and a neighbor of mine. He had a Sunday morning talk show where he inter-

viewed various members of the public. He interviewed me on the topic of Destiny. Those interviews were classics. Steve also drank the Kool-Aid and trumpeted the Pyramid party line. I truly enjoyed these appearances because it gave me the opportunity to show how ridiculous and unfair the deal was. What troubled me, however, was that after one show was over, Kimatian tacked on to the program an editorial comment basically trying to take apart my arguments, without the benefit of my response.

I tried to get the message out in any way that I could. That included an appearance on an afternoon program on public television hosted by George Kilpatrick. One of the shows was a live call-in where I was asked questions by various callers to which I responded. It was a great opportunity and I truly enjoyed it. To this day I remember a Pyramid rendering that George had on the set showing the Tuscan Village with goats on the hill. I took the opportunity to show how naive people had to be to believe a simple rendering as proof of a project. What's fun, to this present day, is whenever I see George, I always ask him whether he has been to the Tuscan Village and seen the goats on the hill yet.

There were years of interviews, years of newspaper articles and electronic media stories on Pyramid and Destiny USA, and years of criticism of me for my conflicts of interest and my inability to understand the importance of such a wonderful project for our community.

When the pilot agreement was finally passed by the city council and county legislature, Bob Congel publicly stated at a county legislature meeting that "now we have everything we need, and if the project fails it's because of us." When he said this he seemed to wipe away a tear from his eye. But Pyramid wasn't done yet. Congel didn't have everything he wanted because he approached the state government for more benefits. I did have some say on this decision.

DESTINY II

Despite Robert Congel's emotional thank you to the County and City for giving Pyramid everything it needed to complete the project, Congel wasn't quite done. Pyramid had the 15-year Carousel Mall PILOT extended to forty-five years; it had a thirty-year PILOT for the new portion of the development; and it had Empire Zone benefits including property tax benefits and tax credits for new employees, together with various sales tax exemptions.

Under the theory of "there's no harm in asking" and, with the unwavering support of the media, no doubt hoping for new advertising revenue, why not continue to ask? Congel next requested the state government to guarantee the amount of Empire Zone benefits that Pyramid would receive on the unenforceable verbal representation that Pyramid would complete the entire 3.2 million square feet of Destiny USA. Without putting a shovel in the ground, Pyramid was looking for guaranteed Empire Zone payments on the value of the planned development, as if it was completed. Under Pyramid's latest request, this guaranteed money could also be used for paying off Pyramid's existing mortgages on the Carousel Mall. It's amazing that Congel would have the brass to ask for this, but it was even more amazing that government officials were considering doing it.

John O'Mara, a well-respected and well connected attorney, became one of the many lobbyists for Pyramid on this proposal. John met with me to help try and convince me of the merits of this newest request. I pointed out to him that nothing had been built, and asked how anyone could guarantee Empire Zone benefits for a concept? I also said that if the payments were guaranteed, Pyramid could pay off its existing mortgage and not do the full build out .

I also was asked by John to have a meeting with Mike Lorenz, the then mouthpiece for the Destiny USA project. I agreed to meet despite the fact that Lorenz had about as much credibility with me as – well, there isn't an adequate word to describe it. In my opinion, Mike would say just about anything to support the project. Facts were irrelevant to his advocacy. The meeting was held. Also attending on behalf of Pyramid was, Bruce Kenan, its underwriters, its lawyers, its lobbyists, and others. I had one staff member with me at the meeting which occurred in my Senate conference room in Albany.

One of the comments that was made publicly and repeatedly, was that Pyramid had actual plans and specifications drawn up for Destiny USA. I always questioned it and, in return for scheduling this meeting, I insisted that Pyramid personnel bring these plans and specifications with them. Having been educated as an engineer and having handled many pieces of construction litigation, I was very familiar with plans and specifications.

Once Mike Lorenz began his pitch, he brought out another rendering of what Destiny USA would look like. I immediately interrupted him and asked him for the plans and specifications. He provided me with drawings of a few thousand square feet of a project that could not be identified as Destiny USA or anything else for that matter. As suspected, there were no plans and specifications. What Pyramid was selling to the public were these conceptual drawings that seemed to change

daily and become more and more extravagant.

After looking at the so-called drawings, I looked at Bruce Kenan and said, "I'm not listening to Lorenz any longer. He has no credibility with me." This was a show stopper. Most there were surprised that I would be that direct. But, Lorenz didn't say anything for the rest of the meeting.

What I next wanted to find out was what guaranteed monies Pyramid was looking for and how they justified the amount. Pyramid's underwriters told me that the purpose of the guarantee, was to have a guaranteed flow of income that would insure investors that if they bought the project bonds their investments would be secure. The amount of money that was projected to be raised on the sale of these bonds was 600 million dollars. And again, that 600 million dollars could be used, not only for construction, but to pay off the existing mortgages on the Carousel Mall even though the agreement did not require the full build out... Pretty sweet deal, huh?

Obviously, I was interested in knowing what dollar amount the annual payments from the state would be in order to determine how much the state was being asked to guarantee on a unspecified, undefined project. The underwriters told me that the periodic payments would be in the amount of about 20 million dollars a year. This 20 million dollars a year was for the Empire Zone tax payments that the state was being asked to guarantee up front. The underwriters said they based this amount that they were asking for from the state, on the fair market value of the property and what the taxes would otherwise have been if there was no PILOT. What? I thought there was no cost to the taxpayer?

It was amazing to hear Pyramid tell the world that there was "no cost to the taxpayer" when it was seeking the sweetheart deal from the city and county, but when it was seeking guaranteed payments from the state the projected annual taxes, by way of the PILOT were now being represented

to be approximately 20 million dollars a year.

When I first began advocating against the deal, I repeatedly said that the city and county would lose approximately $10 million a year in property taxes that they would have gotten after the fifteen-year PILOT on the Carousel Mall expired. I was told repeatedly, as was the general public, by Pyramid representatives that the mall was not worth that amount, and it was already being overcharged in the existing PILOT payments. Now $10 million wasn't enough, but rather that mall plus a 800 to 900 thousand square foot addition, would be so valuable that it would generate $20 million a year in tax payments and justify guarantees in that amount from New York.

I looked over at Kenan and said that I guess I was a little low in what I said the city and county were losing in property taxes by extending the 15-year PILOT on the existing mall. Bruce simply looked at me and did not say a word. Needless to say, Pyramid's explanation, rather than convincing me, hardened me against the deal.

I was informed that Governor Pataki and Assembly Speaker, Sheldon Silver were in support of the proposal. Unbelievable! When the Senate Majority Leader, Joe Bruno, asked me my opinion, I told him that I would not, under any circumstances, support this proposal and I proceeded to explain to him why I was against it. The Senate did not back the proposal.

After the regular legislative session was over that year, I got an interesting call. It was from Charlie Vinal, a person who I had known a long time and who I really liked. Charlie knew everyone, including Bob Congel, and he told me "as a friend" that he wanted to provide me some information. He said that Congel and the Pyramid Companies were going to raise hundreds of thousands of dollars and support football star and author Tim Green, against me in my next election campaign.

Charlie didn't mentioned Pyramid's true objective, namely, to get me to change my mind on the guarantee legislation that Pyramid wanted, but that objective was very clear to me. Green would have been an outstanding candidate with all of his accomplishments. And the threat that he would run against me was a credible one, since Green, at the time, was a close friend of Congel's son.

I asked Charlie if he would be talking to Congel soon, and he said "yes." I told him to please tell Bob three things. First, if I lost the election, I would be spending winters in Sanibel, Florida, as opposed to Albany, New York. Second, I was not going to lose the election. And third, "tell him to kiss my ass."

About a week later I received a call from Bob. He said that he had heard that I wanted to talk to him. I replied that I didn't remember making the request, but I would be more than happy to talk to him at any time and at any place he wanted. He offered to come to my law office. I told him that instead I would stop by his office, which was located in the renovated federal courthouse that house Pyramid's headquarters. The circumstances surrounding the tax benefits received on the purchase and renovation of that building is another story.

In any event, I met Bob at his office a couple of hours later. It was a meeting that I will never forget. He first started out by telling me how much he respected me, especially in view of my successes against his attorneys in court. He then told me how this project was not about the money, but it was about the future of Syracuse. In an emotional plea, he said he wanted Syracuse to be like it was when we were growing up for his grandchildren. He told me he had twenty- plus grandchildren and it was for them.

I told Bob, at that point that this was the problem. He asked, "What do you mean?" I told him that I had grandchil-

dren too, and I didn't want my grandchildren to have to pay his grandchildren's mortgage. He just shook his head.

He then asked me if I would look at another proposal to see whether I would support it. Unbeknownst to Bob, I was well versed on this other proposal. My predecessor in the state Senate was Tarky Lombardi. I had already been informed by other members of the Senate, who represented other large cities in the state that Tarky was running around Albany trying to convince them that this type of deal should be available to each of the five major cities of the state in order to promote economic development. However, I didn't let on to Bob that I already knew what he was going to try to sell.

I just committed to Bob that I would read the proposal, which he handed to me, and that I'd get back to him. On the way out I asked Bob "Do you really respect me?" He said that he did. At that point I was standing at the top of a long and steep set of stairs in the former federal courthouse and I said to him, "Then you really must think that the city and county leaders that you have been dealing with are morons for backing your proposal." Bob, again, shook his head and walked away saying, "You're unbelievable."

I did call him a couple of days later and told him that I did not agree with the new proposal. He asked "why not". I told him that, if approved, "it would result in five shit deals that the state would be saddled with, rather than just the one in Syracuse." The legislation that he was looking for never passed, and it was a good thing since the 3.2 million square foot project was never completed.

Later, CitiBank, the prime financer of the project, stopped providing payments to Pyramid claiming that it was not complying with the construction loan. That ended up in another Pyramid litigation, which was ultimately settled around January of 2011. Pyramid refused to disclose the terms of the settlement so finally, after 12 years of shilling

for Pyramid, the *Syracuse Post Standard* newspaper, through the Freedom of Information Act, asked for copies of the documents.

When the documents were finally made public, the world learned that Citibank agreed to write down its mortgage by $189,000,000 and to eliminate Bob Congel and Bruce Keenan's personal guarantees. In short, by not paying the loan and through litigation, Pyramid got a $189,000,000 write-down of its mortgage. Citibank also released loan funds to pay off some unpaid contractors and allowed an extension of three years to refinance the loan with another lender. Citibank must have really wanted out of dealing with Pyramid.

While Pyramid was attempting to get the state to guarantee Empire Zone payments, it had a slight credibility problem in that it hadn't broken ground yet. Of course, that was an easy thing to rectify. Pyramid put on its PR full court press again. The event was trumpeted by WSYR radio's Jim Reith, the *Syracuse Post Standard*, and all of the television and radio stations as the kick-off for the most important thing to ever happen to central New York. All the elected officials were invited for this historic groundbreaking. Tents were constructed, hotdogs and french-fries and other foods were available for the general public and, of course, there were many speeches by dignitaries.

I didn't go to the groundbreaking since I knew it wasn't real. I knew this since I checked on the permit that was obtained for this "groundbreaking" and it was for a parking garage, not a "Destiny." In any event, for a couple of weeks after the "groundbreaking," which I didn't attend, WSYR radio aired an editorial comment by Joel Delmonico, its station manager. That editorial comment was directed at me and criticized me for my being an obstructionist to this wonderful project. A month or so later, as I was waiting in the WSYR lobby to go on Jim Reith's program, Joel, who I had known since high school,

passed through the lobby. I asked Joel whether I was going to get an opportunity to rebut his remarks. He just smiled.

I then told him that I had some very interesting information, and knowing he was an unbiased individual who wanted to make sure that his programming was fair and balanced, that he might want to put this on the radio in the form of an editorial remark. He asked me what I was talking about.

I told him that a few days earlier I received calls from two individuals. These were individuals who supplied the hard hats, the shovels and the baseball caps that were given out during the groundbreaking. They told me that they hadn't been paid by Pyramid. I gave Joel some more specifics but again, he just smiled.

As expected, nothing was said on the radio, but interestingly enough, I received a call about a week later and was informed that the individuals who called me had been paid. I am sure that the timing of these payments was coincidental. Yeah, sure.

At present, there is a "Destiny" in Central New York, but it bears little likeness to the Destiny that was promoted in return for the outrageous tax breaks and other benefits Pyramid received. Pyramid only completed Phase 1 of the project, which amounted to an expansion of 900,000 square feet, the same size as the Pyramid's original proposal---a tax-paying big box development. Big surprise!

Also, two large area malls that Pyramid competed with, the Shoppingtown Mall and the Great Northern Mall, are on their last legs and virtually empty due, I believe, in part from their inability to compete with the government subsidized Destiny Mall.

It is clear that the City of Syracuse really needed the tax revenue that it gave up in the Pyramid deal, since the city has been and still is close to insolvency. From the date that

the first 15-year original Carousel Mall PILOT should have expired, the City of Syracuse and the County of Onondaga have been losing millions of dollars a year in property taxes from Pyramid and this will continue for a total of 30 years. "No cost to the taxpayer" – yeah right!

Interestingly, Jim Reith, the Pyramid pied piper lost his show at WSYR radio. He was later hired to host a public TV show, which was on the air for a short time. Surprisingly, I was invited on the show despite Jim knowing that I would bring up "Destiny." When I was introduced by Reith and before I said anything, he said, "I was wrong and you were right about Destiny, and there is nothing else to say about that, so let's get on with other topics." Unfortunately, his epiphany was much too late for central New York taxpayers.

THE SITING OF A STADIUM

While serving in local government, as a member of the Syracuse school board, and city Council, I didn't have many dealings with the Metropolitan Development Association (MDA) and with its chairman, Stephen Rogers, Sr. Quite frankly, when I was elected to the Senate, I had little idea what its role was in central New York.

After I was elected to the Senate, I found out a lot about the MDA, and learned of its reason for being. Interestingly, in 2010, the MDA merged with the Greater Syracuse Chamber of Commerce and, the people of central New York literally lost nothing by eliminating one.

The MDA was formed around 1959, and was the brain child of Stephen Rogers, Sr., the publisher of the Syracuse newspapers, (at that time the *Herald Journal* and the *Post Standard*), and State Senator John Hughes. The stated purpose for the organization was to get leaders in all the major businesses together in an organization in order to promote business in central New York. From 1992, when I was first elected to the Senate, to 2010 when the MDA merged with the Syracuse Chamber of Commerce, the MDA sought to take credit for

most of central New York business development but didn't always have much to do with it.

During that period its executive director was Irwin Davis, who put politicians to shame with his ability to tell everyone what they wanted to hear in order to get what the MDA wanted. His primary jobs were to obtain money from government, convince businesses to join and pay dues, and make certain that the MDA took credit for any positive economic development that happened in the community. His chief reason for being, however, in my opinion, was to advocate for the agenda of Stephen Rogers Sr.

When I was elected to the Senate in 1992, I didn't know how closely the agenda of the MDA was to that of the Syracuse newspapers' publisher, Stephen Rogers, Sr. It didn't take long for me to get a first-hand glimpse when it came to making a decision on where the new Syracuse Chiefs' AAA baseball stadium would be located.

During the late 1980s and 1990s, there was a frenzy to build new baseball stadiums with state aid and assistance. There were innuendoes, and, in some cases, outright threats by major and minor league baseball team owners to move franchises to other states, unless they received state dollars. Unfortunately, this state-against-state competition was also occurring for other businesses as well. One state would come up with a tax break and then another state would try to beat it. All of this did very little to help the economy of the United States, but some states used this incentive technique better than others and grew jobs, at least temporarily.

Well, the Syracuse Chiefs wanted a new stadium and the prime mover to get state funds to help pay for this stadium was Assembly Majority Leader Michael Bragman, who represented the northern part of Onondaga County in the state Assembly while Governors Mario Cuomo and George Pataki were in office. After several false starts, a pot of money

was set aside in the state budget for assistance to baseball franchises to build new stadiums.

The hot button issue in central New York was the location of the stadium. You didn't have to be an expert in market research to realize that all new stadiums that were being built at the time were being built in the center cities for several reasons. One was to help revitalize cities that had been ignored for years after the flight to the suburbs. Another was that most thought that people who worked downtown would stay downtown after work, have dinner and then go to a baseball game, rather than flee to the suburbs at 5:00 pm.

Stephen Rogers, Sr. felt that the stadium should stay exactly where it was on the northside of the City of Syracuse. At the time there was much talk, primarily spearheaded by Michael Bragman, to develop the area around the Regional Market near the existing stadium, and that a new baseball stadium would complement that development.

Now who was going to make the decision and how was that decision to be made? Enter the MDA. The objective of the MDA, which I didn't realize at the time, wasn't where the best place for the new stadium would be, but rather how it could remain on the near northside where Stephen Rogers Sr. wanted it. I believe very few members of the MDA, as I, really had any clue about the MDA (Rogers) agenda.

There was a straw poll done by members of the Downtown Committee of the City of Syracuse, which consisted of businesses that were located downtown and who were interested in weighing in on the issue. Needless to say, the Downtown Committee members overwhelmingly voted to have the stadium built downtown, which was consistent with what was happening throughout the country. In fact, there wasn't only a straw poll, but there were pledges from many businesses to purchase boxes or seasons' tickets at the new stadium, to show that there was real support for a downtown

stadium. In fact, most of the general public felt the same way.

There was no doubt in my mind that the economic impact of putting the stadium downtown was much greater than building it at the northside location. I felt this way even though the downtown locations that were being discussed were not in my Senate district, and the location on the near northside was in my Senate district. Be that as it may, using other state money that the MDA had secured, the MDA decided to conduct a study to determine which location would have the best economic benefits for central New York.

It was becoming more and more obvious to me what was happening, but I naively thought that there was no possible way that the study could ever show anything other than downtown being the proper location from an economic standpoint. When the long awaited date came for the report to be released, the report wasn't ready. At least that is what everyone was told. I am convinced that the report was ready, and that it showed the downtown location to be a better one for the economy of central New York. However, that wasn't the conclusion that the MDA wanted. So the report was delayed.

Not surprisingly, when the report was finally issued, it indicated that there would be an equal economic impact, whether the stadium was placed downtown or at the near northside location. The report was the most convoluted nonsensical analysis that I had seen up to that point in my political career. However, remember that my time in the Senate had just begun. I got to see many more manipulated studies thereafter.

Now we had this information, but who was going to make the decision? Well, the MDA decided that there were five stakeholders that had to jointly make the decision. This was a stroke of brilliance on behalf of the mover and shaker behind the MDA. The five stakeholders that the MDA "suggested" in-

cluded the Mayor of the City of Syracuse, Tom Young, and the County Executive Nick Pirro. These two were obvious choices that should have been part of the decision making process.

The other choices were Tex Simone, the then general manager of the Syracuse Chiefs, and the state legislator from each house of state government who were helping to get the funding, namely, Michael Bragman, democrat Majority Leader of the Assembly, and the newly elected member of the Senate republican Majority, yours truly.

A meeting was then set for a discussion among these five "stakeholders." I knew where Michael Bragman stood, since he always stood as close behind Stephen Rogers, Sr., as was possible. I knew where Tex Simone stood, since he publically stated that he wanted the new stadium in the same location that it had always been. I knew where I stood and so did everyone else because of my public statements that the stadium should be downtown, and I knew where Mayor Tom Young stood, since he felt the same way I did. I wasn't sure where Nick Pirro stood on the issue.

In any event, it was decided by the power behind the MDA that this would be a closed door meeting and that the press would not be allowed in. This was odd, since at the time and ever since, the Syracuse newspapers has railed against closed door meetings of government leaders, since the public "had a right to know." However, certain meetings were apparently exempt, especially when the publisher of the newspaper would be present and was right in the middle of what was happening.

Well, the meeting took place and the five "stakeholders" were there, but we had a couple of visitors. The visitors were Stephen Rogers Sr., and Irwin Davis. During the discussions, Rogers made it very clear that he thought the stadium should be on the near northside, and not downtown. When I disagreed and pointed out the support of the down-

town businesses, the likelihood that people would stay in the City and spend money after work, and the obvious trend throughout the country, Rogers responded that the stadium couldn't be downtown because the people from the suburbs wouldn't go to the games because of the "people down there." It was obvious that Mr. Rogers was not happy with me when I asked "What do you mean by the people down there?" He never responded, at least verbally.

Well, once the oracle had spoken, Nick Pirro stated that he wanted the stadium on the northside as well. I could never understand this since the county had just built, with substantial government money, a new downtown convention center. A new stadium would have greatly complimented the convention center. It would have helped the county get conventions to Syracuse since, in addition to baseball games, the stadium could also have been used for other sporting activities and concerts. In any event, Nick cast his vote for the northside location. With Bragman and Tex Simone this made a majority.

When the doors were opened, the press descended upon the parties to this closed door meeting asking questions. That evening I received a call from a very honest, talented and experienced reporter of the Syracuse Newspapers, Mike Fish. He simply asked me whether or not Rogers participated in the meeting. I asked him why he wanted to know. He candidly told me that he wrote an article for the newspaper about the meeting which included the fact that Rogers was at the meeting. He was told that that was not true and he had to take Rogers' name out of the article, and if he didn't, he would be in jeopardy. So much for freedom of the press.

I not only told him that Stephen Rogers Sr. was at the meeting, but I also told him what Rogers had to say, and how the meeting resulted in a vote for the near northside location. He thanked me profusely. I am not sure how he wrote the

article, but, not surprisingly, Stephen Rogers Sr.'s name was not in the article. My guess was that it was eliminated by the editor.

So, it was a done deal. The stadium was going to be located on the near northside. Not so fast. As most things with state government, the funding for the stadiums throughout the state was held up. And while it was held up there was an election for governor, and a little known New York state Senator, who I started my service in the Senate with, George Pataki, surprisingly beat Mario Cuomo. George Pataki came into the Senate the same year I did in 1992, but had served thirteen years as a state Assemblyman before that and was well aware of the workings of Albany. Moreover, I became close to him since philosophically, we were pretty much aligned on most issues.

Since the stadium money had not been released by the state as yet, and the state was not a party to the decision that the stadium site had to be decided by the five-headed stakeholder model, I spoke to the new governor about its location. In fact, when meeting him at the airport one day and driving with him near the location of the old stadium, I explained to him where the new stadium should be built. He indicated to me that he thought that made sense, but it had to be a local decision. I asked him whether, if I could get local support, would he have any problem in changing the location of the stadium to downtown. He told me absolutely not.

So my first step was to contact a developer who previously proposed building the stadium in the downtown area. When I explained my discussion with Governor Pataki, he seemed to be pleased and encouraged. I asked him to get me copies of downtown proposals so that I could discuss them with local and state officials. After a couple of weeks, not having received anything, I called him again, but he never returned my call.

Approximately two days later there was an editorial written by the editorial board of the Syracuse newspapers criticizing me for being a legislator that had numerous conflicts of interest. The article berated me and made it sound like I was personally gaining in my law practice by my decisions as a state senator. Of course, the stadium was not mentioned at all in the editorial. There was another interesting thing about the editorial. My photograph was on the editorial page. For those who are not familiar with the Syracuse newspapers back then it was very rare that a photograph was placed on the editorial page. I would have had no objection, but as you can imagine, it wasn't the most flattering of photographs.

I then realized why the developers never got back to me. The word was out that Rogers, through the MDA, wanted the stadium in the location that the five-headed stakeholder model selected. The last thing a developer needed was to be vilified in the Syracuse newspapers. With the loss of developer interest in downtown, and no others continuing to advocate for a downtown stadium, the new stadium was built on the same northside location. Not surprisingly, the attendance at the new stadium has been no different than the attendance at the old stadium. Simply put, the stadium siting decision was a wrong one.

This episode was the first of many in my political career involving the MDA, and it was the first of many where the free press went after me because I disagreed with the agenda of the MDA.

THE RISE AND FALL OF ELIOT SPITZER

T here were five governors during the time I served in the senate. For twelve of those years George Pataki was governor. Prior to George Pataki, for my first two years in state government, the governor was Mario Cuomo. And during these first fourteen years there weren't really many shocking political developments or any major scandals. But in the next four years, 2007 through 2010, there were enough to last a lifetime.

Eliot Spitzer came on the Albany scene in 1998 when he was elected Attorney General of the state of New York. Eliot came from a well-heeled family and never really had much concern about money. He also was the beneficiary of the best education possible having attended Princeton University for undergraduate school and Harvard law school. He then began the practice of law with the well-known and well respected Wall Street law firm of Paul, Weiss, Rifkind, Whorton & Garrison. Spitzer also worked in the Manhattan District Attorney's office under legendary Robert M. Morgenthau, where he was assigned to the organized crime unit. He gained notoriety for his pursuit of the Gambino crime family.

After leaving the District Attorney's office, he spent

some years in the practice of law until he was elected New York state Attorney General, defeating republican incumbent, Dennis Vacco. As Attorney General, Spitzer concentrated on the prosecution of white-collar crimes, and went after American International Group (AIG) and other major Wall Street players.

He also brought suit against Richard Grasso, the former chairman of the New York Stock Exchange, claiming that he did not disclose fully to his board of directors a lucrative compensation package. Spitzer gained a populist reputation for cleaning up Wall Street and advocating to bring ethical conduct to that segment of the economy.

Spitzer worked himself into an enviable position to run for and become governor of New York. As a democrat in a predominantly democrat state, with the notoriety that he had earned as Attorney General, it was Eliot Spitzer's election to lose in 2006. The polls during the campaign from start to finish showed him leading by wide margins over an underfunded, relatively unknown republican candidate, John Faso. No one was surprised when, in November of 2006, Spitzer won with 69 percent of the vote. After winning, he promptly proclaimed that there was "a new sheriff in town."

Spitzer was bright, articulate, and ambitious and appeared to be standing on the high ground as far as ethics was concerned in view of his record as a prosecutor in the Manhattan District Attorney's office and as Attorney General. However, to an extent not matched by any of his predecessors, Eliot Spitzer felt that he should control and run everything in Albany. In fact, he affectionately called himself, "the steamroller."

During Spitzer's abbreviated time as governor, the Senate Majority Leader was Joseph Bruno, a tough businessman and politician, who never had been, nor ever would be steamrolled. The friction between the two started almost immedi-

ately after Spitzer took office.

The new "sheriff" apparently believed that the state police was his personal political investigative arm. He had the state police follow Bruno and record his comings and goings, believing that it was just a matter of time before he would get something on him in order to force Bruno under his control. Well, it didn't quite work out that way. Spitzer took his first political hit when this state police activity was uncovered and disclosed.

I had no idea that Spitzer was using the state police to tail Joe Bruno, but it was obvious to everyone that there was the strongest dislike, if not hatred, between the two. Spitzer believed that Bruno was impeding Spitzer's total control of state government. And he was.

Spitzer's initiative to give illegal aliens driver licenses was, in my judgment, not only wrong, but dangerous for national security. Spitzer took action by way of an Executive Order requiring the Department of Motor Vehicles to simply issue these licenses. There was no legislative debate and no bill even considered prior to the Executive Order. Bruno and most republicans and many Democrats believed that Spitzer was stepping over the line by attempting to govern by himself.

One day at the height of the Spitzer/Bruno friction, I received a call, while I was on the Lakeshore golf course in Cicero, New York. I was playing a round of golf with a good friend, County Court Judge Anthony Aloi, when the call came in on my cell phone that Governor Spitzer wanted me to phone him. The dilemma I had was that I was on the third hole of the course and would not be finishing any time soon. But I called him after I hit my drive.

I mentioned to my friend that I had to make this call because the governor wanted to speak with me. I had no idea what the call was about, but I did know that Spitzer was mak-

ing the rounds in the Syracuse area the week before, basically berating all legislators, including myself and Assembly democrat William Magnarelli. In addition to Bruno, Spitzer was trying to steamroll other legislators.

During his stop in Syracuse, coincidentally on my way to my law office I saw a gathering of reporters. I asked them what was going on and learned that the governor was three doors from my law office after holding a news conference in front of it. At the news conference he criticized me and other legislators for being in their home districts when they should have been working in Albany. This criticism made little sense, since there was no legislative session that day and legislators were usually in their districts when they weren't in legislative session.

However, I parked my car and walked into the coffee shop in which he was holding court, went up to the governor, and welcomed him to my district. He seemed a little bit uncomfortable, but he handled himself well. We had a plesant short chat, which made it difficult for him to continue with his criticism. In fact, when I left, several of the reporters followed me and I explained it was great to have the governor in town, but he was off base in criticizing legislators for being in their home districts on a non-legislative day. This seemed to defuse the issue.

So when I called Spitzer back on the golf course I was assuming it was a follow-up to this news conference and our impromptu meeting. But it wasn't. He was literally asking for my help to try to convince Joe Bruno to be more receptive to Spitzer's priorities. In asking for my help, he praised me for being one of the few reasonable legislators.

Needless to say, this amazed me in view of his news conference a few days earlier calling me out for not doing my job. Now he was privately praising me and asking for my help. Something was truly wrong with this man. In fact, during the

phone conversation, he told me that he was sitting at his vacation home on some lake having a drink and that he hoped that I could join him there some time. Prior to this conversation I had spoken with Spitzer only a handful of times and now he was acting as if he was my best friend.

The humorous part of the call was that I continued to play the hole as the discussion went on. I simply put the phone on speaker, put it on the ground, and let him talk when I was taking my swings on this long par five. My third stroke resulted in the ball landing adjacent to the green on the other side of a sand trap. As the governor was talking about his vacation home on the lake, I put the cell phone on the ground and chipped over the sand trap near the hole. I then picked up the phone and concluded the conversation. Amazingly, I made the putt and parred the hole, which was a rarity. Judge Aloi suggested that I should have more talks with the governor while playing golf because it improved my game.

This phone call, asking for my help a few days after berating me in the media was strange but I still had no idea how strange things would become. No one knew that at that time Spitzer was violating the same laws that he so relished enforcing against others.

Aside from his criminal behavior, Spitzer imploded over some of his directives. As mentioned earlier, in September of 2007, he issued an Executive Order directing that the department of motor vehicles issue driver licenses to illegal aliens. To add insult to injury, he directed that applicants would not have to prove legal immigration status and could use out of country identifications to get their drivers' licenses.

This was not very popular. A bill was drafted to stop the plan from being implemented and, as a member of the senate, I voted for the bill, which was passed by the vote of 39 to 19. At that time the senate was controlled by republicans, but some democrats joined in the vote. After this vote, Spitzer

revised his plan, but the political damage was already done. By the end of his first year in office his approval ratings had plummeted. He was no longer considered unbeatable. In fact, potential gubernatorial candidates began coming out of the woodwork and making noises.

On March 10, 2008, I was in a republican closed-door conference where we were discussing the senate calendar, when members started going in and out of the room. There was a buzz about Spitzer going down. Prior to that, I had heard absolutely nothing about Spitzer having any troubles with the law.

The republican conference was never concluded, since everyone hurried to television sets to see what was going on. I remember watching the reports, totally amazed at what I was hearing. There were people around the room with their mouths open in disbelief. It was reported that Eliot had patronized a prostitute named Ashley Dupre, whose hourly charge was over one thousand dollars. Apparently, there were similar liaisons with other high priced prostitutes. But what was most unbelievable was that he violated the federal Mann Act by transporting a woman across state lines for prostitution purposes, and he also laundered the money that he paid the prostitutes for their services, and possibly for bribes.

Now some would defend Eliot Spitzer to the present day saying that sexually-related allegations are things that we shouldn't really be concerned about, especially in the post-Clinton years. Even though Spitzer didn't raise the famous "I didn't have sex with that woman" defense based on the Clinton definition of "what sex is," he did violate laws that he had zealously prosecuted others for violating.

Put in the vernacular, he was a phony. A person who was born into great wealth and privilege, posed as someone with unquestioned ethics and integrity, and as the new sheriff who would root out corruption in Albany. Having prosecuted

those who violated the law, he believed and acted like the law didn't apply to him.

One of the most disturbing things was that when he first appeared before the cameras about the allegations, he dragged his then wife, Silda, to the podium with him. From everything that I knew about her, she was and is a wonderful accomplished woman. To watch her face and the agony she was going through while Eliot leaned on her in his time of trouble was disgusting.

Spitzer resigned on March 17, 2008, just over a year from when he took office with an approval rating that was off the charts. This was simply shocking. An individual with his abilities and with his election landslide had the opportunity to become a great governor. Unfortunately, this did not happen.

It's also interesting to note that Governor Spitzer was never indicted for his criminal activity, in stark contrast to his zealous pursuit against others while in his prosecutorial positions. What was also shocking was that Eliot Spitzer was later rewarded by the CNN television network, by making him a host of a television program. Only in America!

The program began airing in October of 2010 and was co-hosted by Kathleen Parker, Spitzer's conservative counterpart. Parker didn't last long, leaving the show four months later. Spitzer made it through to July 2011, when he was bounced. In fact, he spent less time as a talk show host than he did as governor.

The aftermath is just as interesting. In New York state, if the governor dies in office or vacates that position for any reason, the lieutenant governor becomes the governor of New York until the next election. The lieutenant governor at the time was David Paterson. David and I had served in the Senate together for fourteen years. David was sight-impaired, but it never stopped him from making some of the most eloquent

extemporaneous speeches that I heard in my years as a member of the Senate.

The relief was palpable among legislators once David took office, since everyone believed he was a good man, had substantial legislative experience, and would work in a cooperative and constructive way with the legislature. In fact, he was a good man and did attempt to work in a cooperative way. The problem, however, was that he was ill-equipped to become governor of New York. One of the Albany reporters dubbed him the "accidental governor." He was, in fact, the accidental governor, but in short order he was referred to by other names as well.

The Governor Spitzer affair happened at the worst possible time, since we were in the throes of trying to put together the 2008 budget. That budget was due on April 1st. Spitzer resigned on March 12, 2008, so we were in the final weeks of the budget process.

The legislature and Governor Paterson did work together to complete the budget without as much wrangling and friction as was normally the case. Most of the legislators, including myself, were relieved that we had one of our own in the governor's office who would work with us, rather than trying to control everything.

The problem wasn't the lack of civility, the problem was the lack of consistency. A perfect example is when Patterson presented his own first budget the following year, he spoke of the dire financial situation that New York was in and the need for deep budget cuts. This was in January of 2009. His budget speech was right on the money and the republican Senate Majority was with him since we also wanted to put New York's financial house in order.

Unfortunately, between the budget speech and the actual passage of the budget, Patterson caved to the democrat Assembly Majority and its leader, Sheldon Silver, and substan-

tially increased spending, doing nothing to deal with the projected budget deficit. On one day the governor said that he would not sign a budget unless there was reduced spending but he took a 180 degree turn the next day. This phenomenon happened not only in budget matters, but with many other issues that faced the state.

It got to the point that within a year after Governor Paterson took office he had little credibility. No one believed him when he made a pronouncement, since they knew that it was just a matter of time before he backed off it. Many blamed it on the fact that many of the Spitzer advisors had left and Patterson only had second tier people left in place to advise him. To me, that's absolute nonsense. If you were a legislator for twenty years and Lieutenant Governor for over a year, you would have had to have had some knowledge of the process and have some independent consistent philosophy to follow as you govern.

Then, to further add to the problems of the state, Joe Bruno, resigned from office on June 24, 2008. Although it had not been announced, as yet, it was apparent he was being investigated by the federal government for alleged double dealing and benefiting himself from actions that he took in his capacity as Senate Majority leader. Upon his resignation, Dean Skelos, the then deputy majority leader, was selected by his fellow Republicans to become majority leader.

Bruno was indicted on January 23, 2009. Eventually he went to trial on the charges and was acquitted of five felonies and convicted of two others. Shortly after the conviction, however, the United States Supreme Court, in rulings in cases where the defendants were prosecuted under similar statutes, found that the statutes were unconstitutionally vague. Because of this, those convictions were overturned. More about this later.

So, as of mid-2008, two of the three political leaders

of the state of New York were new. Fortunately, however, the rest of the year was relatively uneventful. It's good that it was, since everyone needed a break to prepare for 2009 and 2010, in my mind, the lowest point for the New York state legislature during my tenure.

COURTS ARE APOLITICAL

There has been an ongoing debate in New York whether judges should be elected or appointed. To make the appointment process sound more wholesome, those who favor appointments call the appointment process "merit selection." I was involved in these debates many times, especially when I was chairman of the Senate Judiciary committee.

Most are familiar with the elective process, whereby a party nominates an individual to run for office and the individual that gets the most votes at a general election wins the position. That's also true with judges, with some exceptions. The most notable exception is the Court of Appeals, the highest court of the state, whose judges are appointed.

New York state has a judicial screening committee to review the qualifications of judges who are being considered for appointment to the Court of Appeals. The committee reviews the candidates being considered by the governor and rates them. An applicant can be ranked "highly qualified," "qualified" or "not qualified". But who selects the committee members who make these rankings?

The governor has four appointments to the commit-

tee, the Chief Judge of the Court of Appeals has four appointments, the senate Majority Leader and the Speaker of the assembly each have one appointment, and the senate and assembly Minority Leaders each have one appointment. Obviously, if someone is appointed by an individual in a high political position, it would stand to reason that that appointee has political leanings that correspond to the person who named him or her to the committee. Likewise, the governor is not going to submit names of potential judges for review by the committee that he or she would not want to be on the bench. So to believe that this is merit selection and that this process is less political than the voters making the decision as to which judges are ultimately elected is naive at best.

Let me give you my favorite example. A vacancy occurred in the Court of Appeals during my first term as a New York state senator. Mario Cuomo was the governor at the time, who publicly stated that he wanted to appoint an Hispanic to the highest court of the state. As I recall, he had someone in mind who later decided to withdraw his name from consideration. As a result, the judicial selection committee went back to work and reviewed the qualifications of other potential nominees selected by Governor Cuomo. The nominees included a black man, who was at the time a member of the Supreme Court, Appellate Division, a court directly under the Court of Appeals, a caucasian man and woman, both of whom were members of another Appellate Division, and an Hispanic woman, who was a trial level judge two rungs below the highest Court.

The committee determined that three of the four judges were "highly qualified" and the fourth judge, the Hispanic woman was simply "qualified." Governor Cuomo chose the Hispanic woman to serve on the highest court of the state, the Court of Appeals. Since he had already announced that he wanted an Hispanic on the Court, you might ask what the selection committee's role was and whether this was really

"merit selection".

When a Governor nominates an individual to the Court of Appeals, the New York state senate has to confirm that nominee before that nominee actually assumes the position. At the time I was a member of the senate Judiciary committee. I learned of these rankings and learned more about this Hispanic judge through independent research. The most amazing fact that I learned was that six months earlier this judge was reviewed by another judicial screening committee to determine her qualifications for appointment to the Appellate Division , the court one rung below the Court of Appeals. At that time, the review committee determined that she was "not qualified." In merely six months Governor Mario Cuomo's nominee who was unqualified for a lower appellate court position, became qualified for the highest court of the state. So much for "merit selection."

It is obvious that the reason she was selected was because of her ethnic background and the governor made no secret of it. There are only seven judges on the Court of Appeals and there are simply not enough spots for every ethnic group.

I remember before speaking against this nominee on the senate floor, that I really wanted to argue that I was upset that the nominee wasn't a left-handed Lithuanian lesbian, since left-handed Lithuanian lesbians were grossly under represented on the Court of Appeals. Fortunately, I had better judgment, and I simply argued that we had four "highly qualified" candidates of different ethnic backgrounds, with experience on the Appellate Division, who were passed over for someone who was wasn't qualified six months earlier for a lower Appellate Court position. The judge was confirmed.

The Chief Judge of the Court of Appeals at the time was Judith Kaye. While she was Chief Judge I often commented that she was the best politician in Albany. She definitely knew how to gain support among legislators, as well as support

from the media for her initiatives. I didn't call her the best politician in Albany in a derogatory way but, quite the contrary, as a compliment. It seemed that most everything that she argued for was supported by those who had to, and she rarely didn't get that for which she advocated.

On a personal level, I can attest to what a great politician she was. Several years after the Hispanic judge was confirmed to the Court of Appeals at a time when I was chairman of the Senate Judiciary committee, Judge Kaye invited me to an event in New York City put on by the New York state Bar Association. There was a wonderful dinner and Judge Kaye invited me to sit at her table. Guess who she sat next to me? You're right, the Hispanic judge who I voted against – Judge Carmen Beauchamp Ciparick. Pretty slick!

Quite honestly, Judge Ciparick was a wonderful woman and served well while on the bench, although her decisions tended to be more liberal than I would have liked. However, I stand by my vote since appointments to the highest court are suppose to be, and should be based on merit.

Fast Forward. Judge Ciparick turned 70 and, due to the mandatory retirement age, retired at the end of 2012. That left an open seat on the Court of Appeals for the governor to fill. Ironically, the governor at the time was Andrew Cuomo, Mario's son.

It was assumed that Governor Andrew Cuomo would appoint an Hispanic to this open seat. Why an Hispanic? Because it was then viewed as an Hispanic seat, having been previously occupied by Judge Ciparick.

If anyone doesn't believe that history repeats itself, he or she should pay attention to what happened in 2013 with respect to this Court of Appeals appointment. The individuals that the governor sent to the screening committee were one Hispanic man, two Hispanic women, an African-American woman, an Asian-American woman, and two caucasian men.

Without knowing who the Governor was going to appoint, I would have bet anyone that it would have been one of the Hispanic women. Well, that turned out to be the case. Governor Andrew Cuomo nominated Professor Jenny Rivera.

Ms. Rivera was a professor at the City University of New York law school. She worked for several organizations, such as the Legal Aid Society, and ran an organization out of the law school dealing with minority rights. She had no courtroom experience and no judicial experience, but she was selected by the governor to be the next judge on the state's highest court.

The African-American woman nominee was a judge for 20 years. The Hispanic man was a judge for 18 years, the last four years of which were served on the Appellate Division. One caucasian man was in private practice for eight years and was a judge for 17 years, and at the time he was also serving on the Appellate Division.

The Asian-American woman was a partner in a large law firm with 32 years of litigation experience. The other caucasian male had 33 years of litigation experience. Finally, another Hispanic woman had five years of litigation experience, but she was viewed by the New York state Bar Association to be "not qualified."

Despite having questionable qualifications by any objective standard, Jenny Rivera was one of the nominees the governor had the Judicial Screening Committee screen. Because she was Hispanic? Do ya think?

Being still a member of the Judiciary committee of the state senate, I began doing some research on Professor Rivera. I found that she also clerked for a Federal Court of Appeals Judge, who at the time of Rivera's review, was a member of the U.S. Supreme Court. However, Professor Rivera only served one year as a clerk. I found a video of a television interview with Jenny Rivera. During this interview the way she de-

scribed her services as a clerk was that she got papers ready for the Judge and kept the motions calendar. She sounded to me to be a ministerial court clerk rather than a law clerk. She didn't write any of the decisions for the Judge.

Most disturbing to me, however, was her legal writing. It may have been my deficiency, but I could not understand what she was trying to say in several articles, all of which dealt with "equal rights." One of her theories was that "equal protection" should be brought down to sub-classifications, so that the courts should consider not only whether Hispanics in general had been discriminated against, but also should consider separately the sub-categories of Latinos, Mexicans, Puerto Ricans, etc, to determine whether each sub-class was treated equitably as compared to the other sub-classes. You can't make this up.

During the Judiciary committee hearing, I asked Ms. Rivera questions on these topics. I also asked questions of the then president of the New York state Trial Lawyers Association, as well as the president of the New York state Bar Association. It seemed incredible to me that both of these lawyers spoke on behalf of Professor Rivera's appointment to the state's highest court, when she had no litigation or court experience, and her writings were suspect, at best. Maybe it was politics?

Let's not forget that this process is called "merit" selection of judges. Individuals must go through screening committees to determine whether they are qualified to serve on the highest court of the state of New York. Again, I would take elected judges over this flawed political process any day. At least voters would be able to review the qualifications of the candidates and pick who they thought was the most qualified individual to serve on the highest court of the state. And by doing so, it wouldn't be just one man or woman making political decisions on who should serve on the state's highest

court.

Others asked questions of Professor Rivera, and when a vote was about to be taken, the vote was held up at the direction of the senate republican Majority Leader. I believe that if the vote had been taken at that time, the nominee would have been rejected, and she then could not have gone on for a full senate confirmation vote.

By the following day there were enough votes to have her recommended by the committee to the full senate, and a majority of the senators voted for her. Political? Do you think? She is now on the highest court of the state of New York. At the time of her confirmation she was 52 years old, which means she will be making court decisions for 18 years, that will have to be followed by lower courts and attorneys. Good luck.

When the nomination came to the floor, I was very vocal mentioning that there should not be a Hispanic seat, or any other ethnic seat on the state's highest court. The most qualified person should be nominated by the governor and the nominee should have either trial experience, or judicial experience, but preferably both, and have distinguished him or herself in the law.

Democrat Senator Ruben Diaz, who is of Puerto Rican descent, also spoke. He stated that it was wonderful that the governor thought that a Hispanic nominee would be the choice. But he then rattled off a series of Hispanic lawyers and judges that were more qualified. However, none had the most important qualification that Jenny Rivera had, namely, she was a close friend of Governor Cuomo's chief legal counsel, Mylan Denerstein.

Many who did not talk on the floor on the nominee privately told me that they agreed with me, but they "had to vote for her." Oh brother!

So, in short, in my opinion, there is no such thing

as "merit" selection of judges in the current system for the selection of Court of Appeal judges. In any event, I feel more comfortable allowing the general public to make the decisions as to who should be on the bench, rather than those decisions being made by some chief executive, whether it be the governor with respect to Court of Appeals judges, or others pertaining to local appointed judgeships.

So, the process is political. You either become a judge by receiving a nomination of a party and getting more votes than the other man or woman in a general election, or you are appointed by someone who is in a high level elected political office. Quite frankly, it is impossible to take politics out of the process, whether the judge is elected or appointed. However, with the general public making the decision, at least the decision is not wired for those who are politically connected to one person - the executive that makes the appointments.

There is another side story with respect to the New York Bar Association event that I mentioned earlier. At that event, I was also asked by Judge Kaye to speak at the judges' luncheon as chairman of the senate Judiciary committee. I was honored to do so. Judge Kaye put me at the head table. Also at the head table, among others, was former Court of Appeals Chief Judge, Solomon Wachtler. Judge Wachtler was appointed to the Court of Appeals in 1972, and was chosen to be the Chief Judge of this court by Governor Mario Cuomo in 1985.

While he was Chief Judge, he was mentioned quite frequently as a possible nominee for governor if Mario Cuomo decided not to run for re-election. He was handsome, articulate and a well-respected judge. But it turned out that he had a dark side as well.

Judge Wachtler was appointed co-executor of the estate of one Alvin Wolosoff and trustee of four trusts arising out of Wolosoff's estate. One of the beneficiaries of the trust was

one Joy Silverman. As the story is told, Judge Wachtler and Ms. Silverman began having an affair in 1988, and Judge Wachtler became totally obsessed with her. There were stories that he actually stalked her when she wanted to call off the relationship. Moreover, there was an investigation concerning extortion and blackmail, which eventually resulted in his arrest in November of 1992 and his subsequent conviction and jail sentence. Judge Wachtler ended up serving fifteen months of that sentence.

I never met Judge Wachtler before, and I was quite shocked to see him at the head table at that luncheon, which was held not too long after he was released from prison. He subsequently wrote a couple of books and became a professor of Constitutional Law at Touro law school. In October 2007, he was reinstated to the New York state Bar.

Even though Judge Wachtler was sitting on the dais a few seats away from me, I didn't approach him to talk to him. I don't know if I was simply embarrassed, or I was embarrassed for him, but I didn't know what to say to him at the time. I wish I had, since this was an incredible story of an individual who got to the highest position in the court system and then reached the lowest, but ultimately bounced back. I'm pleased that things went well for him after his downfall.

So there are politics in the "merit selection" of judges, but certainly there couldn't be politics in decisions by judges. Not so fast.

When Governor Paterson ascended to his position as governor as a result of the fall of Eliot Spitzer, the lieutenant governor position was vacant. This had happened several times before in New York state history. The reason no governor to date had appointed a new lieutenant governor when the lieutenant governor's office was open, was that the New York state Constitution does not provide a procedure for such an appointment. It is completely silent. As a result, in prior

instances where the seat was vacated for any reason and the lieutenant governor became governor, the position was left vacant.

Despite this, Governor Paterson decided to appoint somebody as the new lieutenant governor, namely Richard Ravitch. Richard Ravitch had a long and distinguished career in government service. President Lyndon Johnson appointed Ravitch to the United States Commission on urban problems in 1966. He was also named President of the Citizens Housing and Planning Council in 1968. Thereafter, New York Governor Hugh Carey appointed Ravitch as Chairman of the New York state Urban Development Corporation which, at the time, was found to be insolvent. Thereafter, in 1979, Governor Carey appointed him as Chairman of the Metropolitan Transportation Authority. As Chairman, he did not accept a salary. When he received the lieutenant governor position, after the Paterson appointment went through the courts, he also refused to take a salary. It wasn't who was being appointed that was the problem. The problem was whether or not the governor had the authority to appoint anyone.

Governor Paterson decided to make this appointment, I believe, since there was so much confusion in the state senate concerning leadership. Up to 2009 the Majority Leader and the President Pro Tempore were the same person. However, a coup occurred in the senate, which resulted in the separation of those positions. This story is worthy of a future chapter in this book.

What is relevant, at this point, about the coup is that on July 9, 2009, Pedro Espada, Jr., about whom you will learn a lot more, was appointed the new President Pro Tempore of the New York state Senate, the person next in line to be governor if there was no lieutenant governor in place. No doubt there was grave concern about the prospect of Pedro Espada, Jr. possibly becoming governor of the state. I hasten to add,

that I have no direct knowledge whether this was Governor Paterson's reason for appointing a lieutenant governor, but this theory made a lot of sense to me.

In any event, no matter who was in the position of president pro tempore of the senate, there was no procedure in the state Constitution for the appointment of a lieutenant governor when that position became vacant. It seemed obvious that the governor alone could not make such an appointment. Even the commissioners of the various agencies and departments of government, appointed by the governor, had to be confirmed by the senate according to the New York constitution. It would stand to reason that if commissioners appointed by the governor were required to be confirmed by the senate, that a lieutenant governor, who holds a higher position, would have had to be confirmed as well. However, such an appointment and confirmation process had to be written somewhere in the Constitution, and it wasn't.

Most legal scholars thought that there was no authority for the governor to simply make an appointment of lieutenant governor, and predicted that the Court of Appeals would similarly reject the appointment and find that it was improperly made. Again, not so fast.

On September 22, 2009, the Court of Appeals held that the governor did have such authority. What was most interesting to me was that Court of Appeals Judge Susan Reed voted with the majority. Judge Reed was appointed by republican governor Pataki and was considered to be a conservative judge and a strict constructionist. For her to find grounds for such an appointment, when there was no language in the Constitution to allow it, was truly remarkable.

So, was this decision political? Was it made with sufficient legal underpinnings? Or was it simply made to prevent what some felt would be a very undesirable person, Pedro Espada, Jr., from possibly becoming governor.

The irony of this situation was that once Governor Paterson appointed Richard Ravitch as lieutenant governor, Ravitch was totally ignored by Paterson. It became a joke in Albany as to what Ravitch actually did. He would from time-to-time appear in the state senate chambers to preside over the senate, which was one of the roles of a lieutenant governor. However, the governor ignored Ravitch's advice, despite the severe budget problems that were facing the state of New York. I am sure Ravitch wondered many times about why he agreed to accept the appointment. However, the Court of Appeals' decision is still good law and, short of a legislative change, the governor of the state of New York can now appoint a lieutenant governor when there is a vacancy in that position.

I saw another exception to the general rule that courts are apolitical. It came right on the heels of the lieutenant governor decision, and it had to do with judicial pay raises. In New York state pay raises for legislators and judges were always done legislatively at the same time. I believe it was done this way to give legislators political cover when giving themselves their own salary increase.

The last increase for judges and legislators was about fifteen years before. I remember, at that time, arguing about the foolishness of the system, whereby people have to vote on their own salaries and that it would be better to allow for cost-of-living increases for judges and legislators just like in many other government positions. However, that argument was ignored when the last salary increase occurred.

There never is a good time for legislators to vote for a salary increase for themselves. As a result, years went by with no proposals for increases. Unfortunately, judges were tied to this time-honored tradition, and their salaries were remaining the same, while their staffs were getting increases. In fact, some of the higher level administrative positions in the Office

of Court Administration carried salaries greater than the salaries that judges were earning. Amazingly, many first year associates at Wall Street law firms, just out of law school, were also paid more money than judges. It was not right and it made no sense.

As a result, in Spitzer's first year of office, I introduced a bill which would have called for an independent commission to review salaries for judges and make recommendations to the legislature. The senate republicans were in the majority at that time, but I was also able to get all democrats to co-sponsor the bill. As a result, the bill was unanimously co-sponsored by senators of both parties and it was put on the calendar for a vote.

Assembly Speaker Sheldon Silver also had introduced the same bill in the assembly, which he agreed to pass. The timing was perfect, since the following Monday was the annual Law Day ceremonies to be held at the Court of Appeals building, where Governor Spitzer was going to be the featured speaker. Quite frankly, I thought the governor was going to make mention of the fairness of the commission and the proposed process for judicial pay increases. Well, I was wrong.

Early that morning I received a call indicating that Governor Spitzer was going to oppose the legislation unless he got concessions on other totally unrelated legislation. Despite this, I moved the bill to the floor for a vote. Amazingly, all the democrats asked to have their names taken off of the bill as co-sponsors, but I refused to let them, and they then all voted "no." To their credit, all the republicans voted "yes." I thought it was wrong for Spitzer to hold the judicial pay process hostage for some unrelated piece of legislation that he wanted from the legislature.

Democrat Assembly Speaker Silver, despite his prior commitments, did not put the bill on the floor of the assembly so it never was even voted on. As a result, the process that

would have ended this pay problem for judges in the state of New York was dead. In fact, it remained dead in 2008, 2009 and 2010.

Well, needless to say, the judges were not happy. Even though I sponsored the bill and had it passed in the senate, I was severely criticized by some judges, even some friends of mine, for not having passed judicial pay raises. There was no talking reason to any judge. They didn't care to know that I agreed with them and had taken substantial steps to accomplish what they were seeking.

Eventually, several of the judges brought a lawsuit claiming that it was unconstitutional for the legislature to withhold pay increases and to tie those increases to legislative salary increases. Several cases worked their way up to the highest court of the state and ultimately one of the cases was heard by the judges of the Court of Appeals who obviously had deep personal interests in the outcome, namely their own pay. A decision was rendered.

One of the Court of Appeals judges that I respected the most, Judge Eugene Piggott, wrote the decision for the Court of Appeals, and the decision was that the legislature had to "consider" a judicial pay raise. What does that mean? This made little sense, since the mere fact of not legislating a pay increase is considering one – in the negative. Moreover, to strictly comply with the decision all the legislature would have to do is to put a bill on the calendar and vote "no."

In addition, isn't there a conflict of interest for judges to order the legislature to consider pay raises for the judges themselves? To avoid the conflict, shouldn't the case have been decided by the federal courts? In any event, it didn't mean anything since the legislature did not introduce any bills after this decision was made until years later. The decision was simply ignored and there was no way the courts could enforce it.

Fortunately, as part of the budget that was passed on April 1, 2011, an independent body finally was formed to review and recommend judicial pay increases which were approved, and the political hot potato of judicial pay was finally put to rest. However, pay raises for legislators continued to be part of the political game. In 2014 Governor Andrew Cuomo refused to agree to a vote on a legislative pay increase unless the legislature agreed to certain legislation including approving public financing of campaigns, and again in 2016, he refused to support a legislative pay raise unless the legislature passed some "reform" legislation. Sounds like extortion to me.

Eventually, an independent body, like that formed for judicial pay raises was formed for raises for legislators. It recommended a substantial pay raise for legislators and pay raises were granted beginning in 2019. The legality of the commission's decision on raises is now being litigated ! And the beat goes on.

So, although most Court decisions are not political, the above cases are clear exceptions.

THE COUP

According to the Webster dictionary, there are different definitions of "coup." One definition is that a coup is a "brilliantly executed stratagem; a triumph." Another definition is "a sudden appropriation of leadership for power; a takeover." And a "coup d'état" is defined as a "sudden and decisive change of government illegally or by force."

At the legislative session of June 8, 2009, when the democrats were in control of the senate, republican senate Deputy Minority Leader Thomas Libous handed up a resolution to Neil Breslin, the unsuspecting senator who was presiding over the senate. Senator Breslin, a democrat from Albany, glanced at the proposed resolution and, without any thought, asked the clerk of the senate to read the resolution.

Once read, Senator Libous jumped up and asked for a vote. It dawned on a few people on the democrat side that something was going on. What was going on was that Libous was calling for a vote on a resolution calling for new leadership in the senate, which would result in the republicans retaking control of the New York senate.

A little background is necessary. For many years, the senate was controlled by the members of the republican party, and the assembly was controlled by the democrats.

In the 2008 Barack Obama landslide, that balance of power changed. The democrats took over by a slight margin, 32 to 30. Moreover, 23 of those 32 members were from New York City. As a result, the New York state Senate, which was traditionally controlled by upstate New York and Long Island, changed to control by New York City democrats.

The assembly already was, and had for many years, been controlled by New York City democrats. And the "accidental governor," David Paterson was a democrat from New York City. Moreover, virtually every leadership position in both houses went to a democrat from New York City. As a result, the New York state government was not only controlled by democrats---it was controlled by New York City democrats.

There is a substantial philosophical difference between upstate and Long Island republicans and New York City democrats. With this shift of two senators, during the 2008 election, there was no longer political regional balance in New York state government.

This was demonstrated quite clearly in the 2009 budget, which was passed on April 3, 2009. At his budget presentation, Governor Paterson was warning everyone that the state of New York was in a deep fiscal crisis and there were structural deficits built into the budget in the billions of dollars which made it necessary to cut the budget substantially. Within weeks the budget passed, which added, yes added, billions of dollars in new spending and billions of dollars in new taxes. This was absolutely irresponsible.

At the time, I was the top republican on the Finance committee. Even as the ranking member on that committee, I had about as much authority as the janitor did to change anything in the budget, since the democrats had total control of the process. My only avenue to try and change anything was to debate the budget bills on the floor. There were many videos

on YouTube of these "debates." They amounted to me asking the then senate Finance chair, Carl Kruger, various questions about the budget. To be kind, I will characterize his answers as being "non-responsive."

In 2007 a bipartisan budget reform bill was passed that required the assembly and the senate to each adopt separate budget bills by a certain date and then for each leader to assign members to various budget subcommittees to debate the differences in the budget bills publicly. This process was designed to lead to an on-time budget on April 1, and also a budget that was more transparent through open public debate.

In 2008, prior to the change in leadership, New York City democrats were controlling the assembly and republicans were controlling the senate, and the budget was adopted on time and, substantially in accordance with this 2007 budget reform act.

The New York City democrats, in 2009, being in control of everything in state government, simply ignored that law and passed the budget without joint public budget committee meetings, which thrust New York state into even deeper financial troubles. The New York City controlled legislature was aided and abetted by Governor Paterson, who demonstrated another one of his numerous flip flops by signing the budget bills, which substantially increased spending and taxes, when only weeks before he was looking for billions of dollars in budget cuts.

The budget wasn't the only problem. There were many actions of the legislature that ignored U

upstate New York and Long Island, and benefited New York City. One example related to the Metropolitan Transportation Authority, the authority that manages the trains, buses, subways, bridges, and highways in the New York City metropolitan area.

The MTA was in deep financial trouble and the New York City dominated legislature passed legislation that bailed it out. Funding for transportation happened every year, but whenever there was money that was spent for the MTA in prior years, with a republican controlled senate and a democrat controlled assembly, road and bridge money that benefited upstate New York and Long Island, matched the funds that were invested in the MTA. When the MTA bail-out bill was passed, after substantial debate, the democrat leadership in the senate promised that by October of 2009, the upstate road and bridge money would be addressed, but it wasn't.

This was the situation that existed on June 8, 2009, when the Resolution was handed up by Senator Libous to Senator Breslin, after which all hell broke loose on the senate floor. Eventually, after much shouting and many accusations, a vote was actually taken and two democrat senators, Hiram Monserrate and Pedro Espada, Jr. voted with the republicans to change leadership in the senate. Espada and Monserrate were New York City democrats. Why would they do such a thing? Very simply, self-interest.

Up to that point, there was one position entitled Senate Majority Leader who was the elected leader of the senate. He also carried a second title, President Pro Tempore. As part of the coup, those titles were spilt and Pedro Espada, Jr. was named President Pro Tempore of the senate and republican Dean Skelos was voted Majority Leader. Monserrate was named chairman of the Consumer Protection committee which, quite frankly, was no big deal.

Prior to June 8, 2009, I had absolutely no idea that this coup was brewing. Senators Skelos and Libous kept the discussions with Espada and Monserrate very close to their vests. I'm not sure who, if anyone else, knew what was happening, but very few did since there were no leaks that a coup was in the works. This, in itself, was remarkable. Loose lips have sunk

many ships in past years. The most notable of which occurred a few years earlier during central New York assemblyman Michael Bragman's attempt to overthrow New York City's Sheldon Silver to become Speaker of the assembly. Loose lips resulted in Bragman losing the bid to become Speaker. It also resulted in Bragman losing his Majority leadership position, and being sent to a small office in the bowels of the legislative office building.

So, from the republican perspective, the coup was a "brilliantly executed stratagem; a triumph," at least for the time being. From the democrat perspective, it was a "sudden and decisive change of government illegally." But it did not come about by "force."

The democrats didn't give up. The secretary to the senate is appointed by the Majority Leader. Prior to the coup, Malcom Smith was the Majority Leader. He had appointed Angelo Aponte as secretary of the senate. Aponte was a control freak and, in fact, was often seen lecturing senate democrats on the floor as to how they should vote. He was the perfect person for the democrats to be in that position after the coup.

The first thing that he did at that time was to shut off live broadcasts of the senate proceedings over the internet. Live internet broadcast was one of the many efforts made in the senate, by prior leadership, to open the process so that the people could view senate proceedings live. But as the coup was unfolding, the internet was shut off. Also, the lights were shut off in the senate chambers, which made it cozy, but not very conducive to performing business. Sounds like a third-world government, doesn't it?

Once the lights were restored and the internet broadcast was put back on, Aponte refused to provide the key to the senate chambers, which also made it quite difficult to conduct business. The senate republicans were not able to get much help from the state police, which was under the con-

trol of the New York City democrat governor. This was the same police force that a couple of years before was tailing Joe Bruno, at the direction of Eliot Spitzer.

When the republicans indicated that they were going to have session at another location outside of chambers, the doors were miraculously opened. However, Aponte held firm on one of his other actions. He basically locked up the bill jackets, which held the bills that were ready to be voted on during the senate proceedings. So the senate could not conduct business.

On some days when session began, none of the democrats showed up. On other days everyone showed up and the democrats and republicans tried to have separate proceedings. At one meeting, the senate republicans called the senate to order and called for the recitation of the pledge of allegiance, which was always the first order of business in a senate session. The democrats, claiming that they did not recognize the session as a legitimate one, remained seated during the pledge. This became a hot political issue in the next election where Senator David Valesky's image was everywhere showing that he didn't stand for the pledge of allegiance. He won his election anyway.

The coup was short lived and leadership changed back in about one month. During this one month period other tactics were used by the democrats. They organized demonstrations against the "illegal seizure of power" bringing hundreds of people to Albany to protest. What was outrageous about this was that the secretary of the senate, who refused to step down, allowed the demonstrators to demonstrate adjacent to the senate chambers.

The situation was so bad that the demonstrators attempted to block senators from entering the senate chambers. Fortunately, this resulted in only jostling of senators, and a lot of bumping and pushing, but no one was injured.

Never before had demonstrations been allowed in such close proximity of the chambers. One could hear the loud chanting of demonstrators outside the chambers while the republican senators were attempting to get bills on the floor and do business.

Moreover, there was no security in the Chambers, unlike on all other occasions both before and since, when there were threats of protestors, who might disrupt legislative proceedings. It was a low point in the history of the New York state senate, orchestrated by those who had lost power by a legitimate, though slick, senate vote.

Pedro Espada, Jr. under intense political pressure, had a change in heart and on July 9, 2009, he decided to change his vote, as did his partner, Hiram Monserrate. He was allowed by the democrats to keep his title of president pro tempore of the senate, which made him next in line to become governor, if Governor David Paterson's seat became vacant.

It was within days of the retaking control of the senate by the democrats that Governor Paterson decided he was going to appoint Richard Ravitch as lieutenant governor. And it was within weeks of him doing so that the Court of Appeals determined that he could, even though there was no provision in the Constitution allowing it.

What about Hirman Monserrate? Well, he was charged with felony assault for allegedly slashing his girlfriend's face with a broken glass. Nice guy. Those charges were pending when this coup occurred. Monserrate was tried, and convicted of a misdemeanor assault on December 15, 2009, and somehow acquitted of two felony assault counts, despite there being video footage in the apartment building where the incident occurred, showing Monserrate forcibly dragging his hysterical girlfriend down the hallway. As a result of the conviction, Monserrate first lost his committee chairmanship, then was expelled by a vote of the senate on February 9,

2010.

Thereafter, Jose Peralta won a special election to fill the vacant seat of Hiram Monserrate. In an act of supreme chutzpah, Monserrate circulated petitions and was on the ballot against Peralta on an independent line. However, the voters had had enough of Hirman Monserrate, and elected Peralta.

What about Espada? Well, the democrats, while they were more than happy to accept Pedro Espada's change in heart and his valuable vote to put the democrats back in control of the senate, arranged for a primary opponent to take Espada out in the 2010 primary. Despite his temporary defection from the senate democrats and despite an ongoing criminal investigation of Espada receiving kick-backs, he, confident as ever, forged on in his primary campaign. However, he lost the primary on September 14, 2010 to Gustavo Rivera and Rivera then went on to win the general election. So the two senators at the center of the coup were gone in short order.

In my mind, the coup was worth the try, despite the two individuals that the republicans had to rely on to change leadership. The state finances were going further down the drain; upstate and Long Island were being totally ignored; and legislation was passed in other areas that was very concerning. Moreover, the temporary takeover, despite the protestations of the democrats, was not illegal, since the republicans had the votes. However, it was only temporary since the loyalties of Espada and Monserrate were only to themselves.

CLEANING HOUSE

When the New York City democrats first took control of the New York state senate in January of 2009, there were democrat senators that joined together, calling themselves the "four amigos ." These amigos were Pedro Espada, Hirman Monserrate, Carl Kruger, and Ruben Diaz. Three were Hispanic and one was a Jewish amigo.

Espada and Monserrate attempted to enhance their positions by first siding with the republicans in the coup and later going back to the democrats. Carl Kruger was much shrewder. He used the leverage of the four amigos but remained with the democrat conference and became the chairman of the senate finance committee. Ruben Diaz stayed with the democrats as well and became chairman of the aging committee, not a very plum assignment, but something that he wanted.

Well, two of the amigos were out of the senate by the end of 2010, Monserrate having been expelled on February 9, 2010 and Espada having lost a primary on   September 14, 2010.

Espada was later indicted and convicted of receiving kickbacks and on other corruption charges and sent to jail for five years. That left two amigos, Diaz and Kruger. In early

2011, Kruger was indicted for alleged kick-backs, at which time he was removed from his democrat leadership position and relegated literally to a back seat in the chambers, from which he never again said a word. Thereafter, in December of 2011, he pled guilty to various felonies involving kickbacks and was sentenced to nine years in jail.

After the news of the Kruger indictment, I passed Senator Diaz in the senate chambers and I said that he was now the last of the amigos. With a big grin and his heavy Puerto Rico accent, he replied "And then there was one!" But things didn't get any better in 2010 after the democrats regained the senate. The democrats continued to ignore the budget reform act, and constructed a budget behind closed doors, without any open meetings of budget subcommittees to discuss the proposed budget. In fact, in 2010, the senate and assembly never even passed their separate budget bills, as required by law.

Eventually, the budget was passed, and despite the rhetoric of then Governor Paterson about the need to cut state government, the budget, crafted behind closed doors and made public just before the vote of the legislature, increased spending and taxes. The end result was that taxes and spending each increased by $14 billion over the two-year term when the legislature was totally controlled by New York City democrats. Those controlling Albany government were truly sending the government down the river to financial disaster. It became patently obvious that the 2010 election cycle was going to be extremely important for the state of New York. The state simply could not continue to go down this path during a recession without a resulting financial disaster.

Also, the scandals didn't end. Governor Paterson who most, including myself, thought was a good person but simply incapable of governing, showed that maybe he wasn't so pure after all. In February of 2010, one of Governor Paterson's staff

members, David W. Johnson, was accused by his girlfriend of assault and other domestic abuse. It was learned that Paterson contacted the woman and had others from his administration, including the state police, do the same to try to have her drop the charges. Considering how David Paterson got the Governor's position in the first place, as a result of Governor Spitzer's criminal activities and abuse of power, this development was truly shocking. Fortunately, in March of 2010, Johnson pled guilty to a misdemeanor and the issue went away.

Thereafter, there were allegations that Governor Paterson, against the ethics rules, accepted free tickets to a New York Yankee game, which he, at first, denied. Now, I know this seems petty, and I think it is too. The ethics rules, in some cases, had become absurd. One example was demonstrated at a state Library Association gathering. At that event a sign was posted that indicated that legislators could have either a cup of coffee or a small pastry, but not both, "by ruling of the Commission on Public Integrity."

In any event, it wasn't so much the acceptance of tickets that hurt Governor Paterson, it was his denial that he received free tickets. He eventually paid for the tickets, and that issue went away as well.

However, the biggest hit came in October of 2010 when the democratic inspector general of the state issued a report concerning dealings pertaining to the Aqueduct Race Track. Basically, it was alleged that democrat senate leaders, Malcom Smith and John Sampson, attempted to deliver a sweetheart deal to a group known as AEG, who wanted to operate the Aqueduct Race Track. It was reported that one of the principals of AEG was Reverend Floyd Flake, who was said to have had very close relationships with senators Smith and Sampson.

The inspector general found that Governor Paterson ignored the advice of his budget director and the director of the

division of the lottery, and disregarded the state's competitive bidding laws. The inspector general also found that the senate leaders, Smith and Sampson leaked bid analyses to AEG giving it an advantage in preparing its bid, and further that senator Sampson pressured AEG to include a New York City contractor that he wanted in the deal in return for his help.

The IG also found that although Smith tried to create a façade that he wasn't involved in the process, he actually advocated for AEG. These leaders' efforts resulted in AEG being selected by Governor Paterson for the Aqueduct operation's contract on January 29, 2010, even though AEG offered the state one hundred million dollars less than the highest bidder! One of the focal points of the investigation was the over one hundred thousand dollars of political campaign contributions by AEG and others to senate democrat campaigns.

These were incredible revelations that were made less than one month before the November elections. But remember there is "freedom of the press." Many newspapers didn't even mention these findings of alleged blatant wrongdoing. The Inspector General actually referred his investigation findings to the Manhattan district attorney for consideration of criminal charges. No charges were brought.

Some good came out of the Inspector General's report, in that Governor Paterson, once he and his senate democrat leaders were exposed, and under intense public pressure, reversed himself on granting the contract to AEG.

During the two-year democrat senate control, there weren't just ill-advised budget decisions and questionable ethical behavior, but also other ill-advised laws passed that never previously saw the light of day. One example was the law that was enacted in 2010 "reforming" the Rockefeller drug laws. At this time anything labeled "reform" was something that was deemed to be good. Change, however, is not always good, and this change in the criminal law was clearly

not. Its sponsor was Eric Schneiderman, who was later elected New York attorney general in the November 2010 election.

Basically, the theory behind the bill was to give drug users and sellers opportunities to make themselves productive citizens. Very few could disagree with that goal. However, the bill went way beyond giving users and sellers the opportunity to rehabilitate. What the bill provided for was that an individual charged with a felony of using or selling drugs could have that record sealed if he or she successfully completed a drug rehabilitation program. One might justify such an approach for drug users – but for drug dealers? However, the bill had more dangerous provisions.

It also provided for the sealing of up to an additional three prior misdemeanor convictions of that same individual. This provision certainly would help an individual to get a job, if rehabilitated. However, what about school districts and senior citizen centers, and day care centers, who were required by law to do criminal background checks of individuals before they were hired, for the protection of the vulnerable? How are employers to know that they are considering hiring someone who could have a felony and three misdemeanor drug related convictions, including drug sales. How are the vulnerable to be protected?

Considering legislation is always a balancing act. There is no perfect legislation and you have to weigh the pros and the cons. The balancing act on this bill was skewed far in favor of the drug user and seller, and against New York's vulnerable.

There were many similar bills that were passed which convinced many, including myself, that the election of 2010 would be one of the most significant legislative elections in New York's history. The direction of the state had to change, not only from a budgetary standpoint, but from a philosophical standpoint. Moreover, there had to be regional balance in state government and a balance in various political philoso-

phies for the good of the people of the state.

Fortunately, in 2010 there was also a gubernatorial race. Mario Cuomo's son, the then attorney general, Andrew Cuomo, was the democrat candidate. The endorsed republican candidate was Rick Lazio, a political retread who lost big to Hilary Clinton in a U.S. senate race several years earlier. Lazio got the nomination, but Carl Paladino, a wealthy businessman from western New York, beat Lazio, and beat him badly, in the primary. However, Paladino's campaign was a total disaster. Cuomo did not even have to campaign. There wasn't much he had to answer for, since republican Paladino, was so weak. Cuomo, like his predecessor Eliot Spitzer won in a landslide.

Cuomo ran, in part, on a fiscally conservative platform insisting that the most important thing for the state of New York was to get its financial house back in order. And when he became governor, at first, he followed through on that pledge. Fortunately, the residents of New York, who believed that the state had to cut spending and stop raising taxes, also voted to give back control of the senate to the republicans. It definitely wasn't by a landslide. Some of the races weren't decided until weeks after the election. But ultimately, the senate republicans regained control with a 32-30 majority.

Also, after the election, four of the democrats decided that they didn't want to align with New York City democrats. These democrats, Jeffrey Klein, David Valesky, Diane Savino, and David Carlucci, formed an Independent Democrat Caucus (IDC) and acted independently. They were sometimes helpful to the republican conference throughout the 2011-2012 legislative session.

It was fortunate for Governor Cuomo, that the republicans regained control of the senate because his fiscal platform at the time was almost identical to what the senate republicans had been advocating, for years. All senate repub-

licans voted "no" on both the 2009 and the 2010 budgets when the democrats were in control, which budgets collectively increased spending by fourteen billion dollars and increased taxes by fourteen billion dollars, at a time when the state was in serious financial trouble.

The senate republicans, during the 2011 budget process, partnered with the governor, not only to get the budget done on time, but much more importantly, to pass a budget which cut $10 billion in spending, and which spent less money than the prior year, for the first time in fifteen years. Moreover, the senate and assembly followed the 2007 Budget Reform Act and set and followed a calendar for the various milestones in the budget process, including passing assembly and senate budgets, appointing conference committee membership, and conducting open public joint conference committee meetings on the budget before a final vote was taken.

It was so gratifying for me to be personally involved in this process having, as senate ranking member on the Finance committee, railed against the budget process and the budget results for the last two years. In 2011, I became the new senate Finance committee chair, and was the senate point person in helping to marshal the fiscally responsible budget through the state senate.

It was noteworthy that after the budget was completed in 2011, I was contacted by an reporter from an NPR radio station in Los Angeles who wanted to speak with me live on the air, about the New York state budget process. Whereas, over the last few years, New York state was criticized as having the most dysfunctional government in the United States, the host of the program was praising New York for being able to pass a responsible budget in a bipartisan manner and on time. This was in stark contrast to the budget fiasco then going on in California.

New York state government was recognized for effi-

ciently passing a responsible on-time state budget. Amazing!
Would this cooperative spirit continue?

INDEPENDENT REDISTRICTING – A CONFLICT IN TERMS

Every ten years the federal government is required to take a census. There are many reasons for it. It provides valuable information to government and businesses alike, as to the growth or loss in population, the migratory trends of its residents, the number of legal immigrants entering the country and information as to where they are settling and the changes in population among the states. It also provides a lot of jobs for the rank-and-file members of the party that happens to be in power. That last reason is somewhat tongue in cheek, but the people who work the census are, for the most part, selected by leaders of the party in power.

The census is extremely important to individual states, since federal aid is distributed, in large part, according to population. It is also important from a political standpoint, since the number of congressional seats for each state is determined by state populations.

Over the last two redistrictings, the State of New York lost congressional seats, since the New York state population

dropped substantially in comparison to gains in other states. In 2001, New York lost three seats, going from 34 to 31 members of Congress. In 2011, the census resulted in New York losing two additional congressional seats. Notwithstanding the fact the US Constitution allows each state two U.S. Senators irrespective of the population of the state, a basic tenet in constitutional law is "one man one vote." Technically, each citizen's vote should weigh the same as any other citizen's vote. This is why when states lose population, they have to lose congressional seats which dilutes their representation in Congress.

Consistent with this "one man one vote" principle, the congressional, and state assembly and state senate districts have to be redistricted every ten years. Each of the senators, based on the 2011 population of the state, represented approximately 300,000 residents, and each of the assembly members represented approximately 120,000 residents.

With all this being said, how is this redistricting accomplished? In New York there is a constitutional provision that requires redistricting to be done by the New York state legislature. Both the assembly and the senate have to pass identical redistricting bills for the state's legislative seats and federal congressional seats. As in every other case where an identical bill passes both houses, the governor can either sign or veto the legislation. If this legislation is vetoed, which very rarely happens, the legislature, by two-thirds vote of each house, can override that veto.

However, that is not the end of the process. There seems always to be a court challenge of any redistricting plan. The court challenge may be based upon issues concerning whether the redistricting plan discriminates against minorities, or whether the plan provides the appropriate balance with respect to numbers of residents in each senate or assembly district. There are usually also other esoteric con-

stitutional challenges that are in reality brought for political reasons.

As was discussed earlier, in 2009 and 2010, New York government was totally controlled by New York City democrats. The governor was from New York City, the Speaker of the assembly and the senate Majority Leader/Temporary President were from New York City. Needless to say, in the event that this make-up continued after the November 2010 elections, it was a virtual certainty that the two congressional seats that had to be eliminated would be in upstate New York and/or Long Island. But you say, how could that be, since the principal is one man one vote? It can happen by creatively drawing congressional district lines, unaffectionately called gerrymandering.

This holds true for redistricting of senate and assembly seats as well. The senate is a good example. If the majority of the state senate, after the 2010 elections remained in New York City democrat control, 23 of the 32 majority members would have been from New York City. The assembly was likely to, and did, remain under strong New York City democrat control. So if the majority in both legislative bodies remained the same, there is little question that there would have been creative drawing of district lines to further strengthen democrat New York City control. Moreover, the district lines in upstate and Long Island could be creatively drawn in order to make it easier for democrats to take some seats outside of New York City and grow their majorities in each house.

Before the coup, New York City democrat Malcom Smith was selected by the democrats, who had the majority of members in the senate, as the majority leader and temporary president pro tempore of the senate. At a political function, before the coup, Malcom Smith was quoted as saying that once the senate democrats retain control of the senate after the 2010 elections, the republicans would be put down for

the next twenty years. Simply stated, the 2010 elections were very important for upstate New York and Long Island, as well as for the republican party.

During the 2010 legislative session, the democrats took an additional step to enhance their New York City regional control. A law was passed over the negative vote of all republican senators and assembly members which provided that prisoners in prisons throughout the state of New York would be counted as residents at the location in which they lived prior to their incarceration. This was not the case up to that point, because prisoners were counted as residents of the area where they were being housed.

Since the vast majority of the prisoners in upstate prisons came from New York City, this law would provide more numbers for the New York City area for the 2011 redistricting. This law was challenged in court as being unconstitutional, on the grounds that most of the prisoners were actually living in upstate prisons. The services that were being provided for the prisoners came, in large part, from the locale where the prisoners was housed, and there was no guarantee that a prisoner would go back to New York City when released. The fact is that many did not.

Moreover, another practical problem was raised. If the prisoner was not a resident of the state of New York at the time he was sentenced, where should that prisoner be counted? Despite these cogent arguments, the court ruled that the prisoners had to be counted, for redistricting purposes, in the locale where they lived prior to their incarceration.

This law passed when New York City democrats controlled everything in state government, and it was passed to enhance downstate population and representation in the state legislature. I repeat, the 2010 legislative races were obviously important from a redistricting standpoint.

Former New York City mayor Ed Koch was well aware of this, so he decided to lead another reform movement in Albany. Leading the reform agenda meant to him that an independent redistricting commission had to be appointed to do the redistricting. The former democrat mayor of the City of New York, of course, had no political agenda. He simply wanted good government. Sure.

Mayor Koch went around the state getting pledges from legislators and candidates for legislative offices. The pledges included various "reform" measures, including a commitment that the candidate would support an independent redistricting commission. I, as well as just about every other candidate, signed the pledge. Quite frankly, I had no problem supporting an independent redistricting commission so long as that commission made recommendations to the legislature, and the legislature made the final decision, since the New York constitution required the legislature to do redistricting.

In November of 2010, after the senate was returned to republican control, the senate leadership proposed and the New York senate passed an independent redistricting commission proposal, as an amendment to the constitution. Republicans were criticized by democrats who argued that this was simply kicking the can down the road, since in order for the constitution to be amended that bill would have to be passed by two consecutively elected legislative bodies and then placed before the voters for a referendum. Obviously, this process could not be done in time in order to affect the redistricting for the 2012 elections. The republicans correctly reasoned that since the redistricting procedure was governed by the constitution, the only way to change the redistricting procedure would be to amend the constitution.

The new, and at the time very popular, Governor Andrew Cuomo, introduced a bill for an independent redis-

tricting commission as well. His bill was not a constitutional amendment. However, what many people involved in the debate did not focus on was that this bill would have resulted in democrat elected officials selecting the vast majority of the members of the commission. This would hardly be independent or bipartisan.

It stands to reason that if there are such high political stakes involved in how district lines are drawn, the individual elected officials making the appointments, whether republican or democrat, are most definitely going to appoint people that have their political leanings. The appointment process under the Cuomo bill was a convoluted procedure that tried to make it sound like the people would be independent. However, in reality, you simply can't keep politics out of politics.

Also, the procedure that the independent commission would follow after the appointments were made escaped most people. The process was as follows. The independent commission would create district lines and send their proposal to the legislature, who could reject it. If rejected, the independent commission would go back and draw another set of lines and resubmit that to the legislature, who could reject it. If rejected again the independent commission would continue to do its work for a third time and come up with another set of lines, which the legislature could amend but, ultimately, would have to approve or disapprove, as amended.

In other words, despite all of the rhetoric about the commission being independent, and being a reform, ultimately, the legislature could amend the independent commission's proposal and pass something more to its liking. Not surprisingly, this proposal had the broad support of the press because the press is always for "reform" and "bipartisanship," even if, in substance, it changes little.

I had no problem voting for such a piece of legislation, so long as the independent commission's recommendations

were advisory only, and ultimately, the legislature had the final decision-making authority, as required by the New York state constitution. In fact, because of the advisory nature of the independent commission's work, this whole independent commission business was much to do about nothing. I still believed that passing a law would not be enough, since the constitution had to be amended to change the redistricting process. So whatever the legislation said, it would be unconstitutional unless it followed the process required to amend the constitution.

Ed Koch continued to insist that the legislature pass an independent redistricting piece of legislation. He gave the legislature a deadline of March 1, 2011. When the deadline wasn't met, he determined that he was going to have robo calls made, which are automatic phone messages into people's homes, criticizing those legislators that violated their pledge to pass an independent redistricting bill. I received many of these calls in my district. So did many other republican senators.

How many democratic senators that signed the pledge had such calls go into their districts? Any guess? Well, if you guessed "none," you'd be correct. This so-called non-partisan former democrat mayor seemed to forget his call for bipartisanship.

The democrat controlled assembly didn't even introduce a bill of any type, by the time the robo calls began. The senate at least passed an independent commission proposal that would change the constitution and which the voters would, ultimately, be allowed to vote on in a referendum. So weren't the democrat assembly members more guilty of violating mayor Koch's pledge? You would think so. But still no robo calls were made in assembly democrat members' districts.

So much for independence and so much for bipartisan-

ship. But, the press carried on the fight on this issue demanding an independent redistricting commission and supporting Ed Koch in his efforts. What the media did not focus on, nor did the League of Women Voters and all the other "good government" groups, was that there actually would be bipartisan and regionally balanced redistricting in 2011. This was because in the November, 2010 elections the republicans took back control of the senate thereby returning the upstate and Long Island voices in the legislature.

In short, there was again a balance in government with the senate controlled by upstate and Long Island republicans and the assembly controlled by New York City democrats. These majorities would have to get together and pass the same redistricting legislation in each house. That bill would have to be both regionally and politically balanced by the different political and regional majorities controlling each house.

Also, if the governor was unsatisfied with the bill passed by the legislature, he could veto it, subject to a two-thirds override vote by the senate and the assembly. And still the courts would no doubt get involved as they have been involved in virtually every redistricting, because someone always contested the redistricting plan.

The regional and political balance of the houses that occurred, as a result of the Republicans taking back the senate in the November, 2010 elections, at least gave upstate New York a chance to save one of its congressional seats rather than both being eliminated by an all New York City democrat controlled government.

Once seated in 2011, the democrats, who controlled the assembly and republicans, who controlled the senate, went on their ways preparing and, ultimately, completing the redistricting plan. The senate prepared a plan for the senate and the assembly prepared a plan for the assembly, and both plans were approved by each house. Similarly, the republicans

controlling the senate and the democrats controlling the assembly worked together to arrive at new congressional districts which, as anticipated, resulted in the elimination of one upstate and one downstate congressional district.

As expected, the court challenges followed. Surrogates for the democrat minority members in the senate brought various lawsuits challenging the state legislative lines, one of which contested the republican majority's creation of a 63rd Senate district, claiming that it was unconstitutional to do so. There was also a republican minority challenge of the assembly lines drawn by the democrat majority in the assembly. As it turned out, none of the challenges was successful.

There were also challenges made to the congressional district lines drawn jointly by the senate and the assembly. In fact, one of the most vocal members of Congress, who criticized the plan, was central New York Congresswoman Ann Marie Buerkle. She should have been complaining. Her seat was changed substantially, which would have resulted in her losing areas of her district that voted heavily for her, and gaining a new county which voted heavily for her opponent in the last election. Other members of Congress had similar complaints. As it turned out, a federal district court judge redrew the lines for Buerkle's district, and the redrawn lines were upheld on appeal. Congresswoman Buerkle was very happy about the court ruling. Other members of Congress were not. However, the decision was finally made and everyone was on to his or her next election with new district lines.

So as partisan as redistricting always was and always will be, everything seemed to turn out as well as could possibly be expected. Both upstate and New York City lost one congressional seat. The central New York Congresswoman, Anne Marie Buerkle had a fairer district than was proposed in which to run for reelection, and the senate and assembly were both able to redraw district lines that theoretically would

help their incumbents and help take back some other seats. Moreover, a 63rd seat was created in the senate which the republicans thought they could win.

However, theory only goes so far. The people would vote in the November, 2012 elections and decide who would represent them. As it turned out, Buerkle lost convincingly to former Congressman Dan Maffei, primarily, as a result of President Barack Obama's landslide victory in New York state.

Similarly, as a result of President Obama's victory, the republicans lost the majority and, theoretically, lost control of the state senate. As of election night, the democrats won 32 seats and the republicans won only 30. Moreover, the carefully drawn 63rd Senate seat was too close to call since the democrat candidate won by only 19 votes. This happened despite the best efforts of the republicans in drawing the lines!

However, it turned out, control of the senate was nowhere near being resolved for weeks after the election. "How can that be?," you ask, with 32 democrats and 30 republicans, with one race undecided. I'll tell you.

One of the democrats that won was a philosophically conservative candidate running in a New York City district that was called by some as the "Super-Jewish" district. The winning candidate, Simcha Felder, won his race handily. Prior to the election, he hinted that, despite being a democrat, he might sit with the republican conference in the senate. Shortly after the election, he formally announced that he would become part of the republican conference. This being the case, the margin became, 31 in the democrat conference and 31 in the republican conference, with one race undecided. The newly created 63rd Senate District was still too close to call. During the counting of the paper ballots, the candidate who was leading changed almost daily.

While that was going on, discussions were held between the republican senate leadership and four democrats.

No, these weren't the "four amigos." Three of those four amigos were out of the senate by that time, one serving a jail sentence, and one awaiting sentencing.

These four democrats that were negotiating with the republicans were members of the Independent Democrat Conference (IDC). They broke away from the democrat conference when the republicans took back control in 2011. These democrats were Jeffrey Klein, the leader of the IDC, David Valesky, David Carlucci, and Diane Savino.

In 2011, these independent democrats chose not to sit with the democrat conference, partly because of philosophical differences, but mostly due to the dysfunction of the democrat conference. There was a history of working with the republicans. This independent democrat group, during 2011 and 2012, chose to vote with the republican majority on many important issues. This gave the republicans a cushion with extra votes, needed when republican members were either absent or voted against the conference's positions.

Over these two years substantial trust developed between the republican majority members and the IDC. As a result, it was natural for discussions to begin to see if a coalition leadership could be created for the next two-year term.

Simultaneous with the discussions between republicans and the four democrats, the vote count was going on in the newly formed 63rd senate district. Needless to say, there were high stakes involved, in that, if George Amedore, the republican candidate, won the race, the republicans conference would be up to 32 votes, a majority, and therefore would not need the four independent democrats to choose its leaders. On the other hand, if Amedore lost the race, the bargaining power of the four independent democrats would be substantially greater. Each group, therefore, had an incentive to come to an agreement before the race was ultimately decided.

Because of this uncertainty, the republican and independent

conferences reached an agreement, later referred to as a co-alition majority – 30 republicans, 1 democrat, (Simka Felder, who joined the republican conference) and the five members of the IDC. As it turned out republican George Amadore lost the race in the newly created 63rd senate district race.

You may be wondering if I made a mistake in saying the independent conference had five members. Well, it was no mistake, since democrat Malcolm Smith joined the IDC by the time the agreement was reached. Ironically when the democrats first took control of the senate in 2009, Malcolm Smith was the democrat majority leader! More about Malcolm Smith later.

This coalition majority was certainly a group of strange bedfellows. This again points out a cardinal rule in politics – never burn bridges. Whether this bipartisan coalition majority would work remained to be seen. However, one thing was clear, namely that "independent redistricting" is a conflict in terms.

A PRESIDENTIAL
CANDIDATE?

Before Andrew Cuomo completed his first six months as governor of New York, political pundits were predicting that he would be a democrat candidate for President in the future. Smartly, Cuomo just shrugged off any such comments and simply said repeatedly that he was elected governor of New York and had a big job to do to get New York back in fiscal order. He was right.

He did an outstanding job during his first six months in office. When he arrived, the state had a $10 billion structural deficit, and hadn't had a timely budget in two years. Cuomo also had to deal with a government that was the laughing stock of the nation. To say it was dysfunctional was an understatement.

During Cuomo's first six months in office, he showed leadership in working with the senate in substantially reducing the deficit, helping to enact a budget which called for less spending than the previous year (for the first time in fifteen years), and leading the charge for the enactment of an ethics reform law. Quite frankly, it was exactly what the people of New York wanted. He showed great leadership in getting most of what he wanted done.

In his first budget, he proposed cutting the public workforce by 7,500 jobs, but gave the public unions the alternative to negotiate their contracts to accomplish savings to the state in ways other than layoffs. He was able to get concessions, with two of the largest public unions in New York, the Civil Service Employees Association (CSEA), and the Professional Employees Federation (PEF). If Cuomo continued in this fiscally conservative direction, he would have had many republicans supporting his candidacy for any office, including President of the United States.

The other major item of his first legislative session was the enactment of same-sex marriage law, accomplishing another of his campaign promises. Whether you agreed with him or not, he showed incredible resolve in garnering ther votes necessary for that bill to pass. This legislation clearly helped him to bring back much of his liberal democrat base that he was losing because of his fiscal conservatism.

But, from a legislator's standpoint, one of the most important things that he was able to accomplish was to restore some faith in state government. He worked in a bipartisan way and had an excellent working relationship with leadership in the state senate, including myself. It was truly refreshing after having experienced the likes of Eliot Spitzer, on one extreme, who wanted to dictate everything and David Paterson on the other extreme, that didn't know what he wanted to do from day to day. So, Andrew Cuomo, was being talked about as a potential presidential candidate.

It was amazing to see the state being transformed from the most dysfunctional state government in the country to a state government that was looked on as a model. I was shocked when I received that call, after the budget was passed that year, from a reporter from National Public Radio in Los Angeles, California, asking that I be on the live talk show to discuss how New York state was able to accomplish a

balanced budget with a democrat governor, a democrat controlled assembly, and a republican controlled senate. The host could not believe how New York state representatives could work in a bipartisan matter to get the job done, when the state of California was mired in political bickering and conflict.

All five governors that were in office during my time in the state senate thought they were going to become President of the United States. Well, that may not be quite true. I doubt that Governor Paterson thought that he would be President, since he probably realized that he was in over his head as governor of New York. Also, it's not quite true since Eliot Spitzer's didn't think he was going to be President, he knew it.

The first governor I served with was Mario Cuomo, Andrew's father. Mario Cuomo came to national attention in 1984 when he gave the keynote address at the democrat party national convention in San Francisco. His speech was entitled the "Tale of Two Cities." It was an incredible speech that was talked about for months. However, he never quite made it as a presidential candidate, probably because his liberal views were much too far to the left to be successful in a national election at that time in history. Mario died on January 1, 2015, the same day Andrew Cuomo was sworn in for his second term as governor.

Interestingly, Andrew Cuomo was very actively involved in his father's campaigns and clearly was a disciple of his father's liberal philosophy then, and in future years when he ran for the office of New York attorney general. There is no doubt, in my mind, that Andrew believed that we had to get the state of New York in good fiscal order, and that's why he worked so well with the republicans in the state senate, who had been calling for that for years. However, there likely were political reasons as well, namely, to get more to the center and not repeat the political mistakes of his father.

The second governor that I served with, while in the

state senate, was George Pataki. George was first elected to the senate the same year I was, after he had served in the assembly for several years. He was not the favorite of then senate majority leader, Ralph Marino. In fact, Marino barely tolerated Pataki since Pataki took a very conservative fiscal approach to state government, and he refused to vote for parts of the state budget during his two years as a senator. That, to put it mildly, did not endear him with Marino.

It soon became apparent that Pataki's real goal was to become governor of New York. At first, I thought it was simply wishful thinking, but as time passed, it became a real possibility. The reason was that at that time, the state was in a fiscal crisis. Jobs were leaving the state, the tax base was dwindling, and business leaders were openly critical of Governor Mario Cuomo's policies. Mario Cuomo's solution was to raise taxes and to spend beyond the means of New York state taxpayers. That turned out to be fatal to his political future in that the political battle cry became "anybody but Cuomo." I think Andrew Cuomo definitely learned a lesson from all of this, since he inherited a state with similar fiscal problems as those during the last years of his father's tenure as governor.

In 1993, Mario Cuomo invited the legislators to the Executive Mansion, which is the Albany home of the governor provided by the state. While there, for a short time, Governor Cuomo was speaking with three Senators: one was John Scheffer from Buffalo, and the other two were first term senators, namely, George Pataki and me. Someone took a photograph of the three of us looking at the governor as he was speaking. That photo, is a classic. It shows Pataki glaring at Cuomo with a look in his eyes that seemed to say "I'm going after you." And he did!

The then senate Majority Leader, Ralph Marino did everything he could to torpedo Pataki's efforts to become governor. In fact, he backed a conservative party member,

Herb London, for the nomination. Early on I, and a handful of state senators, backed Pataki, much to the chagrin of Senator Marino. However, it was definitely the right thing to do.

During Pataki's first two years as governor, he cut taxes, reformed welfare, and really made significant progress in regulatory reform, which the business community was demanding. This resulted in a much better business climate and New York started to recover.

To accomplish his agenda, Pataki had to get support, not only from the republican controlled senate, but also from the democrat controlled assembly, which, was led by Speaker Sheldon Silver. It was an incredibly difficult job, because Silver fought Pataki every step of the way. In order to get some of his agenda passed, Pataki had to give up something to Silver. For example, one budget was weeks late because Silver would not agree to workers' compensation reform unless he got an extension of the Loft Tenants' Law. That law, which basically was rent control for tenants occupying lofts in the City of New York, was set to expire, and without Governor Pataki agreeing to a renewal of that law, workers' compensation reform that year would not have happened.

Pataki did not have the luxury that Andrew Cuomo later had of working with the opposition republican party that actually agreed with fiscal austerity measures. However, Pataki, despite the resistance from Sheldon Silver, did do an incredible job to get New York state's fiscal house in order, at least during his first two terms.

Pataki served three four-year terms, and there was no doubt that, during the third term, his eye was on the presidency. His name was floated and, even though a formal campaign committee was not formed, he was out testing the waters. When it became apparent that George W. Bush was going to be the nominee, Pataki wisely supported his nomination and was granted a prime speaking role at the republican

convention in Philadelphia. He gave a great speech.

George Pataki's presidential aspirations did not end there. Barack Obama was the democrat presidential nominee in the election of 2008. Pataki was definitely out there again, with a host of other republican candidates. His candidacy never caught fire, but, his aspirations didn't fade.

During the first term of Obama's presidency, Pataki formed an organization called "Revere America." The organization was created to advocate for the repeal of the Obama health care law known as "Obamacare." It became obvious that there was another objective as well, namely to keep his name in the national spotlight for 2012. This became apparent to me when in 2010, he came to Syracuse to campaign for Ann Marie Buerkle, who was challenging democrat incumbent, Dan Maffei, for a congressional seat in central New York.

When Pataki came to speak on Buerkle's behalf, he spoke very briefly about Buerkle, and spoke a lot more about how the country had to change direction from where it was headed under the new president. And that wasn't an isolated case, since Pataki continued to support various congressional candidates and was occasionally on national talk shows, not as an official candidate, but as someone who hoped that many would see him as such. What he was doing was staying out there and available in case a strong republican candidate didn't emerge. In other words, he was available to be drafted for the job, but it didn't happen. Similarly in 2016, Pataki appeared in a few republican presidential debates but never caught fire.

So Andrew Cuomo's future as a presidential candidate was not as far-fetched as some might have thought. This would have been especially true if he continued his fiscally conservative policies, and helped bring New York back to a leading state in cultivating business and creating jobs. But he took a sharp pivot to the left in his second term in office.

A CONSTITUTIONAL CONVENTION

During the height of the dysfunction in Albany and at other times when there was dissatisfaction with state government, the rallying cry for many was for a constitutional convention. At times the charge was led by "good government" groups whose purpose purportedly was to make government work better.

The movements always included several legislators who proposed legislation calling for a constitutional convention. In New York, proposing and introducing legislation to change the constitution is easy, much easier than legislators actually solving the underlying problems themselves. Moreover, introducing legislation gives legislators doing so "cover" and an easy answer to their constituents, namely, that they are trying to do something by passing legislation to allow the people to decide on the overhaul of government at a constitutional convention.

This sounds good and it diverts attention from the legislators who are causing the dysfunction. But it is not easy to convene a constitutional convention and it's even more difficult for delegates of a constitutional convention to change anything in a real way. Let me explain.

The first step in having a constitutional convention is to pass legislation that calls for a referendum at the next election on the question, "should there be a constitutional convention?" If the electorate votes "no" that ends the matter. If the people vote for such a convention, then delegates to the convention must be elected at the next November election. The New York state constitution provides that three delegates from each senate district (presently there are 63 districts) and fifteen delegates statewide are to be elected to serve at the convention. Any individual, who is eligible to vote, can run to become one of the delegates. Once the delegates are elected, the constitutional convention is convened.

The state constitution also provides that each of these delegates receive the same salary as a legislator, and that the delegates can appoint assistants and fix their salaries. Administrative costs that are necessary for the convention are also provided for in the constitution. In other words, the process is similar to electing another legislative body with many of the associated costs.

The constitution further provides that within six weeks after the adjournment of the convention, whatever proposals that are passed at the convention must go to the voters to decide whether or not the constitution should be amended in accordance with those proposals. It sounds like democracy at its best and a sure fire way to end Albany dysfunction.

I wasn't so convinced, especially since I had the good fortune of sitting next to Senator John Marchi from Staten Island during the 14 years which our senate terms overlapped. John knew, from his nearly 50 years as a New York state senator a lot about the workings of government. In fact, there were very few things that happened during my tenure that Senator Marchi hadn't already experienced. One of his experiences was being in office at the time of 1967 New York state

constitutional convention. He, therefore, had had a birdseye view of the last convention and didn't have to rely on theory.

I graduated from the Duke University School of Law in 1971. When I graduated I received an employment offer from Simpson Thacher & Bartlett, a large, prominent Wall Street law firm. Rather than fight subways and the chaos of Manhattan, my wife and I, with two young children at the time, rented an apartment on Staten Island.

Immediately after having taken up temporary residence there, I learned of John Marchi, who by 1971 had already had an incredible political career. He was first elected to the New York state senate in 1957, when Dwight Eisenhower was President! So as of the time that I took up residence in Staten Island, he had already been a member of the senate for many years. Moreover, by that time he had already run for mayor of New York City on two occasions.

In 1969 he ran in a republican primary against the very popular John Lindsay and won! Unfortunately for the City, Lindsay was also on the liberal line and won the election for mayor over both democrat candidate, Mario Procaccino and John Marchi on the republican line. Marchi ran again for mayor in 1973, but lost to Abraham Beame.

But this probably turned out best for New York City. During the mid-70's, New York City was on the verge of bankruptcy and they looked to New York state for help. Fortunately for the City, John Marchi as a state senator helped craft the financial package that saved New York City from bankruptcy. His other legislative achievements are too numerous to mention, but suffice it to say, that John was a well-respected legislator during his entire tenure, but most of all he was a true public servant and a true gentleman.

I never heard John Marchi say anything bad about anybody. He was also one of the few legislators that was truly an intellectual. He loved the classics and spoke fluent Italian.

When he spoke on the senate floor or privately to me while we were enduring some long legislative days, he spoke from knowledge and experience and a love of the institution.

I didn't realize until his death in 2006, at age 87, that he served our country in World War II in anti-submarine duty in the Atlantic, and in the Okinawa campaign. His other public service is too extensive to relate here but it is easy to find. It seemed fitting that this renaissance man died while vacationing in Lucca, Italy, the home of his ancestors.

So rather than following the tide that was rapidly coming to shore calling for a constitutional convention, I went directly to someone who knew, John Marchi. Having been there, he had firsthand knowledge of the workings of the 1967 constitutional convention, and those workings were not something of which to be proud.

First, delegates had to be elected by the people. The people most likely to be elected would be those who had some name identification or some political affiliation enabling them to raise money and win elections. As a result, many of the delegates turned out to be officials who were already in office, or had been previously elected to office. A majority of the rest that weren't current or former elected officials, were present or former staffers for elected officials, all with extensive political histories and affiliations.

As a result, some legislators and staffers could draw not only their salaries in their government positions, but also salaries as delegates to the constitutional convention. Moreover, the state was saddled with the additional expenses of the offices, employees and assistants appointed by the delegates for the operations of the convention.

One might say that this is a small price to pay for overhauling an outdated constitution. However, it is naïve to think that there would be an extensive overhaul when current or former elected and party officials, their staffs, employees,

and supporters were delegates. The delegates did pass various reform proposals, which included additions to the Bill of Rights, the repeal of the 1894 Blaine Amendment which prohibited the direct or indirect aid to denominational schools, and anti-discrimination measures. Other approved reform proposals included the authorization of economic and community development projects for cities, the takeover of the operating costs of the judiciary in favor of a statewide court system, and something that is still an issue today, the transfer of the costs of welfare programs from the local governments to the state.

Democracy at work? Not so fast. What the delegates decided to do was to lump together the proposals into a few amendments calling for "yes" or "no" votes. This assured the defeat by voters of all of these proposed amendments in the referendum that followed the adjournment of the convention since everyone seemed to be against at least one of the components of the few proposed amendments. As expected, all proposals were defeated. In short, the 1967 constitutional convention turned out to be a colossal waste of time and money.

This analysis did not escape the "good government" groups that were calling for a constitutional convention at the height of the state's governmental dysfunction. The members of these organizations argued that the problem wasn't the convention, but rather the manner of selecting delegates. They argued that this could be corrected if there were truly independent citizens making these decisions and not delegates with political baggage. So some of these groups proposed that all that had to be done was to prohibit elected and other government and party officials and their staffers from becoming delegates and, thereby stop them from controlling the convention. This, of course, sounds good, but there is one small problem. That small problem is that the New York state constitution simply provides that three delegates shall be selected from each senate district and 15 at-large delegates shall

be selected state-wide. The constitution does not, in any way, limit who can or cannot be delegates.

Sound familiar? It was the same situation as "good government" groups calling for independent redistricting, not redistricting by the legislature, as provided for in the constitution. Picky, picky, picky. Let's not let the constitution get in the way of good political rhetoric.

I should point out that the New York state constitution also provides another way to have a constitutional convention. It provides that every 20 years, there will be a question on the ballot as to whether or not there should be a constitutional convention. What's interesting, and what is largely ignored by the "good government" groups is that if the constitutional convention is such a good thing, why have the voters decided against convening one when the question has been on the ballot every 20 years? The last "no" vote on whether there should be a constitutional convention recently occurred in 2017. So, in government, what sounds like a good solution to government dysfunction might not be as good as it sounds.

So what can be done when government becomes dysfunctional? The answer is to elect new legislators and a new governor, and that is what happened in 2010. After that election, the state government, at least at the start of Andrew Cuomo's first term, became functional again.

ENDING
CORRUPTION BY
COERCION

L et me start with a hypothetical. Let's suppose a governor of some far away jurisdiction decides that the most important thing that he can accomplish during his time in office is to eliminate all gun control laws then on the books, in order to secure every citizen's second amendment right to bear arms. Let's further suppose that the legislature doesn't believe that that is the proper policy and resists the governor's efforts. Let's be even more specific and suppose that the governor submits a bill to do the above two weeks before the end of legislative session, and threatens that if the legislature doesn't pass the bill before the end of session, he will impanel a commission to investigate each and every member of the legislature who earns outside income from services not related to his or her legislative duties.

Continuing this hypothetical, let's say that the legislature doesn't pass the legislation and the governor impanels a commission comprised of prosecutors with subpoena power to subpoena all records of outside income, the source of that

income, and records concerning the individuals with whom the legislator does business. And further assume for the purposes of this question, that upon impaneling the commission, the governor explains that he is doing so since the legislature failed to pass the legislation eliminating all gun control laws. Do you think that the governor, under the above circumstances, has abused his power? Do you think that maybe the press might rail against the governor for his heavy-handed approach in seeking the repeal of all gun control laws? Would you be offended by these actions?

Let's just change one fact in the above hypothetical. Let's suppose the bill that the legislature failed to pass, which aroused the ire of the governor and resulted in the creation of a commission, was a bill that would require greater gun control statutes in New York state. Well, if you are an advocate for gun control, you probably would not be offended. But, should the governor's actions be less objectionable if you agree with what the governor is attempting to accomplish? Does the end justify the means in a democratic government?

Well, a version of the above hypothetical actually happened. In June of 2013, Governor Andrew Cuomo introduced the so-called "Public Trust Act," which created new felony offenses for official misconduct, eased the burden to prove the crime of bribery, sought the so-called "reform" of certain voting procedures, and increased restrictions on campaign financing. When he did so he stated "either the legislature will be passing a piece of legislation that cleans up Albany, or I'll do it on my own through a Moreland Commission. Life is options, and those are the options." Well, the legislature did not pass his bill and the governor appointed a commission.

The Governor appointed 25 Moreland Commission members, the co-chairs of which were prosecutors, accompanied by the clear threat that the prosecutors would have the authority to bring criminal charges against any wrong-

doer that the commission uncovered. Letters were sent out to each senator and assembly member that earned outside income of over the arbitrary number of $20,000, demanding that the legislator provide detailed information about the sources of his or her outside income, what services the legislator provided for this income, and information about the individuals with whom the legislator did business.

There was no probable cause, reasonable suspicion, or any other standard met for these demands or for setting this arbitrary amount as a basis for the the demanded disclosure. Granted that all legislators were required, by law, to make extensive annual financial disclosure but there were no allegations against anyone who received letters from the commission that he or she was suspected of violating the state disclosure laws.

Only a few legislators voluntarily produced any documents in response to the letter. The same day that the vast majority of legislators declined to provide the requested information, the commission spokesperson, Michelle Duffy, announced in a press that the legislators' lack of response implied that they had something to hide. Her exact words were "as the old adage goes, if you've done nothing wrong, you have nothing to hide." She went on to say that the legislators' position was "legally indefensible, ethically repugnant, and disrespectful to the public's right to know."

This "enlightened" position of the commission, who had no evidence of any wrongdoing, further demonstrated how the rule of law was immaterial to this witch hunt. There were not only defensible legal positions, but strong policy reasons why this effort by Governor Cuomo had to be fought and fought strenuously.

Michelle Duffy also stated "There are a number of avenues through which the commission can obtain the information being sought, and we will pursue them." The governor con-

curred with the spokesperson of this "independent" commission, by saying that "they [the panel] are prosecutors. When they say they have other avenues, it means that they have other avenues that they are going to pursue." And they did so by issuing subpoenas.

Shortly thereafter, the commission co-chairs proclaimed that the commission would continue to "aggressively move forward in compelling the production of information into specific matters the commission is investigating." So, it became patently obvious that the Moreland Commission was set on pursuing legislators, without any evidence of wrongdoing. This "McCarthyist" approach was applauded, rather than criticized, by the media on the grounds that the governor and the Commission were aggressively attacking corruption in government.

The subpoenas that were issued to the "targeted" legislator (all legislators with outside income of $20,000 or more) demanded the following, among other things:

1. Documents and Communications relating to professional services provided by the targeted Senator.

2. Any contract, agreement, appointment or offer letter, business card, letterhead, attorney business or professional profile in any Document, including correspondence, describing the targeted Senator's position.

3. Records of the targeted Senator's compensation, including in-kind benefits.

4. Invoices, billable hour reports, time sheets, expense reports, reimbursements forms related to the targeted Senator.

5. Documents and communications relating to the solicitation and engagement of any and all clients by the targeted Senator, including pitch books, marketing materials, engagement letters and retainer agreements.

6. Clients advised or represented by the targeted Senator and a general description of the services provided by the targeted Senator to such clients.

7. Building access records (electronic and otherwise), and sign-in sheets reflecting the targeted Senator's access to the Petitioner-employer's office.

8. Documents and communications showing any relationship, business (including receipt of funding), litigation, lobbying or other contacts on the Petitioner's own behalf with, before or against the State of New York, or any of the states affiliated entities or bodies.

9. Documents and communications showing clients that have any relationship, business (including receipt of funding), litigation, lobbying or other contacts with or before or against the state or any of the affiliated entities or bodies.

10. Documents and communications showing any clients that have engaged the Petitioner in connection with requests for funding, lobbying activity, legislation, or any other legislative or political activity.

11. Documents and communications relating to monies, benefits, or campaign contribution from the Petitioner, its members, or close relatives of its members, or any political organization or committee associated with the Petitioner to elected state officials, political candidates, political entities, campaigns, political action committees, political party organizations, or political clubs.

Once again, there was no evidence of wrongdoing by anyone, and not even an allegation that any of the elected officials had violated the existing disclosure laws of the state of New York. If the breadth of the subpoena and the four-year time period for which records were sought did not demonstrate that this was a groundless fishing expedition to coerce legislators to pass the governor's bill, the definitions of

"communication" and "document," which were being sought, clearly showed it .

"Communication" is defined "in the broadest sense of the term,including, among other things, conversation, discussion and other transmittal of information or message, whether transmitted in writing, oral, electronically or by any other means"; and "document" is defined in the "broadest sense of the term and means each and every writing of whatever nature, whether an original, a draft, or a copy, however produced or reproduced, and each and every tangible thing from which information can be processed or transcribed.

The subpoena noted specific examples of items that fell within this definition,

"such as plans, records, charts, grafts, diaries, analyses, instructions, voice mail, memoranda, notes, recordings (audio, visual or digital), credit card charge slips, USB flash drives, diaries, studies, calendars, photographs (positive prints and negative), computer printouts and programs, microfilm, and marginal comments appearing on any document."

My favorite demand from the subpoenas was for "business access records (electronic and otherwise), and sign-in sheets reflecting the targeted senator's access to his Petitioner-employer's office." What possible relevance could that have to the commission's investigation, other than to harass the person subpoenaed? And how, could anyone respond to each and every one of those requests, in good faith, and continue to operate his or her outside business or profession?

Generally, a subpoena cannot be issued unless it has some relevance to a legitimate investigation. The commission couldn't even justify how it determined which elected officials to subpoena. The reason given for subpoenaing legis-

lators with more than $20,000 of outside income was that "a review of 2012 financial disclosures indicates that average household incomes of legislators is significantly higher than those of the state general population." So what? Does that mean that the legislators illegally earned the outside income? Does that mean that legislators who have this amount of outside income are more likely to be corrupt, and that legislators who have no outside income can not be corrupt?

It was impossible to show the relevance of documents and information subpoenaed if you couldn't even describe what the investigation was all about, other than "to root out corruption in government."

Also, for lawyers or law firms that had been subpoenaed, substantial issues of confidentiality of clients' documents arose. One of the co-chairs of the Moreland Commission, William Fitzpatrick, explained that "we simply want to know what you do for these retainers... and we would like to know from those who are honest legislators, who have trial firms, what do you do to earn it." What? What business is it of the commission to know what honest legislators do to earn their honest wages? Clients have cases that are confidential to them. In fact, lawyers are bound by the ethics' rules of the legal profession to keep matters confidential. And, the more basic point is that if there is no suspicion of wrongdoing, how could the commission have the authority to demand these broad documents or communications "simply [because the commissioners] want to know what you do for these retainers?" So there were substantial bases for contesting the subpoenas and the fishing expedition of the commission. And the subpoenas were vigorously challenged.

Moreover, there were important policy issues that demanded that the legislature contest the subpoenas and the legitimacy of the Moreland Commission itself. First, there is a basic principle in government, namely that there are three

independent branches of government, and that there is a separation of powers between those branches, to provide checks and balances among them.

If Governor Andrew Cuomo, or any governor, for that matter, was allowed to demand legislation, and if the legislation was not passed, was allowed to investigate legislators and harass them without probable cause until they pass the requested legislation, the concept of separation of powers would be eviscerated. But this is exactly what was being done through the Moreland Commission.

The principle of separation of powers and an independent legislature is essential. It was amazing to me that this principle was lost on the media. I'm not sure why I was amazed, since many in the media were only concerned about controversy and maybe some juicy news about some legislator that got caught-up in the net during this fishing expedition. The principle of separation of powers seems to me to be something that was worthy of concern.

There's another reason why these subpoenas were improper. Simply stated, the Moreland Act, which Governor Cuomo was using as a basis for impaneling this commission, did not give him that authority. A little history is in order.

In June of 1907, the legislature of New York, at the request of then Governor Charles Evans Hughes, passed legislation giving the governor the power and authority "to centralize control over the state administration in the Executive Office in order to insure administrative responsibility." The law, thereafter known as the Moreland Act, allowed the governor or his appointee "to examine and investigate the management and affairs of any department, board, bureau, or commission of the state." By the wording of the statute, the governor was not given the authority to investigate the legislature, a separate branch of government, but rather only to investigate his administration.

Over the years, many commissions were appointed under the authority of the Moreland Act. Some of these commissions were as follows:

1. 1915 – Commission to examine and investigate the management and affairs of the Office of the Fiscal Supervisor of State Charities, the State Board of Charities, the Sites, Buildings and Grounds Commission, the Building Improvement Commission, and the Salary Classification Commission. This Commission was appointed by Governor Charles S. Whitman.

2. 1928 – Commission for the investigation of Workmen's Compensation Law Administration, appointed by Governor L. Smith.

3. 1953- Commission to study, examine and investigate state agencies in relation to pari-mutual harness racing, appointed by Governor Thomas Dewey.

4. 1961 – Commission concerning bingo control, appointed by Governor Nelson Rockefeller.

5. 1962 - Commission on welfare, appointed by Governor Nelson Rockefeller.

6. 1963 – Commission on the alcohol beverage control law, appointed by Governor Nelson Rockefeller.

7. 1976 – Commission to investigate nursing homes, appointed by Governor Hugh Carey.

8. 1987 – Commission on government integrity, appointed by Governor Mario Cuomo.

9. 2012 – Commission to investigate New York utilities' response to Hurricane Sandy, appointed by Governor Andrew Cuomo.

As can be readily seen, none of these commissions was appointed to investigate another branch of government. Each was appointed "to examine and investigate the management and affairs of [a] Department, Board, Bureau, or Commission of the state."

The Moreland Commission, appointed by Governor Andrew Cuomo in 2013 was the one and only commission appointed purportedly pursuant to the Moreland Act to investigate the legislature exclusively. In fact, several of his commission members readily admitted that they were not appointed to investigate the governor, even though the governor, being the chief executive officer, had substantially greater opportunities to be part of a corrupt enterprise.

Most instructive are the comments of Governor Mario Cuomo, Andrew Cuomo's father, and his counsel, Evan A. Davis, upon the appointment of the 1987 Commission on Government Integrity. Governor Mario Cuomo, upon advice of his counsel, stated quite clearly that "the panel's powers to investigate practices in the legislature would be limited by legal separations between the branches of government." The only testimony taken from members of the legislature was from then assembly speaker Mel Miller and senate majority leader Ralph Marino. Both testified before the commission voluntarily, and not under the compulsion of subpoenas. In fact, the chairman of this commission, John D. Feerick, wrote that "the Moreland Act authorizes the governor, by establishing a commission, to investigate the management and affairs of any Department, Board, Bureau, or Commission of the state – not other branches of government, however."

Again, it seems quite surprising that not one member of the media questioned the authority of the Moreland Commission to investigate the legislature, most likely on the broad theory that "the people have a right to know." It's like the statement of the Moreland Commission spokesperson that "as the old adage goes, if you've done nothing wrong, you have nothing to hide." However we are ruled by laws. The rule of law includes that individuals do not have to answer broad subpoenas because prosecutors or the public want to know more about their fellow citizens. The commission has to be authorized by law to act, and the Moreland Act did not so au-

thorize. Subpoenas do not have to be answered unless there is some basis, such as probable cause or reasonable suspicion to believe that something wrong has been done or is about to be done, and the subpoenas have to be drawn to only elicit relevant information about a legitimate inquiry.

As it turned out, the governor ended up issuing an Executive Order terminating the Moreland commission shortly after the passage of the New York state budget on April 1, 2014. The stated reason for terminating the Moreland commission was that "it was never meant to be a permanent commission," and the legislature did do some legislation as part of the budget that he felt would help restore the public trust in government. These reforms included the appointment by the governor, with the advice and consent of the senate, and the assembly, of an investigator for the state Board of Elections, increasing the penalties for attempted bribery, requiring additional disclosure from various entities, and a pilot public financing program for the state comptroller's race in 2014.

It was, and is, my opinion that each of these so-called reforms were much to do about nothing, but gave the governor a reason to terminate the commission before a court ruled that it was not legally created and its subpoenas were not enforceable. But even if these reforms did amount to something, they were accomplished by coercion, not by a democratic process. Actually, the commission was a corrupt way to obtain anti-corruption legislation.

When the governor announced that he was going to end the commission, the media went ballistic, as did some of the members of the Moreland commission, who believed that the commission should continue in order to root out corruption. Again, no member of the media ever questioned the legitimacy of the inquiry or the broad scope of it. But why did the governor end this Moreland commission? Were the subpoenas getting too close to him and his contributors?

TURNABOUT IS FAIR PLAY

The Moreland Commission was announced in July of 2013. At the news conference, a casual observer would have no choice but to believe that this commission, backed by the powerful governor of New York state, would root out any and all corruption in the state of New York. It was touted as a completely independent body with subpoena power granted to it by the attorney general of the State of New York, Eric Schneiderman.

In fact, in the following weeks, when there were questions being raised about the independence of the commission, the governor stated the commission would be "totally independent." Moreover, he said "they could look at anything they want to look at..., they can look at me, the lieutenant governor, attorney general, comptroller, any senator, any assemblyman...." The fact of the matter was that anyone who had any dealings with the governor, knew, without question, that the governor had only one management style and that was to micromanage every aspect of state government to make sure that he had control over every decision in his administration.

An excellent and comprehensive article written by Susanne Craig, William K. Rashbaum and Thomas Kaplin, entitled "Cuomo's Office Hobbled State Office Inquiries" ap-

peared in the *New York Times* on July 23, 2014. The article was based on personal interviews, numerous emails, and other documents. It outlined numerous examples of interference by Governor Cuomo and his staff in the operations of the Moreland commission. Moreover, the commission's executive director, Regina M. Calcaterra, was reported in the article as having routinely conveyed to the governor's most senior aid, Lawrence S. Schwartz, information about the private deliberations of the commission.

It was reported that she even gave the governor's office advance notice of when subpoenas were going out and to whom the subpoenas were going. In some cases when those subpoenas were targeted at individuals and organizations with whom the governor had substantial political dealings, Mr. Schwartz intervened to stop the subpoenas.

Since it was becoming obvious that the commission was far from "independent," Governor Cuomo changed his spin. In fact, he stated that the commission had never been intended to be independent of him. He stated to a reporter from Crain's *New York Business* in April of 2014, that "I can't interfere with it, because it is mine, it is controlled by me." I challenge the most competent of linguists to reconcile the statement that the governor made at his initial Moreland commission press conference announcing that the commission would be "totally independent" and the statement he made after the commission was shut down by him, namely that "it is controlled by me." It simply can't be done since this Cuomo-speak is irreconcilable.

Upon the creation of the Moreland commission, Cuomo wanted to be known as the person who ended corruption in Albany. In order to be known as that person, he would have had to create a truly "independent commission." When he was caught controlling the commission, he tried to defend the "independence" argument but it didn't work. It didn't work because commissioners and others involved with the commission, were leaking information and complaining

about the governor's control of the process. This control included suggesting what subpoenas should be issued, stopping subpoenas that he was uncomfortable with, and even being involved in the writing of the preliminary report by the commission to make it look favorable to the governor. However, once Cuomo disbanded the commission, U.S. Attorney Preet Bharari demanded that all records be turned over to him for his review and his investigation.

Again, Cuomo's spin was irreconcilable. The only common theme of the two statements was his efforts to rationalize an action depending upon from where the heat was coming. Even though the U.S. Attorney did not indict the governor, the governor's credibility took a huge hit. But, the governor's lack of credibility was not limited to this Moreland episode.

Beginning in 2013, the senate had a new political conference. Instead of just a republican and a democratic conference, some democrats peeled from the democrat conference and formed their own conference, the IDC. For all of 2013, the governor raved about how well state government was working in a bipartisan fashion under his leadership. Quite frankly, it was operating well, despite the split leadership in the state senate shared between the senate republicans and the IDC. It certainly wasn't easy, in that the IDC members had much more liberal positions than the republicans, especially on social issues. However, the IDC and the senate republicans worked together in order to avoid going back to the totally dysfunctional government of 2009 and 2010.

Beginning in 2014, a new powerful element was introduced to New York state politics, namely, the New York City mayor, Bill de Blasio. To label Mayor de Blasio a liberal is an understatement. Democrats in both the senate and the assembly, now had a new role model for their liberal causes. One such cause was known as the Dream Act, which would provide illegal aliens (or to be politically correct, "undocumented residents") with college tuition assistance. As you

might expect, the republican senators believed that, since there weren't enough dollars to spread around to provide adequate college aid to citizens, it was wrong to provide college tuition assistance to illegal immigrants.

It was simply amazing that the republicans were able to stop the bill from getting to the floor for a vote in 2014. However, universal pre-kindergarten classes, paid for by the state, which primarily benefited residents of New York City, made it into the budget. This occurred as a result of Mayor de Blasio's pledge to increase taxes on the wealthy in New York City in order to fund universal pre-kindergarten there. Governor Cuomo insisted that that would not happen. His solution was to provide universal pre-kindergarten throughout the state and have the New York state taxpayers pay for it. There were many more such proposals made by de Blasio that didn't pass, but clearly de Blasio moved Governor Cuomo farther to the left in the political spectrum.

At the beginning of 2014, in preparation for the governor's re-election race, the governor ran ads extolling the virtues of his leadership by making a bi-partisan government work, which was unheard of in the past. As the party nomination process was coming to a close, he switched directions 180 degrees. Under the pressure of de Blasio's liberal democrat followers, most importantly the public employee unions and the working families party members, Cuomo moved still farther to the left. In fact, in order to get the working families party nomination, he pledged that he would support democrats in the senate races and also get the IDC members to come back into the fold to make a democrat majority in the senate. That commitment worked. Cuomo received the nomination of the working families party, in an attempt to solidify his liberal democrat base. Bi-partisan government commercials immediately were taken off the air.

No doubt some will say that Cuomo should not be criticized because of his adept political moves. But abrupt changes in moving to the most expedient political position show a

lack of core values and lack of credibility. His only consistent value seemed to be self-interest and personal advancement.

At the beginning of the campaign, Cuomo had an approval rating of over 60% and was leading in the polls by more than 30%. His final vote on election day was: Cuomo 54%, the rest 46%. To get that slim majority he spent over $35 million on his campaign! His main opponent, Westchester County Executive Republican Rob Astorino spent about one million dollars.

The public seemed to figure out that Cuomo had few core values and that he would do just about anything and say just about anything to try to run up his vote totals. The opposite occurred. Cuomo alienated the same liberal base that he was trying to win over to become the top "progressive" in New York state.

During the campaign he infuriated the working families party (WFP), controlled by New York labor unions. Many party members, at the beginning of the campaign, did not want to consider Cuomo as their standard bearer. However, once the WFP extracted various commitments from Cuomo, he obtained the nomination.

This decision did not sit well with many rank and file members of the WFP. As a result, petitions were circulated for Zephyr Teachout, a New York City professor. Enough signatures were obtained so that she was placed on the WFP primary ballot. Instead of leaving well enough alone and just beating her in the primary, Cuomo decided to challenge the legality of the petitions and try to knock her off the ballot. Despite his bravado, he lost the legal battle and the primary went forward.

Not only was the primary run, but Teachout obtained approximately one-third of the vote. This was absolutely amazing. Approximately a month earlier no one even knew her! Needless to say, the true progressives in the WFP saw through the Cuomo-speak.

The strategy to tell everyone what they wanted to hear

and then do something else simply didn't work. This held true for the teachers' unions as well. Cuomo, for whatever reason, decided to state that one of the main issues that he would deal with, if re-elected, would be reform of the education system. This was like sticking a pencil in the teachers' unions' members eyes. This comment immediately resulted in a letter from the president of the New York state United Teachers' union (NYSUT) speaking favorably about Cuomo's Republican opponent, Rob Astorino, and negatively about the governor.

Another amusing thing about the Andrew Cuomo/ Zephyr Teachout battle was that she did something else that made Cuomo look foolish. Teachout released a book that she had written before she was a candidate for governor. Naturally, less than a month before the election, Andrew Cuomo released his own book. The press got great chuckles out of reporting the sales for each book during a two to three week period after Cuomo's book was released. Teachout's book was outselling Cuomo's!

Cuomo's release of his book less than a month before the election showed the chutzpah of the man. What was supposed to be a boost to his campaign became a Cuomo misstep. While all of this was going on, the campaign for governor became tighter. In fairness, there was no way that Rob Astorino could win since there were third party candidates in the race that would siphon some votes and because of the lukewarm support by the republican party. The republicans were more concerned about not having Cuomo spend some of his millions of campaign dollars against the republicans in the senate races.

Yes, turnabout is fair play, but the turnabout by Cuomo by stepping away from his bipartisan government theme and publicly seeking a New York City democrat majority in the senate, hurt him. What should have been a substantial victory was not.

As it turns out, the republicans took back a pure majority in the senate so that they would not have to totally rely on

the IDC during the next term. Also for at least two years, until the next election, there would be some checks and balances over progressive government championed by Mayor Bill de Blasio, and now also, apparently, by Andrew Cuomo.

The senate victory was truly remarkable. The republicans won every race run by an incumbent except one. That one race was for a seat in the Buffalo area held by Mark Grisanti. The teachers' union heavily funded the republican candidate that opposed Grisanti because it believed that if the other republican candidate could damage Grisanti in the primary, either republican candidates woud be weaker in the general election. The union was right since the democrat candidate won the general election. However, the other 21 republican incumbents who had opponents were reelected.

In addition, there were four open republican seats, the incumbent either having decided not to run for reelection or having decided to run for Congress. Republicans won all four of those seats and even more impressively, three republicans defeated incumbent democrats. For the first time in years, the republicans had seven new faces in the republican conference, and a majority of 32 republicans members. In addition, democrat senator, Simcha Felder, remained part of the republican conference, giving the republicans a majority of 33 in the senate.

As a result, in an election year that was supposed to end in a landslide victory for the governor, propelling him to being seriously considered as a presidential candidate in 2016, did not occur. Similarly an election that the senate democrats were salivating over believing they would take over the Senate majority, also did not come to pass.

GUILTY UNTIL PROVEN INNOCENT AND OTHER LEGAL PRINCIPLES

When Elliot Spitzer was the New York state attorney general, he named himself the "Sheriff of Wall Street." He was so enamored with his self-proclaimed "sheriff" title that when he was sworn in as governor, he proudly proclaimed that "there is a new sheriff in town." Little did anyone know that, at the time, he was violating some of the same laws that he had prosecuted others for violating. Eventually everyone learned of these offenses, including the crimes of transporting a prostitute across state lines and hiding the sources of the payments for her services. But despite these offenses, Elliot Spitzer was never charged. Rather he simply had to resign from office.

Before these violations of the law were uncovered, and while playing the role of the "new sheriff in town," he got into an ongoing battle with the New York state senate majority leader Joseph Bruno. In order to bring law and order to Albany he had the state police tail Bruno and investigate Bruno's use of a state aircraft. Spitzer fully expected Bruno to roll over to

the pressure, admit some wrongdoing and resign from office. He thought Bruno would react this way based on the reactions to his pressure that he saw by so many of his targets while attorney general. He would charge corporations and their chief executives with substantial wrongdoing, demand astronomical fines and admissions, but just before the case would go to trial, he would extract admissions to lesser charges and penalties to close the case.

Joe Bruno was one of the few who wouldn't fold to Spitzer's antics and pressure. Being from the old school and tough as nails, Bruno battled Spitzer to the end. Interestingly, then attorney general Andrew Cuomo had the state police actions against Bruno reviewed, and lo and behold, the result was that Cuomo admonished Spitzer's administration for ordering the state police to track Bruno's travel and travel records. The investigation by Cuomo concluded that Spitzer's actions were meant to cause political damage to Bruno and had no legal basis. It was shown that Spitzer's communications director was in the middle of the planned strategy to embarrass and harass Bruno in the media.

Spitzer had tried to justify his investigation of Bruno on the grounds that there were Freedom of Information Law (FOIL) requests made by the press and that the documents being turned over were in response to legitimate media requests. However, the 57-page report by Cuomo showed that the documents concerning travel weren't even requested by the press at the time they were turned over. In short, Cuomo concluded that Governor Spitzer had used the state police to follow the senate majority leader and had travel documents provided to the press to embarrass Bruno, and to try to create political consequences and possible criminal charges against him.

However, the Albany County district attorney decided not to bring any changes against Spitzer for either his role in the Bruno matter or his criminal activity which resulted in Spitzer's resignation as governor. Were no crim-

inal charges brought because Albany County district attorney, David Soares, was a true blue democrat politician, swept into the office partly due to substantial financial contributions of benefactors from the liberal wing of the democrat party?

This didn't end it for Joe Bruno, however. A separate, unrelated investigation continued against Bruno by the United States Attorney for the Northern District of New York. On January 23, 2009 Bruno was indicted on eight counts of corporate, mail, and wire fraud and for providing illegal services to individuals through his senate office. Bruno pled not guilty, and did not budge from that position despite offers by the United States Attorney for Bruno to plead to lesser charges.

Unrelated illegal services charges were brought against others in other states as well. Coincidentally these other charges were being contested before the United States Supreme Court on the grounds that the statutes were unconstitutionally vague and unenforceable.

Once it was announced that the United States Supreme Court was going to review these cases arising in other states to determine whether the statutes were unconstitutional, Bruno's attorneys made a motion to District Court Judge Gary Sharpe, asking that the trial be postponed until the Supreme Court ruled on whether the statutes were constitutional. Sharpe, a former federal prosecutor, ruled against Bruno and forced Bruno to go to trial.

On December 7, 2009, Bruno was convicted of two felony counts and was acquitted of five others. The jury was hung on the last count. The trial cost Joe Bruno a fortune. Shortly after the trial, the United States Supreme Court handed down its ruling that the illegal services statutes were unconstitutional. Accordingly, the two counts that Bruno was convicted on had to be set aside, which meant that the trial was a colossal waste of everyone's time and Joe Bruno's and the taxpayers' money. Bruno spent more than a million dollars. Had the trial judge simply postponed the trial to await the Supreme Court's

ruling, substantial time and expense would have been saved.

Now you might think that prosecutorial discretion might result in the United States Attorney not trying an 80 plus-year old Bruno again, or you might think to try him again would be double jeopardy. Not so fast.

The two charges that Bruno was convicted of were dismissed based on the Supreme Court's ruling but the United States Attorney brought other charges to the grand jury and Bruno was indicted on two counts of bribery. There was nothing that would have prevented the prosecutor from also indicting Bruno on bribery in the first indictment but he didn't do so. Bruno's attorneys vigorously argued that it was double jeopardy to now go back and charge him with a more serious charge that he could have been indicted on at the start . Well the United States Court of Appeals disagreed and allowed the prosecutors to go forward with a second trial.

So Bruno and his attorneys went through a second costly trial. Joseph Bruno was finally acquitted of the two bribery charges on May 16, 2014. This five-year marathon cost Bruno around three million dollars. It cost the federal government probably three times that amount.

So what was Joe Bruno's remedy once acquitted? The law provided that he would get indemnified by the state for "reasonable" attorneys' fees as determined by democrat attorney general, Eric Schneiderman. Eventually, after many delays, Bruno ended up receiving an agreed-upon two million dollar reimbursement for attorneys' fees and costs from New York taxpayers.

What remedy did Joe Bruno have against Judge Sharpe for denying Bruno's motion to postpone the trial for only a couple of months to see if the Supreme Court would find the charges unconstitutional and avoid a needless first trial on those charges? None. What remedy did he have against the United States attorney for having orchestrated the unsuccessful and repeated prosecutions? None.

About ten years before Bruno's ordeal, the state of New

York passed legislation that would allow for the taking of DNA samples from individuals charged with crimes. A DNA database was set up originally only for people charged with felonies. This was later expanded to people also charged with misdemeanors. This database became available to be used not only by prosecutors to solve crimes but also by defense attorneys to determine whether there was evidence that could exonerate a client from a charge. The database was also used to reopen some cold cases either to belatedly find a perpetrator or to prove that someone was wrongly convicted.

Over the years that the database has been in place and in use, many crimes were solved and many innocent people were exonerated. Moreover, numerous individuals who were convicted and serving jail time were found to have been wrongfully convicted.

An analysis of many of these cases showed that prosecutors violated the Brady rule, which contributed to the wrongful convictions. The Brady case established the principle that a prosecutor has a duty to provide exculpatory information to defense counsel. That is, all information that would tend to exonerate a defendant must be provided to defense counsel. By not doing so, a defendant is deprived of a fair opportunity to fully defend himself. As a consequence, many of those who were wrongfully convicted brought civil lawsuits against the state of New York after their criminal cases were overturned, and were successful in recovering millions of dollars from the state because of this prosecutorial misconduct.

What are the consequences to the prosecutor who violated defendants' rights and deprived them of their liberties? None. Prosecutors are immune from lawsuits and immune from paying money damages out of their own pockets, for wrongful convictions. There are no other real consequences either.

This is why I introduced a bill in the senate in 2014 and assemblyman Nick Perry introduced the same bill in the

assembly, which would create a commission to review allegations of prosecutorial misconduct, and impose real consequences if misconduct is proven.

Needless to say, this bill created a firestorm among the district attorneys of the state and many law enforcement agencies. I offered to those who opposed the bill, the opportunity to make recommendations for changes to the bill. None did. Finally, years later, in 2018, my bill passed the senate and soon thereafter passed the assembly. It was also signed by the governor after the senate and assembly agreed to make amendments to it. As of the time of this writing, the enforceability of the legislation is being challenged in the courts by the state district attorneys' association. Coincidentally the president of the state D.A.'s association, who is leading the charge to have the courts find the law unconstitutional, is Albany County D.A. David Soares.

The commission, once constituted, would review complaints against prosecutors to determine whether the prosecutor violated any ethics rules or laws in the prosecution of a defendant. The determination by the commission could exonerate a prosecutor, or find the complaint to be meritorious, and, if so, the prosecutor could be sanctioned from merely a reprimand, or censure, to removal from office. If and when finally implemented there will at least be a remedy against prosecutors for prosecutorial misconduct.

The protests of prosecutors, in my judgment are not well founded. There has been an almost identical commission that has reviewed complaints against judges since the 1970s. In New York, the commission is ably run by Robert Tembeckjian and his staff. Judges are exonerated, judges are censured, and judges are removed from office but at least there is an independent body to review complaints of misconduct against judges. When first enacted, the Commission on Judicial Conduct met with severe opposition, but, in time, the commission was shown to work and still works well.

Without such a process to hold prosecutors account-

able, there is little question that those prosecutors that are more concerned about convictions than justice, are going to continue to pile up convictions, some of which obtained by unethical or illegal means, resulting in some being wrongfully convicted and spending years in jail. It will also result in millions of taxpayers dollars being used to settle wrongful conviction lawsuits.

HERE WE GO AGAIN

When US Attorney, Preet Bharara, announced an indictment of then assembly Speaker Sheldon Silver, he concluded by saying that the general public should "stay tuned." Well, the public didn't have to wait long because on May 4, 2015, the majority leader of the senate, Dean Skelos, and his son, Adam, were arrested on charges alleging a scheme to extort money to benefit Skelos' son. Skelos and his son were each charged with two counts of conspiracy, two counts of extortion and two counts of solicitation of bribes and gratuities.

The general thrust of the criminal complaint was that Skelos pressured business owners to arrange for his son, Adam, to be paid tens of thousands of dollars in return for influence in the senate. More specifically, the complaint alleged that Skelos illegally obtained a $20,000 payment for his son from a large real estate developer which sought assistance from Skelos for various tax breaks. Additionally, it was alleged that, Adam Skelos, received $10,000 in monthly payments from an environmental technology company seeking government funded contracts in New York.

Investigations of Dean and Adam Skelos by Preet Bharara had been rumored for several months. Needless to say those rumors and the ultimate arrests cast still another shadow on the New York state legislature. However, both

defendants firmly protested their innocence. In fact, Skelos, stated that "I'm not only 'not guilty' but I am innocent."

There is a basic tenet in the law, namely, that one is presumed innocent until proven guilty, but this was not so for legislators at this time in history. The problem is that guilt or innocence isn't determined for many months, and in former Senator Joe Bruno's case, a verdict of "not guilty" took many years. But the effect is immediate and continuous for someone holding public office.

A few days after the Skelos' arrests, I appeared on *Capitol Tonight* with Liz Benjamin, a television talk show host in Albany. During our discussion Liz came just short of saying that "we know he is guilty." Other reporters were more subtle but just as firm in their beliefs, which showed in their reports. Their reports clearly shaped public opinion much more than the legal principal of being presumed innocent.

The Skeloses were arraigned on the criminal complaint in Manhattan on May 4, 2015. This was a legislative day in Albany, so needless to say, nothing much got done. However, the senate republican majority scheduled a private conference for 8 o'clock that evening.

Earlier that night the long-scheduled annual senate staff appreciation party took place. The timing couldn't have been worse. Dean arrived at the tail end of the party and upon his arrival he received a resounding round of applause and encouragement. No doubt this was based on the staff's concern for Dean and his family, but also on their worry over their own futures.

Immediately following the party, the senators went back to the Capitol building for a conference, during which Dean Skelos protested his innocence and vowed to fight on. Several senators spoke at the conference encouraging him and pledging their support. However, roughly half said nothing and a couple of senators actually sent out press releases call-

ing on Skelos to resign for the good of the senate.

Based on the presumption of innocence, I spoke on Dean's behalf with the following caveat. I looked at Dean and said words to the effect that "however, if by staying on, you are damaging the survival of the republican senate majority, you have to do the right thing." Dean said in reply, "John, you know me, and you know I will do the right thing."

We completed the legislative days on Tuesday and Wednesday. On my way home on Wednesday, I began receiving calls from several senators who were very concerned about the negative atmosphere in their districts because of Dean not being removed. They were torn as to whether they should stay with Dean or do what they considered to be the right thing, namely call for his resignation. I simply told them that they needed to do what they thought was right. Thereafter, several sent out releases calling for his resignation. All throughout the state, editorial pages were demanding Skelos' resignation from that point forward. And still more releases were sent out by others senators calling for Skelos' resignation.

Again, despite the presumption of innocence it is almost impossible for a leader to stay on as a leader while facing criminal charges. It was just a matter of time, in my mind, that he would have to step down

On Wednesday, May 6th a few of the senators who were calling me asked if I would please contact Skelos and try to arrange for an early conference before they made final decisions about sending out releases. So I called Dean and explained how things were breaking up, and that people were under pressure and that it would be very difficult for him to stay on as leader. He indicated that we will have our conference, at the regular time, the following Monday.

I said that that would be too late and that I thought it was a huge mistake. I reminded him of the fact that he said

he would "do the right thing," if the conference was breaking up. He said that he never said that and what he said was that he would do the right thing when he couldn't lead anymore. I didn't know quite frankly what the difference was between what he remembered and what I remembered but the conference was clearly breaking apart, and he couldn't lead anymore.

Dean then asked me to sign a statement supporting him and I replied that I needed to know the exact wording of the statement. He then emailed it to me and I reviewed it. It basically said that the signatories were 100% behind Dean Skelos staying on as leader. I called him back and told him that I couldn't sign it.

I again recommended to Dean that he get the conference together immediately to see where he stood and make a decision as to where he would go from there. I told him if half of the conference wanted him to stay on as leader and the other half was sending out press releases for him to resign, the conference was irretrievable broken. His next statement shocked me. I knew he was under a lot of pressure but when I told him my opinion he said, "They started it," meaning those senators who were calling for his resignation. I responded that his comment clearly showed that the conference was breaking apart and he would have to "do the right thing," as he had said he would.

Before the conversation was over he said he would really like me to sign the support statement and that senator Mike Nozzolio would not sign the letter unless I did. I told Dean that it was up to Mike Nozzolio to decide what he wanted to do but I simply could not sign the letter. The fact that so many were calling for his resignation was an obvious indication that his support was dwindling and the release of the letter signed by less than a majority of the conference would show this weakness. He disagreed and sent the letter

out.

The response was immediate. Additional senators sent out releases saying they were calling for him to step down and the press was commenting on how Skelos' hold on the conference was falling apart as evidenced by only 16 people out of 32 republicans senators signing the letter. The heat kept rising on Dean.

It was obvious at this time that Dean could not survive as leader. Now the focus turned to who was going to succeed him as majority leader of the senate. The main beneficiaries of the contest were AT&T, Verizon and Sprint. Senators were constantly calling each other. The supporters of one candidate or another were calling other senators and reporters were doing their jobs trying to find out what was going on. It became clear that the two contenders were down to John Flanagan from Long Island and yours truly from central New York.

The difficult part of this process was pinning an individual down as to who he or she was really supporting. But it was clear early on where 24 of the 32 senators stood. There was no doubt in my mind that John Flanagan would get all nine Long Island senators plus the three New York City senators for an even dozen. I was certain that about another dozen were absolutely in my corner from the outset. That left nine people to count, and a vote from five of the nine to win the position.

It was very difficult to pin down this uncommitted group. None of them were from Long Island or New York City so I believed I had an excellent opportunity to get five. One of my supporters, central New York senator, Joe Griffo, tried to keep me informed of where the uncommitted group actually were leaning. However, the undecided were getting calls from Flanagan's backers with the message that if Flanagan doesn't win, Skelos would not only resign as leader but also

resign from the senate. Then, I heard that Simcha Felder, the democrat that conferenced with us, would probably go to the democrat conference if Flanagan didn't win.

Obviously, that put tremendous pressure on those undecided, because if Felder left the conference and Dean resigned from the senate, our conference would go from a majority of 33 to a minority of 31. Compounding this problem was that Tom Libous was convalescing from operations and treatment he was having for cancer, and was not likely to return for the remainder of session. Libous was also facing criminal charges of his own for allegedly lying to an FBI agent. He had a trial scheduled for July 13, 2015.

In other words, this "nuclear option" as it was called by the *Daily News* in its Sunday paper was a not-so-veiled threat that if senators didn't vote for Flanagan we would lose the republican majority. This petrified many senators young and old. In addition, despite the governor's denial, he was making calls on behalf of John Flanagan. That didn't surprise me since I'm sure the governor felt that I would be his biggest nightmare, since I would never hesitate to express my opinion, whether he agreed with it or not. That didn't bode well for me.

And, as it turned out, the vote ultimately went for John Flanagan, 18-15. He got votes from some upstate senators that most would have thought would have had an allegiance to the upstate senator in the race. What really was surprising to me was that Mike Long, chairman of the New York state conservative party released a press statement the morning of the vote that said the conservative Party could work with either candidate. This was truly remarkable in that I had close to the top, if not the top conservative party rating during my time in the senate. Politics is an interesting endeavor.

Just before the meeting to select Skelos' successor was called to order, one of my supporters came to me and said that John Bonacic, who I considered my best friend in the senate,

had told her that he was voting for Flanagan. This literally threw me for a loop, since before the conference, Bonacic had told me that he would "do the right thing."

John Bonacic was not in the conference at the time I was informed of his intentions, but I located him, and told him how disappointed I was that he led me to believe that he was going to vote for me. I'm sure that, at the time, he thought that he would be doing "the right thing" but I was devastated that he did not tell me directly. Well, at that point, I knew the writing was on the wall, and that I should be prepared for a loss.

Something else occurred before the vote that showed me the true character of senator Mike Nozzolio. I was waiting in the room adjacent to the conference room when Mike walked towards me with a stern look on his face. When he got to me he said, "Why didn't you call me over the weekend?" I asked him why ? He responded that I should have called him to ask for his vote. I answered that the call would have been fruitless since he was openly supporting Flanagan, and was actually making calls on his behalf. He deflected my comments with some non-responsive phrase or two.

He then said I should have also called Kathy Young, a senator with whom he was very close, to ask for her support. I gave him the same answer, namely that Kathy Young was not only supporting Flanagan but also calling other senators for him as well. She was so forceful in these calls that she actually badgered one female senator into tears.

Yes, Mike and Kathy are two peas from the same pod. Maybe that's why they were so close. Apparently, they both thought that the best defense was a good offense. They tried to make me feel that I lost their vote by not reaching out to them. Even after the vote they were informed some constituents that the reason they didn't vote for me was because I didn't ask!

Just before the roll call was going to be taken, I asked to be heard. I stood up and expressed how disappointed I was that people were not truthful to each other. Totaling the votes that Flanagan thought he had and those that I thought I had resulted in a count of 38, when there were only 33 senators! I also said that if everyone had been truthful, John Flanagan and I could have resolved the whole situation in about two minutes, counting heads and going into the meeting like gentlemen and electing a new leader by voice vote.

The night before the vote John and I had met at my apartment in Albany basically to map out various ground rules to make sure the conference was conducted professionally and that people acted in a respectful way. We also agreed that we would abide by the results without fanfare or hoopla.

It was a very cordial meeting. The day of the vote John came out with a great quip. When the press asked him if we had met, he told them that we met at my apartment Sunday evening. He added that I served him frozen pizza. He had the quote of the day when he said "No self-respecting Italian would serve frozen pizza to anyone other than an Irishman." I though the comment was great to help alleviate any tension that might come at the conference.

As I walked into the conference room for the vote, I was mobbed by a group of reporters. I basically told them that this was going to be resolved in a professional way and I mentioned John's comment and made a quip of my own. I told the reporters that if they were looking for some theater, they were not going to get it because the conference was going to stick together no matter how the vote turned out. And that is exactly what happened.

After the vote was taken, I walked out to the press with John and we made brief remarks and then went into session and I carried the resolution to nominate John as the next majority leader. Dean Skelos had already submitted his written

resignation as leader. The discussion on the floor was a true show of unity, which we had to have because our senate majority was razor thin with only a one vote majority since Tom Libous was absent due to his cancer treatments.

All members wanted desperately to maintain a senate republican majority, and all said the right things. Unfortunately, it was the "nuclear option" that scared votes over to Flanagan, namely Skelos' threat to resign entirely from the Senate and the rumor that democrat Simcha Felder would leave the conference if Flanagan didn't win.

When I spoke to Felder, the day before the vote, he denied ever having said that he would leave the conference if Flanagan didn't win, and he assured me that in the event that Skelos stepped down as leader and I was elected majority leader he would support me.

Keeping the conference together was not as easy as one might think. It was in the interest of all of us to maintain that majority and I pledged to, and did everything possible to make that happen. However, after the vote, many of the upstate senators who opposed me were threatened by their county republican leaders with primaries in the 2016 elections. In fact, one individual announced his candidacy against long-serving Senator Hugh Farley the day after the vote. As it turns ed out, Farley retired and there was no primary.

Although this backlash was expected, I don't think anyone expected it to be so intense. At the time, I shared representation of Cayuga County with two other senators, Jim Seward and Mike Nozzolio. When it came out that they both voted against me, and actually could have turned the vote around for me to become majority leader, the *Auburn Citizen* blasted them immediately after the vote was disclosed. After the vote I was bombarded by news reporters asking how I felt about the result, what happens next, and if the republican majority was broken. Over and over again I explained how

important it was to maintain the republican majority, with a more conservative fiscal philosophy than the democrats, and I was part of that team.

Interestingly, late in the afternoon on the day after the vote, I received a call from Governor Cuomo. He told me that he was sorry that I did not become majority leader, and that I would have made a great leader if the vote had gone the other way. He added some other insincere platitudes.

I replied by saying that if he thought I would make a great leader why the hell did he make calls on behalf of John Flanagan. He forcefully responded that he stayed out of it and made no calls. I told him "Do you think that I'm a moron," and that I knew that he had made calls because some of the senators that he called informed me of it. What followed was an embarrassing silence. He then went on to a totally different topic, unrelated to the majority leader selection.

I lost the majority leader position, but I think I gained respect from a lot people on how I handled that loss since I did everything to keep the republican majority conference together. I also did everything I could to dissuade primaries from upstaters who thought that their representatives should have supported me. As it turned out no one primaried the upstate senators who didn't vote for me. So the republican majority was maintained, at least for the time being, giving upstate at least some voice in New York state government. However, I have often wondered how things would have been different if I had become majority leader.

GUILTY

Sheldon Silver and Dean Skelos were both found guilty at their trials. Needless to say, the cries for reform in Albany reignited after each trial and continued through the end of 2015 and into the 2016 session.

This reform mantra was aided and abetted by prosecutor Preet Bharara. He called for reforming the system by not allowing legislators to make outside income, and by calling for the old chestnut, term limits, among other things.

Governor Cuomo, again joined the bandwagon, which is quite ironic in so far as at the time Preet Bharara had initiated investigations of Cuomo's own staff. The governor promised to have proposals for serious reform in his January 13, 2016 state of the state message.

Only Cuomo knows whether his new reform move was intended to be a good defense. But there were several news stories while the Silver and Skelos trials were going on that investigations were ongoing into whether there was wrongdoing in the governor's awarding of contracts in the "Buffalo Billion" dollar program and others. He touted this "Buffalo Billion" initiative since it was announced in his first year in office. Basically, the Governor pledged that he would make available $1 billion to Buffalo to move the city from a state of near depression to a vibrant economy. The real reason for dishing out this money to Buffalo, in my opinion, was that in his first election, the governor got hammered in western New

York by his weak republican opponent, Carl Paladino, and he needed to repair that damage before his next election.

The news stories suggesting that the governor was being investigated by Bharara concerning his role in awarding these contracts escalated. But what really caught everyone's attention was while the governor was announcing his latest round of state economic development grants in November 2015, Preet Bharara tweeted in a now familiar "Preet Tweet" the words, "Stay tuned." Those were the same words that Bharara used at the end of his news conference announcing the indictment of Sheldon Silver. What followed shortly thereafter was the indictment of Dean Skelos. Even more specific rumors were floating around to the effect that Cuomo was going to be indicted in early January of 2016. Was Andrew Cuomo's newest pledge to have real reform in the state of the state message of 2016 simply an anticipatory defense?

No one can argue with those individuals and "good government" groups that called for reform in view of the numerous convictions and guilty pleas of state officials since 2002. A list of those convictions follows:

□ Dean Skelos (R) Majority Leader of New York state Senate: Convicted of federal corruption charges in 2015 related to the hiring of his son by companies who had business with the state; the case is on appeal.

□ Sheldon Silver (D) Speaker of the New York state Assembly: Convicted of federal corruption charges and receiving kickbacks in 2015; the case is on appeal.

□ Tom Libous (R) Deputy Majority Leader of the New York state Senate: Convicted of lying to the FBI in 2015 pertaining to the hiring of his son; he was sentenced to six months of house arrest, probation, and a $50,000 fine. He died shortly thereafter. Since his appeal was pending at the time of his death, the conviction was set aside.

□ John Sampson (D) Minority Leader of the New York state Senate: Convicted of obstruction of justice and making a

false statement in 2015; He was sentenced to 5 years in prison.

☐   Malcom Smith (D) Minority Leader of the New York state Senate: Found guilty of conspiracy, wire fraud, bribery and extortion in 2015 in his attempt to bribe a Republican party official to put him on the ballot as a Republican candidate in the 2015 New York City Mayoral race; He was sentenced to 7 years in prison.

☐   Gabriella Rosa (D) State Assemblywoman: Pleaded guilty to entering into a sham marriage to gain United States citizenship in 2014; She was sentenced to one year in jail.

☐   William Boyland (D) New York state Assemblyman: Convicted of bribery in 2014; Sentenced to 14 years in jail.

☐   Eric Stevenson (D) New York state Assemblyman: Found guilty of bribery, conspiracy, and related charges in 2014; He was sentenced to 3 years in jail.

☐   Nelson Castro (D) New York state Assemblyman: Convicted of perjury in 2013; He was sentenced to 2 years' probation after cooperating with federal investigations of two other elected officials.

☐   Shirley Huntley (D) New York state Senator: Convicted of mail fraud in 2013; She was sentenced to one year in jail.

☐   Pedro Espada Jr. (D) President Pro Tempore of the New York state Senate: Found guilty of embezzling money from a federally funded health care clinic in 2013; He was sentenced to 5 years in jail.

☐   Vincent Leibell (R) New York state Senator: Convicted of felony bribery, tax evasion, obstruction of justice in 2012 relating to kickbacks; He was sentenced to 17 to 21 months in jail.

☐   Nick Spano (R) New York state Senator: Convicted of federal income tax evasion in 2012; He was sentenced to

16 to 18 months in jail.

☐   Alan Hevesi (D) New York state Comptroller: Convicted of a "Pay to Play" scheme in 2012 in relation to the New York state pension fund; He was sentenced to 1 to 4 years in jail.

☐   Carl Kruger (D) New York state Senator: Pleaded guilty to corruption and bribery charges in 2011; He was sentenced to 7 years in jail.

☐   Efrain Gonzalez Jr. (D) New York state Senator: Convicted of fraud and embezzling $400,000 from a West Bronx neighborhood association in 2010; He was sentenced to 7 years in prison.

☐   Brian McLaughlin (D) New York state Assemblyman: Convicted of racketeering in 2009; He was sentenced to 10 years in jail.

☐   Hiram Monserrate (D) New York state Senator: Convicted of misdemeanor assault in 2009; He was sentenced to 1 year probation.

☐   Gloria David (D) New York state Assemblywoman: Convicted of bribery in 2003; She was sentenced to 5 years probation.

☐   Guy Velella (R) New York state Senator: Pleaded guilty in 2003 for accepting money in return for public-work contracts; He was sentenced to 1 year in jail.

The breakdown of the above state officials convicted of wrongdoing since 2002 is as follows: 16 of the 20 were democrats; 16 of the 20 were from New York City; 12 were senators; 7 were assembly members, and one was the state comptroller. I am not sure what conclusions can be drawn from these statistics, but they are worth noting.

As far as the crimes are concerned, virtually all of them pertained to using the representative's office to benefit either

him or herself or a family member. Hence, the cries for cleaning up Albany and reforming the system were understandable. The real question is what reforms should occur.

First, every one of the convictions was based on violations of existing law. In other words, prosecutors were able to convict 20 Albany elected officials in 13 years based on laws that were already on the books. What additional laws should be passed to "clean up Albany?" Put another way, what additional laws are necessary in order to stop individuals from using their offices to commit crimes for the benefit of themselves or family members?

Many have asked for more disclosure by representatives on their financial disclosure forms. I would suggest that anyone who believes this is necessary should review the current disclosure forms that each elected official is required to complete. In fact, members of various boards and commissions in the state, whether paid or unpaid, have to make the same disclosure. All income sources must be disclosed, together with the amount of income from each source; all assets must be disclosed, whether they are the elected official's assets or those of his or her spouse; all memberships to boards must be disclosed by the elected official for he or she and the official's spouse; and the list goes on.

When I was first elected to the senate the disclosure form was held privately by an ethics organization so that every bit of the elected official private financial life was not immediately disclosed to the public, but still available to investigators who might be investigating wrongdoing. That disclosure was expanded so that by 2012 these disclosures were online for anyone, with an inquiring mind, to be able to find out everything about the elected official's financial status by a click on a link to the state Board of Elections website.

In 2014 and 2015, there were rules drafted that would require elected officials who are attorneys to disclose the names of their clients and the types of cases that the elected official was working on for his or her clients, despite at-

torneys being ethically bound not to disclose client consult-
ations.

Moreover, to require this type of disclosure for someone who is being appointed to a non-paid public service job
such as a board or commission, is over-the-top, and has a
chilling effect on finding good appointees. Most importantly,
no matter what the rules of disclosure are, if someone is intent
on violating the law to benefit him or herself, this disclosure will simply be ignored and not complied with by them.
You don't have to come up with a hypothetical case to show
this since this was exactly the case with Sheldon Silver, who
did not disclose some of the clients that he brought to a law
firm, for which he received fees, alleged to have been illegal
kickbacks. So if there are already extensive disclosure requirements, what other reform is needed?

As mentioned above, some have called for an often repeated reform, namely term limits. Well let's look at term
limits. New York City already has term limits for its mayor
and members of the New York City council. So, how does that
work in practice? The present *modus operandi* is for an official
to serve for the number of terms that he or she is allowed to
in city government and when that time is up, to run for the
state legislature or something else. This is simply a recycling
process of candidates bouncing from public office ito another.
Most importantly, if the constituents of an elected official believe that the official is doing a good job, why should they be
deprived of that official by an artificial term limit?

Some have called for preventing legislators from being
able to have an outside occupation or business and income
from that occupation or business. This is suppose to reform
Albany? Up until approximately 2012, I practiced law, doing
mostly litigation, and made a nice living from that profession,
while serving in various public offices including the city of
Syracuse school board, the city of Syracuse common council,
and the New York state senate.

I feel very strongly that my law practice gave me total

independence on how I voted on various issues. My livelihood did not depend on whether or not I won an election. And I repeatedly showed that independence by taking stances that often were against public opinion. However, I kept getting re-elected.

If the rules change to "reform" the system, to require politicians to be full time politicians and their only source of income is from their political office, it would seem logical that the official would be more likely do anything and everything he or she had to do to win reelection, so that he or she would not have to start a totally new career after an election loss. Barring outside income would also stifle the independence of that elected official and almost insure that his or her votes would be based upon the mood of the public at any particular time, rather than on what was right and wrong. Finally, barring outside income would deprive the public of elected officials with diverse backgrounds and expertise in many areas.

However, this issue may ultimately be moot, at least for attorneys and other professionals for if the disclosure laws are broadened even further, attorneys, doctors and other professionals who are ethically bound not to disclose attorney/client or doctor/patient relationships, won't run for office. Fewer and fewer professionals will become elected officials. Similarly any person who has a successful business – realtor, contractor, store owner, etc, would be less likely to run for office. It seems the last thing we would want to do in this country is to create the full time profession of "politician."

Some have called for public financing of elections. The taxpayers are taxed too much already. Requiring taxpayers to pay for elections, or for government to direct some of its precious resources to finance campaigns would be the wrong way to go. It would be objectionable to require a taxpayer to have his or her tax dollars used to support a candidate who he or she would never support because they had opposing views. Some have said that this is nothing new since tax dollars are

already supporting things that some taxpayers don't agree with. I agree that we can't direct our tax dollars to only things we agree with. However, public financing of elections would require a taxpayer to pay for the election of candidates with opposite political views who, if elected, would be making decisions on all issues with a philosophy contrary to that of the taxpayer.

But there is an even more basic issue. We do not have to speculate on what public financing of elections would look like; we just have to look to New York City which has public financing for local races including mayor, comptroller, public advocate, and city council. For every dollar a candidate raises, the taxpayer has to kick in $6 in New York City. True, the amount that each individual or corporation can contribute is limited, but there have been many violations of this requirement by groups dividing up large contributions and reporting that many individuals gave smaller contributions rather than being bound by the contribution limits. Moreover, the elections are overseen by an appointed body that is woefully behind in their enforcement of the public financing laws in New York City.

Even more basic, one of the rogues of Albany that isn't on the above list because he wasn't charged and convicted, was Vito Lopez. Vito, a former assemblyman, was accused of groping some young female staffers in his office. This was kept totally quiet by the then speaker of the Assembly, Sheldon Silver. In fact, a private settlement was made between each of these victims with Lopez paying part of the cost from his campaign account, and Silver kicking in the rest out of public funds. Due to pressure from the public, Vito Lopez resigned from the assembly. But what did he then do? He ran for New York city council and took advantage of the public financing system. He raised funds for the city council race under the city's public financing ordinance. His first check of taxpayers' dollars from that office was $68,000. Public financing would not be a "reform." It could result in taxpayers pay-

ing for elections of disgraced candidates who should not be in public office.

There is no doubt there will be other "reforms" that will be seriously considered. However, for each such proposal an honest appraisal must be made on whether or not the "reform" would make it less likely that a dishonest elected official would use his or her office to benefit him or herself or members of his or her family. This should be the litmus test. Calling something a "reform" doesn't make it so.

IS IT TIME?

It's noon on December 31, 2015. In twelve hours I will have served 38 years in elected office: four years as a member of the Syracuse city school board (including one year as president); 8 years as a city of Syracuse councilor at-large, three years as president of the Syracuse city council and 23 years as a member of the New York state senate. Is it time?

I am now 69 years old. Never in my wildest dreams, did I believe that I would still be in elected office at this age. Over the years I've seen many senators age while serving and have asked myself, "why is he or she still here?" Presently, there are members of the Senate that are in their 80s. Incredibly, Senator William Larkin, representing portions of Orange, Rockland and Ulster Counties is 88 years old! Senator Hugh Farley, of Schenectady County just turned 83 years old! Hugh is in fabulous physical and mental health. Bill is in good mental condition but his body is failing. Bill says that he is running again, but it is going to be very difficult for him to do so.

During a substantial period of my time in the senate, I had the good fortune of sitting next to Senator John J. Marchi, from Staten Island, who was a member of the senate for about 50 years. He retired in his mid-80s and died three years thereafter. I also was honored to sit next to Owen Johnson, who served until he was in his mid-80s and died two years after he retired. Is it the right time for me to leave?

From the above examples it's oblivious that age alone is not the determining factor. Those that served into their

twilight years continued to have the capability to do so and, loved what they did. But serving as long as they did, left them with little time to enjoy life after elected office.

I still enjoyed what I was doing and I liked being an independent voice in state government. My constituents seem to be satisfied, if this can to be judged by the size of my victories. However, whenever I hear the question about when I am going to retire and enjoy life, I think back to senators John Marchi and Owen Johnson, who didn't have much time to do other things after they finally left the senate.

The first time I really thought about not running for reelection was in July of 2014. My health always had been good. I have also prided myself in being in good shape and have always enjoyed sports and physical activity. I played full court basketball pickup games at the YMCA until I was about 63 years old with much younger people. I still play tennis and golf, and at the age of 67 I joined a hardball baseball team in Ft. Myers, Florida, for a week of hard ball on a team of 65 to 70 year olds. It was like being a kid again, like when I was playing college baseball at Syracuse University.

But about fifteen years ago, I started having TIAs, which are basically mini-strokes. That obviously gave me pause. There isn't much that can be done about this condition other than taking proper medication, staying in good physical shape and not over stressing.

This was under control until June of 2014. At that time I was playing golf with friends. Fortunately, one of them, Chris Farnum, was an administrator at a local hospital. As I was golfing, I could feel myself starting to slur my words and talking gibberish. I also had numbness in my right arm. These were not good signs as I had learned over the years. Chris told me we were going to the hospital. I, quite frankly, fought it, but he and my other golf mate, high school classmate and long-time great friend, Joe Falcone, brought me to the hospital. There they did a series of tests which led to the placement of a Holter monitor. It monitored my heart activity for 48 hours.

This lead to examinations by cardiologists, and to still more tests. As it turns out, I was diagnosed with ventricular tachycardia. This is a rapid irregular heartbeat that I was told can result in sudden death. Within a few days of that diagnosis, I was on an operating table where an attempt was made to perform an ablation to stop irregular electrical activity in parts of my heart. The operation was unsuccessful.

A pacemaker/defibrillator was then implanted that same afternoon. The pacemaker was to keep my heart beating regularly, and the defibrillator was a preventative measure so that my heart could be automatically zapped out of afib, if necessary. Fortunately, since the implants, the defibrillator has not gone off at all and the monitoring of my heart has shown that my heart has been operating satisfactorily.

The timing of my heart episode in June of 2014 couldn't have been worse from a political sense. 2014 was an election year and I had already been nominated by the republican, conservative and independence parties to run for re-election. Petitions were being circulated for that race. When the petitions were filed, I was formally named as the candidate of those parties for the November election. I could have declined the nominations but even though I worried about my condition, I really thought that I was physically able to continue.

What soon became a great concern of mine, was my government pension. There was at that time, and still is, a section in the Retirement and Pension Law of the state of New York that provides that if you die prior to filing for retirement, and while still serving in office, your surviving spouse would receive a small insurance lump-sum payment, which declined as time went on. And despite serving in public office for almost 40 years, and building up a pension, if I didn't file for retirement, my wife of 45 years, at that time, would not have received annual pension payments.

After much thought, I didn't decline the nominations of the republican, conservative and independence parties and

won the election handily. However, since I still had a condition that could result in sudden death, there was a risk that I could pass away at any time during my term of office, leaving my wife without my earned pension.

I contacted the New York state comptroller's office to see what if anything could be done. I was advised that since I was over 65 years of age, there was a provision in the retirement law that would allow me to file for retirement and receive my retirement benefits while serving additional terms in office.

Obviously, this is not the most popular thing to do as a public official. Others who have done it in the past, were soundly criticized. However, the more important thing to me was to make sure my wife was taken care of and received the benefits that I earned over almost 40 years of public service. So, at the end of 2014, two years after I could have filed, I filed the papers and was "retired."

There was strong criticism and negative news media reports about it. Although I could have explained my health condition and maybe allowed more people to at least understand why I did it, I didn't mention my health at all. I would bet that just about anyone who was facing the situation that I was would have done the same thing. It was completely legal and permitted by state law. Moreover, it was completely justified considering my condition at the time.

The answer to the question "is it time?" was "no" but the question would come up again.

"PROGRESSIVE" NEW YORK STATE

The "progressive" movement got a great boost in 2015 when Governor Andrew Cuomo used a wage board to set a minimum wage for fast food workers. The wage was set at $15.00 per hour. Actually, the governor directed his appointed state labor commissioner to impanel a wage board and appoint its members to "study" fast food workers' minimum wage. In reality, this political façade ended with the hourly minimum wage for fast food workers being raised to what the governor sought, namely $15.00.

A lawsuit was filed by the fast food industry challenging the manner of appointment of the members of the wage board and its ultimate "recommendation." The main thrust of the suit was that, despite the requirements in the law, the labor commissioner did not appoint a member to the board who was a person who was part of the affected industry - fast food restaurants. This lawsuit was still pending when the governor announced that he was going to deliver a joint state of the state and budget message on January 13, 2016.

This joint speech was a creation of Andrew Cuomo, for whatever reason. It was a very cumbersome, and an excruciatingly long presentation. More importantly, in the past, when the budget message was given separately from the state of the

state speech , at the conclusion of the message, members of the legislature were able to ask the budget director specific questions about the content of the budget. There was no such opportunity after this joint message. As a result, the joint message was long on rhetoric, even for Andrew Cuomo, and very short on details.

Before Andrew Cuomo, the state of state message was always given in the assembly chambers but apparently this wasn't a big enough venue for him, so he moved the joint message, to the New York convention center. This gave him plenty of opportunities to bring in special interest groups to clap vigorously at the right times.

Not only was the convention center big, but for the 2016 presentation the governor's podium was, to say the least, a bit large. All I could think of when I was attempting to see Lt. Governor, Kathy Hochul who was behind the gigantic podium to introduce the governor, was that we were being spoofed at a Saturday Night Live taping.

The governor is not a small man, but despite that, it was difficult to see him as well. However, the more I thought about it, the podium size was necessary to house his oversized ego.

The main thrust of the speech was to demonstrate his "progressive" credentials for whatever political move he had in mind next. In his speech he announced his $15.00 an hour minimum wage for everyone and a provision for paid family leave. When these proposals were announced, the cheers of the throngs of special invited guests were deafening and prolonged.

Every other time in my 23 years in the senate when there was a call for an increase in the minimum wage there was an analysis and a discussion related to the economic impact of a minimum wage increase. The problem, in this case, was that the $15.00 per hour minimum wage was simply a political number that the "progressive" movement was trying to sell throughout the nation. There was no economic

analysis or basis for such a substantial boost.

The last minimum wage increase was done over a three-year period with a final increase to $9.00 per hour effective December 31, 2015. There wasn't an inflation increase or a justification for a cost of living increase from this date to the date that the governor announced his plan in mid-January, 2016.

The last three-year phase-in increased the minimum wage in New York state by 24%, and New York state's minimum wage after the phase in was 24% greater than the federal minimum wage. The Governor's proposed three-year phase in from $9.00 to $15.00 an hour amounted to an *additional* 67% increase in the minimum wage. Absolutely incredible!

As soon as I left the two-hour state of the state/budget presentation, I was asked by the press my thoughts about it. I stated it was an outrageous increase that had no basis in sound economics. Moreover, I raised what an incredibly negative effect it would have on New York state small businesses, non-profits and young people attempting to get summer jobs.

I knew that this proposal would be a darling of the state assembly that was controlled by New York City liberals or "progressives," whichever the politically correct term was at the time. Because of my opposition, within a week or two the unions that were behind the proposal for a $15.00 an hour minimum wage began commercials targeting me as the face of rich New Yorkers who had no empathy for the poor. The commercial called me the "$6 million man" apparently based on my financial disclosure statements.

Every year that I have been in the senate, there have been cries for more "reforms," and each year legislators and even individuals who were seeking a position on a commission without pay, have had to file more and more details about their personal wealth. I complied with all the requirements each year but it made absolutely no sense to me. What relevance is your total net worth to whether you are acting im-

properly in your position. Do a lot of assets indicate that you are corrupt and you obtained those assets illegally? Does a low net worth mean you are more susceptible to graft because you have little money?

When the commercials started characterizing me as the "$6 Million Man," I finally realized the purpose of disclosing one's net worth---to give opposition groups something to use in commercials to criticize an official with whom the groups disagree. A hatchet job trumps facts when the facts don't support your position.

Shortly after the ads began, I called a news conference. At that new conference, I stated my position, which was supported by other speakers, including a farmer, a small business owner, a CEO of a non-profit organization, an owner of a senior citizens residence, and an owner of a daycare center.

Each of these individuals stated how this $15.00 minimum wage would adversely affect them. Many indicated that the cost of their products would have to go up, or they would have to lay off workers. One powerful speaker was the owner of a daycare center. She indicated that she could not lay off workers because she was required to have a certain number of workers based on the number of children that were under her care. As a result, all she could possibly do was raise her rates for daycare. She explained that she would need to raise the cost of daycare for two children from $10,000 to $16,000 per year!

The nonprofit CEO, indicated that this minimum wage increase would cause the cost of caring for children to skyrocket. His nonprofit was Elmcrest Children's Center which cared for children who have been in and out of foster care, providing a residential setting to help get those children the help they needed. He stated that the cost to his facility would amount to $2 million more a year if the $15.00 per hour minimum wage was passed.

A similar story was told by an operator of a senior citizen facility. The state of New York, through medicaid,

provides funding to health care providers and residential facilities for seniors. Similarly, the state provides funding for children in need such as those housed at Elmcrest. Unfortunately, this funding does not cover the cost of services.

Places like Elmcrest and residential senior citizen facilities, as well as hospitals, were already struggling. And the governor's proposed budget did not include any additional funding to assist in paying the 67% increase to minimum wage workers. Facts like this didn't matter since the governor's real objective was to lead the "progressive" movement, not to set an economically sensible minimum wage.

Later it came out that California was also going through the same process, to raise the minimum wage to $15.00 per hour. Toward the end of the budget process there was a race between Jerry Brown, the governor of California, and Andrew Cuomo to see who was going to have the $15.00 per hour minimum wage in place first. This race was not an economic one, but rather a purely political one, to become the darling of "progressives."

After the governor presented his budget, the senate and the assembly had joint budget hearings in Albany to listen to and question agency heads as well as the general public on their views of the budget. One such hearing was scheduled for local governments. I was present for the testimony of Kathy Sheehan, mayor of Albany, who argued strongly for more state aid since much of the property in Albany was government property that was property tax exempt. She was asking for millions of additional dollars. When it came to the issue of minimum wage she said that Albany, of course, was in favor of it.

I asked her if the city of Albany was in such dire financial shape, how could it pay the minimum wage increase to Albany's employees. She said they would be able to do so. I then asked her about the summer jobs programs and whether she would have to cut a number of young people participating in that program. She said "no" without hesitation.

Also, I heard from the catholic conference, lobbyists for the Catholic church, who were looking for a tax credit for parents who sent their children to Catholic schools. Other lobbyists for various religious and private school systems were pushing for the same credit. Before they concluded their pitch, they said they were also in favor of the $15.00 per hour minimum wage. I asked how they could be in favor of a 67% wage increase while at the same time pleading for tax credits to help Catholic schools remain open. Their answer, without hesitation, was that, they would need more state aid to make up for the increase in the wage. I commented to them that they were obviously men of great principle---in favor of a higher minimum wage as long as the taxpayer paid for it.

While the issue was being discussed with them, there was a rally of union members and other advocates outside the Capitol building pushing for an increase in the minimum wage to $15.00 per hour. One participant who appeared with the governor was Cardinal Timothy Dolan, who excited the crowd by showing his support for the 67% minimum wage increase. No doubt he thought that this was the right thing to do but I suspect he also thought that it would help him get the tax credit the Catholic conference was seeking from the governor. But he must have been disappointed in that the final budget did not include the tax credit. It was rumored that this was the third year in the row that the Cardinal was led to believe by the governor that the tax credit would be included in the final budget, but it wasn't.

The political scene got uglier and uglier. I was asked to meet with the Syracuse leader of a union pushing for the minimum wage, Ann Marie Talaricio. I had known her for many years and I didn't hesitate to meet with her. When she came in, I asked her why she didn't meet with me before the unions started to vilify me in their commercials. She didn't have an answer. Quite frankly, she made a very weak attempt to change my mind about the increase in the minimum wage. To be fair to her, she knew that she couldn't.

Shortly thereafter, Talaricio sent a letter to the mayor of Syracuse, Stephanie Miner, criticizing her for not attacking me for my opposition to the $15.00 per hour minimum wage. Interestingly, the mayor had already unilaterally implemented the minimum wage of $15.00 per hour for all Syracuse employees. She agreed with the unions on the minimum wage issue and had actually implemented it even before governor Cuomo proposed it for state employees. But what she did wasn't good enough for the unions.

The mayor, who I am fond of and able to work with, even though I am a moderate republican and she is a progressive democrat, refused to attack me. Well what do you think the unions did at that point? They started running commercials attacking the mayor for not aggressively advocating for the 67% increase. You can't make this stuff up. The mayor, who had already implemented in her City what the unions and the governor wanted for the state was being attacked in commercials by those seeking the state minimum wage increase!

Governor Cuomo had his fingerprints all over this one. These attacks on the mayor can partially be explained by the fact that the Cuomo hated Stephanie Miner and refused to work with her. This was a way for him to attack her through the unions.

In any event, the noise got louder as the state got closer to its April 1 budget deadline. I was the poster child, but others were criticized as well. These tactics were not surprising. What was unexpected was what occurred in the republican conference about the minimum wage increase.

A TYPICAL BUDGET "PROCESS" - 2016

2016 was my twenty-fourth year in the Senate which meant my twenty-fourth budget. Virtually every year the budget process was criticized by "good government" groups and the public in general. For the first 18 years the main criticisms were about the secretive discussions among the "three-men-in-the-room" (the governor, senate majority leader and speaker of the assembly), and about the late budgets. However, the budgets, for the five years leading up to the 2016 budget, were all done on time, which was a great achievement by Governor Cuomo.

In 2007, a budget proposal became law that required that after the assembly and the senate passed one-house budgets, joint public conference committee hearings between the senate and the assembly were to be held. Although many of these meetings were uneventful and lacked much substance, there was at least an opportunity for the public to hear what some of the issues were and what positions the senate and the assembly were taking. But everyone knew that most of the important negotiating was being done behind closed doors.

Despite the law of 2007, the public joint senate and assembly meetings did not occur at all in 2016. In fact, even

when the leaders emerged from private discussions, there was little, if any, information given about what had been discussed and what positions each had taken.

During my tenure I always defended the "three-men-in-a-room" process on the grounds that when there are negotiations, for example, between labor and management, all members do not attend the negotiations. Rather, a limited number negotiate on behalf of union and management. Similarly, the senate and assembly legislators discuss the various issues with their leaders, the majority leader in the senate and the speaker in the assembly, and their positions are negotiated among the governor and the two leaders.

The senate experienced a major setback in 2015 with our negotiating team. Robert Mujica was the main staffer in the senate that had negotiated the most recent budgets for the senate republicans. During December 2015, Mujica was hired by governor Cuomo as budget director. This resulted in many problems in the negotiations for the senate. First of all Mujica knew everybody in the senate. He knew the new leader John Flanagan, and his strengths and weakness. Moreover, Mujuca did virtually all the negotiating for the former leader Dean Skelos. As a result, he developed a very close relationship with governor Cuomo while he was representing the senate in negotiations.

To complicate things more for the senate, majority leader John Flanagan appointed Mujica's chief of staff, Mike Paoli as the chief administrator for the senate finance office. Paoli was an outstanding staffer but unfortunately, he really was not a negotiator and did not play a significant role in the negotiations in 2016.

Flanagan had his competent chief attorney, Beth Garvey, carry all the heavy weight in the negotiations of 2016. She appointed Rebecca Wood as her main assistant. Wood was competent as well. However this all resulted in a big hole in the negotiating team. Garvey and Wood had to take on the heavy load of negotiating, especially on the more compli-

cated issues. Moreover, several of the senior finance team had retired, which left other holes in the finance negotiating team. Finally, the senate's new leader, John Flanagan, had not played a significant role in negotiations prior to 2016. As a result, the senate was in a weak staffing position.

As the budget process moved forward, Flanagan had many conferences with the senate republican members in attempts to get a consensus. These meetings resulted in conversation after conversation and restatement of positions after restatement of positions.

From speaking with other members and listening to them in republican conferences, I strongly believed that there was a majority of senate members who did not support the governor's $15.00 an hour minimum wage proposal. I spoke to the press freely about that. Flanagan kept his remarks very vague both in public and in the private republican conferences. All he would say was that the leaders were discussing various options and were trying to come to an agreement. This vagueness led to substantial frustration among the senate membership.

I, and many others in the conference, stated our position that the New York businesses, especially small businesses, farmers, nonprofits and the like, could not absorb a 67% increase in the minimum wage on the heels of a 24% increase that was just implemented. I continually repeated that $15.00 per hour had no sound basis in economics and simply was a political number pulled out of the air by the "progressives" in New York and other states. Again, there was never a definitive comment by the majority leader Flanagan. He simply let people talk for weeks and weeks.

As we got closer and closer to the budget deadline, we seemed further and further away from a consensus. Moreover, I sensed from the negotiating team, as did others, that they also were not clear as to what the ultimate goals of the negotiations were and there appeared to be frustration on behalf of staff as well. Add to this the pressures of the increasing

volume of rhetoric by unions, in favor of the minimum wage increase, and by large and small business groups, nonprofits, farmers, and the like opposed to it. The republican conference became fragmented. All John Flanagan kept saying was that we had to keep negotiating, without identifying what our goal was in the negotiations.

There was one positive unforeseen development. The *Syracuse Post Standard*, which in the past has had little hesitation in criticizing me for many positions that I had taken, actually editorialized against the minimum wage increase to $15.00 an hour. I would have liked to believe that my outstanding presentations at news conferences and other advocacy was the reason they supported me. However, when I came down to earth, I realized that the reason the paper editorialized against it was because the newspaper had low income employees as well, and that the paper was struggling with reduced circulation and revenues in trying to stay in existence. But, other newspapers, including the *New York Times*, editorialized in favor of the $15.00 minimum wage.

My position in the republican conferences was unequivocal that we simply should not do a 67% increase. When we kept hearing from Flanagan that we were still negotiating and "we are still trying to work something out," I would respond that we should be telling the governor that there is a line in the sand that we are simply not going to cross, and that the decision had to be based on sound economics, and not the progressives' political agenda. But, all Flanagan kept repeating was that we needed to continue to negotiate.

One of the most vocal people in the conference was first-term senator Sue Serino from the Hudson Valley. She was very emotional about it and explained that when she went back to her district all she heard was how the senate needed to stop this unreasonable minimum wage proposal. Less emotional but as forceful, was Senator George Amadore who was always a fiscally conservative voice in the confer-

ence. Senator Tom O'Mara, a veteran in Albany, repeated, in no uncertain terms, that he could not support a $15.00 minimum wage.

Some newspapers and commentators were making this into an upstate/downstate battle over the minimum wage, but that was not true. Brooklyn senator, Marty Golden, was as vocal against the unreasonable increase as were upstate senators. Some members of the media were trying to pit Flanagan against me, since there had previously been an upstate/downstate battle for the majority leadership. But, the minimum wage proposal was simply not an upstate/downstate issue.

At one point, Andy Lanza, from Staten Island, mentioned that Staten Island was very similar to upstate, and that it couldn't support an increase in the minimum wage to $15.00. Quite frankly, just about everyone in the conference, at one time or another, expressed that same position. But, I was particularity proud of the first-term Senators who were not sitting around like wall flowers, but were aggressively participating in the debate.

Rob Ortt, a military veteran and a first-term senator from the Niagara Falls area, expressed his opinion on many occasions, namely that it just would not fly in his district and that he was concerned that it was almost a certainty that he would not withstand a "yes" vote on the minimum wage in his first reelection bid. Similarly, another first-term Senator, and military veteran, Tom Croci from Long Island, expressed his concerns, but didn't say a lot until the last week of the discussions when it became more and more apparent where the minimum wage "negotiations" were going.

Some of the main themes of those against the minimum wage were that it shouldn't be done at all; that we should have a separate upstate/downstate minimum wage; that summer youth employees should have a separate lower minimum wage; and that small businesses with less than 50

employees should be exempt from it.

The only position that gained any traction was a separate minimum wage for upstate. As we got closer to the budget deadline, John Flanagan announced in conference that negotiations were heading towards a $15.00 minimum wage, phased in over 3 years, in New York City and phased in over four years on Long Island and Westchester counties; and a separate upstate New York minimum wage of $12.50 phased in over 5 years, and thereafter, up to $15.00 phased in for a period to be determined after an economic review. Immediately, the volume of the conference discussions increased with more senators speaking up.

In particular, Marty Golden from Brooklyn vehemently argued that he would be killed if New York City had a $15.00 wage phase in over 3 years and upstate didn't have to reach $12.50 until 5 years later. He stated, in no uncertain terms, that he would not vote for the deal on the table. Senator Andy Lanza from Staten Island also said the same thing. This was surprising since up to that point he seemed to go along with everything that Flanagan was saying. Of course, it was easy to go along with Flanagan up to this point since before this discussion, he never said anything specific other than that they were negotiating.

Senator Croci made it clear that Long Island needed to have the same deal as upstate New York. Frankly, I couldn't blame him for insisting on that. He had been a town supervisor on Long Island before coming to the senate and had done some great work bringing small businesses to his community. He argued that there was no way he would support the disparate minimum wages because he would be damning the very businesses that he worked so hard to bring to his town.

What was very apparent was that the discussion now wasn't whether we should do a minimum wage increase at all but rather how much and over what time period. This didn't

sit well with me since I think we caved for no reason. I thought we should have just said "no" and that we wouldn't raise the minimum wage at all until there was an economic study. I believed that the governor wanted an on-time budget more than anything, and if he had to move the minimum wage discussion outside the budget process he would have done so. Many others in the conference agreed with me. But John Flanagan continued on with his "need to negotiate" mantra.

At the time, the republican conference had a slim majority, actually comprised of only 31 republicans and one democrat, Simcha Felder. I wasn't quite sure why, but Felder was not at any of these knockdown, drag out conferences. Since Andy Lanza had served with him on the New York city council, and was a close friend of his, I asked Lanza about Felder's position. He said he would definitely be voting "yes" for the increase in minimum wage because of his strong feelings about helping the poor. I assumed Lanza was being forthright with me, and maybe he was, but as it turns out when the floor vote took place Felder ended up voting "no".

Two weeks before the vote, Flanagan scheduled a meeting for the leadership of the senate majority. As second in command, I was obviously there, and all the other senators with leadership positions attended as well. Some of the leaders gave locker room speeches, to the effect that "we have to stay together once we have the best deal possible, as determined by the leader," or "we need this to maintain the majority." I responded by asking what good is a majority if we can't stand by our principles and avoid damaging the state's economy further.

I said many times, that every ten years we lose a couple of seats in Congress. The reason for that was that New York continued to lose population in relation to other states, and the population loss was getting worse. I also emphasized that we were last or next to last among the states in favorable busi-

ness climates and what we were doing with a 67% increase in minimum wage was putting another nail in New York's economic coffin.

The pitch of almost everyone who chose to speak in those leadership meetings was that we had to have an on-time budget and we have to come up with a compromise, and if we didn't we would be beaten in this coming November's elections. To complicate things, on April 19th a special election was scheduled to fill the seat vacated by the Dean Skelos, and winning that seat was crucial to keeping the republican majority.

Although it wasn't said in so many words, it was believed that governor Cuomo had given Flanagan his commitment that he would not interfere in that special election so that republicans would have a better chance to win. It was also implied that the unions would not put their considerable resources behind the democrat candidate for that seat.

Quite frankly, I thought this was a lot of nonsense. Some unions were trying to kill the republican conference for virtually the whole time that I was in the senate. To believe that after attacking us, and pressuring us into agreeing to their $15.00 minimum wage proposal, that all of a sudden they'd be our friends is naïve at best. It made no sense, since if they could get rid of the republican majority they would have an easy avenue to everything that they wanted including other "progressive" changes in New York state law.

Also, both at leadership meetings and at full conference meetings I, and other senators, repeatedly asked Flanagan to talk to Mike Long, chairman of the New York state conservative party, to find out his position. Knowing Long, I knew that he couldn't possibly support this minimum wage proposal as it was crystallizing.

For at least a week, Flanagan said that Long seemed to be fine, but then he would say that he was trading calls with

Long and that he couldn't get through to him. I called Long with about two and one-half weeks left before the due date of the budget and told him that if he didn't advocate strongly against the $15 minimum wage, it was going to happen. He told me he would be more aggressive but I saw nothing that showed that he did so.

At the end of the first leaders' meeting, Ken LaValle, a longtime senator from Long Island, told the group that he had a sensitive question to ask. He then looked at me and asked, "John, as the deputy majority leader, are you going to support the leader and vote for this?" I said that I needed to know what I would be voting on first since there had been no consensus reached. That didn't seem to sit well with the group.

The following week we had another leaders' meeting. By that time there were more details of the status of negotiations. It came out that the State University of New York (SUNY) was not getting an increase in funds in the budget. Ken LaValle had been the chairman of the senate higher education committee for many years and was a strong advocate for the SUNY system. He spouted off about how the governor can't do this to our higher education institutions, and that he was extremely upset and hated that portion of the budget and went on and on and on. I then raised my hand, and when recognized, I asked Ken if I could ask him a sensitive question. I asked, "as a leader in this conference will you support the majority leader on this budget?" That generated a lot of laughter in light of LaValle's question to me at the last leaders' meeting. LaValle never answered the question, but did smile.

We had more conferences and the same arguments were repeated and repeated. I then made the suggestion that I had made in earlier conferences, namely to take the minimum wage proposal out of the budget bill, and allow us to vote for a separate bill for minimum wage. John Flanagan definitely did not want to do this because he wanted everyone to

stick together and vote for his negotiated deal. He explained that otherwise it would be interpreted as an upstate/downstate battle. I am not quite sure how that was the case, but I strongly believed that everyone should vote his or her conscience on the minimum wage issue separate from the budget.

Other senators began asking for a separate vote on minimum wage but as soon as some did, the senior-most members in the conference continued to repeat their speeches that we have to support the leader, that we have to stick together, etc. What was most troubling to me was that Flanagan then started pointing out to each member what items they had in the budget that would not happen if the budget as a whole was not passed.

For example, one senator had a water project for which she had funding in the budget. Another had some money in the budget to help mitigate the closure of a nuclear plant in her district. Another had funding restored for a hospital in his district, and the list went on. It got to the point where Flanagan was either gently reminding or mildly threatening senators of what they would lose in their districts if the proposed budget deal did not pass.

He also said that the governor told him that if we didn't pass the budget, including the minimum wage increase, he would impanel additional wage boards for different industries and raise the minimum wage anyway. I thought that this was absolutely ridiculous. The governor did his wage board for the fast food industry the previous year which was only popular with one group, namely employees of fast food restaurants, and it was very unpopular with business leaders. I argued that it would be impossible for him to keep impaneling these wage boards for individual industries and unilaterally raising various minimum wages without looking like a fool and drawing the wrath of the public.

The conferences got uglier and Flanagan got more and

more frustrated as did everybody else in the room. Each of the senators who wanted to vote "no" were called in one by one to talk with Flanagan. Many did not budge.

When I had my meeting, Flanagan said that I had some $90 million in projects in the budget that were important to me and that they wouldn't happen if we didn't have an on-time budget that included the increase in the minimum wage. I challenged him immediately to break down the numbers and tell me where the $90 million came from, because it simply wasn't true. I also said that I don't give a damn about any of the things that I would have in the budget, since stopping the unreasonable 67% minimum wage increase was more important than any project that any district might get. Flanagan was visibly upset and told me that my position was not helpful and he didn't know what he had to do. I then told him if he was talking about taking away my deputy majority leader position, then he should go ahead and do it. He responded that he never said or implied that.

I did feel sorry for John because he was totally frustrated about what was going on. I told him again that he should do a separate bill and let anyone who wanted to vote "no" do so, just like what was done with the controversial gay marriage and gun control bills that were passed in prior sessions. He steadfastly refused to allow it, saying that we had to stay together.

It got really bad the last couple of days. Senator Tom Croci made it clear that if Long Island couldn't get the same deal as upstate he wasn't going to vote for it. He was visibly shaken when speaking. What happened next was that senator John Bonacic, I'm sure with the full knowledge of Flanagan, talked to Croci and advised him there was one way to avoid all of this and that was that he could stay away from session so he would not be present, and would not have to vote "yes." Croci told Bonacic that he wouldn't run again, and that had he

known that this was how the process was going to work, he wouldn't have run in the first place.

When the bills were printed, there wasn't a separate bill for the minimum wage. Rather, there were only budget bills that had a record amount of education aid for school districts, and other goodies, together with the minimum wage increase and a new paid family leave. So if we voted "no," we were voting "no" against education funding for our school districts and "no" for transportation funding, etc., etc.

Despite everything that went on, everyone agreed to vote for the bill except for Croci and two or three others. More importantly, many stated that if someone else voted "no," he or she was going to vote "no" as well. So another conference was called and eventually everyone left the meeting under the impression that they were going to vote for the minimum wage compromise. So we all went back into session.

My main responsibility as deputy majority leader was to handle the floor during the debate, which can be difficult during the budget debates. At one stage when we were discussing these large bills with everything wrapped into them, a few democrats complained that certain things were not in the budget, and they didn't like other things that were in the budget, but on balance, they indicated that they would support the bills. Some of the speakers were very passionate, and made it sound like they were in an untenable position with all of the items tied together and that we, as republicans, didn't do what we were supposed to do to have a better budget. After hearing this several times, I decided to speak.

I said that the democrats did not have a monopoly on dissatisfaction with various parts of the budget. I indicated that some parts of the budget are good, some parts are bad, and some are truly ugly. Everybody in the chamber clearly knew what I was talking about, namely the $15.00 minimum wage.

My speech prompted Flanagan to immediately call for a republican conference to discuss where everyone was on the bill now that we were ready to vote. I didn't notice that Tom Croci was not in the chambers. I later learned that Tom was ready to resign and that he asked Bonacic to make sure that the senate took care of his staff.

Shortly after the conference discussion began, Flanagan left the room and asked that senator Andy Lanza join him. When they returned, some 15 minutes later, Flanagan indicated that he had called Croci and asked him to please come back to conference. Needless to say, he was not happy. When Croci got back, he asked that he be given the opportunity to talk to the governor about making the minimum wage on Long Island the same as upstate. So we went back into conference and Flanagan and Croci left. We later learned that governor Cuomo was either unavailable, or more likely than not, unwilling to speak to Croci.

We then went back into session and, shortly after reassembling, a vote was taken. Everyone, republicans and democrats alike, voted "yes," on the big ugly budget bill except one, Simcha Felder, who voted "no" on the bill that contained the minimum wage. Unbelievable! Now it was apparent that Felder didn't conference with us towards the end of the budget process because he probably never had the intention of voting for the minimum wage bill. Sadly, all us who shouldn't have voted "yes," did vote "yes." Our session for these budget votes lasted from 4 PM on Thursday through the night until about 9:45 AM on Friday. Everyone was exhausted and all were disgusted.

Governor Cuomo never ceased to amaze me. While we were in the middle of our budget debates on the bills, he held a news conference outlining everything that was in the budget and how it was a wonderful budget. We hadn't even voted on at least half of the budget bills at the time, and we definitely

hadn't voted on the controversial issues, including the $15.00 minimum wage. So when the governor was announcing the budget specifics, it hadn't even passed.

After getting a couple of hours sleep, I drove back to my Syracuse senate office. I got there about 4 PM. Around 5 PM my cell phone rang and I answered it. Guess who? Andrew Cuomo. Amazing!

He told me that it was great that we got a budget done and that it was a wonderful budget. I disagreed with him about the quality of the budget, which was no surprise to him. After I said it was not a good budget, he indicated that we still had the rest of the session to do other good things and hopefully we can work together. Cuomo, the consummate politician, then said that he would be in Syracuse sometime soon and said that maybe we could get together then. Are you kidding me?

The ink wasn't dry on the governor's signature on the budget bills before the reaction started coming in. Predictably, the unions and other advocates for the phased-in $15.00 minimum wage were ecstatic over their monumental victory. Small businesses, nursing homes, non-profits, farmers, and everyone who had to pay for the increased minimum wage and struggle through a declining economic climate in New York, were not happy to put it mildly.

The most interesting reaction was from Mike Long, the state conservative party chairman. On the last day of the budget process, John Flanagan told us that he had spoken with Long and that Long was "in a good place." This representation obviously went a long way to relieve some of the fears of those who were uncertain whether they were jeopardizing their conservative party endorsements for re-election. However, the press release from Long, immediately after the budget was passed, stated that a vote for the minimum wage was like putting a sign on your chest that says "please run against me." He

also said that some conservative party county chairs in the state would not support those who voted "yes" on the minimum wage. It didn't sound like Mike Long was "in a good place," nor were a majority of republican senators.

A few hours before the voting on the 2015-16 budget bills began, we all were given a summary of the terms of the various budget bills by an employee of the republican majority. This was the first time we republicans learned that there were some special provisions hidden in the budget. One was a $2.3 billion medicaid allocation to "offset the cost of the minimum wage" for certain employers. As it turned out, these dollars would be available to some employers who hired the same union members that were the main advocates for the minimum wage proposal. These are the same union people that ran negative ads and electronic media messages against me, mayor Stephanie Miner and others. It was now obvious why at least these employers didn't fight the minimum wage hike – the state taxpayers were picking up that cost.

There was a second surprise provision. During the last five years of Cuomo's reign, the budget had an informal 2% cap on the amount spending could increase in the state budget over the prior year. Tucked away in this budget was another provision allowing the commissioner of health to go beyond the 2% spending cap to implement the new minimum wage law. In other words, Cuomo made sure that he wouldn't be prevented from going over the 2% spending cap, in order to provide state funding to help the state afford the new minimum wage. However, nonprofits, farmers, and other private businesses were left to absorb the additional costs of the minimum wage law by either laying off employees or raising the prices of their products and services. What a result!

INFLUENCE OF THE INDEPENDENT DEMOCRAT CONFERENCE

T he republicans did not win a majority of the senate seats in the 2012 election. It seemed that we were going back to the New York City democrat controlled senate, and would likely repeat the disastrous years of 2009 and 2010, when the New York City democrats controlled the senate.

As discussed earlier, to his great credit, then republican majority leader Dean Skelos negotiated with Jeff Klein, who was a leader of the small band of democrats who did not want to conference with the democratic leadership. This resulted in a very creative governance. The rules of the senate were changed so that there were co-majority leaders. Although there were 31 republicans and only 5 independent democrats, Skelos agreed to share leadership with Klein. Granted, this was not an ideal situation, but at least it promised to be a relationship less damaging to upstate, western, central New York and Long Island than the democrat rule in 2009 and 2010.

Quite frankly, it worked fairly well, considering the potential conflicts. It gave Jeff Klein and his partners substantially more authority than they would have had if they conferenced with the democrats, and preserved the major role for the republicans in the senate. Committee chairs were shared and joint decisions were made as to what bills would come to the floor for a vote.

Obviously, it also resulted in a movement of the majority to the left and it required consideration of several bills that republicans would never have put on the agenda, if they had a pure republican majority.

The republicans gained control of the senate in the elections of 2014. The co-leadership positions were eliminated, with the republicans taking back sole control, but the cooperation between the republicans and the Independent Democratic Conference (IDC) continued. IDC members' roles were diluted but they were still in a position to substantially influence legislation. This relationship continued into the 2016 budget year.

One of the top priorities of the IDC in 2016 was to pass a paid family leave bill. Not so coincidently, the governor had a paid family leave proposal in his executive budget as well. The republican senate majority was neutral about the concept of paid family leave but, if it happened, the majority wanted to make sure that it was reasonable and not an undue burden on businesses and non-profits.

The fact that a minimum wage increase of 67% to $15.00 was also in the budget, made it much more difficult to agree on a paid family leave proposal as well. The thought was that small businesses, especially, could get hammered by the minimum wage increase and it would be wrong to add a requirement for paid family leave as well.

The governor's paid family leave proposal was outrageous. It would have provided that after working for an em-

ployer for a month, the employee could be excused from work for up to two months for the purpose of caring for a seriously ill individual, or for bereavement purposes. If enacted in this form, small business owners would have to find a new employee temporarily to fill the spot of the employee on leave, or alternatively, the owner would have to work more hours to cover for the absent employee. Moreover, when the employee came back from paid family leave, the employer would have to terminate the employment of the temporary employee. That would likely result in a claim for unemployment compensation by the laid off temporary worker, potentially causing unemployment insurance rates to go up.

Even though the republicans technically had a majority without the IDC (31 republicans and 1 democrat, Simcha Felder) there were practical issues whether we could maintain that majority. Bill Larkin, the senator from the Hudson Valley was 88 years old and in failing health, which from time to time resulted in him either absent or having to leave some session days early. Also, senator Mike Nozzolio announced that he had to have open heart surgery immediately after the budget was passed, which would require his absence for a substantial period of time. Similarly, Jim Seward had to undergo an operation after the budget process. To add to all of this, there was a special election to be held 18 days after the budget approval, on April 19, 2016, to fill the empty seat of Dean Skelos who resigned after his conviction.

For all of these reasons, it was important to maintain a good working relationship with the IDC to avoid having control taken over by the New York City democrats again.

The other concern about the paid family leave proposal was that, although the program initially would be paid for through premiums paid by the employee only, most believed that that would not last for long.

Paid family leave programs in other states were ana-

lyzed and it was found that their costs were substantially greater than what the New York proposal estimated and the benefits were less. Most suspected that the employee payment for the initial cost of paid family leave would soon have to be augmented with employer contributions. Again, this was not acceptable to most republican senators, especially in light of the proposed minimum wage increase.

As a practical matter though, it seemed very likely that John Flanagan would recommend that a paid family leave proposal be part of the final budget. The question was what parameters he would negotiate. Up to a couple of days before the passage of the budget, there were absolutely no details discussed in conference about paid family leave. That prompted me to contact Beth Garvey, the senate's lead counsel, asking for a copy of the proposal as negotiated up to that point. After reviewing it I found that it made some important changes but it was still problematic, especially in view of the fact that the minimum wage increase appeared more and more likely. The details of the final paid family leave proposal were not really discussed until the hours before we were scheduled to vote on the first budget bill.

The final details of the proposal provided that an employee would have to have worked for a company for twenty-six consecutive weeks before the employee would be eligible for paid family leave. The cost of the family leave would be born 100% by the employee.

The proposal also provided that the benefits would be phased in as follows: Beginning on January 1, 2018 an employee could take up to eight weeks of paid family leave for the care of a sick family member, bereavement, or the like. For the first year, an employee would receive up to 50% of his average weekly wage, or up to a 50% of the statewide average weekly wage. Beginning on January 1, 2019, employees would be entitled to ten weeks paid family leave and receive 55% of

their average weekly wage, and on January 1, 2020, paid family leave would remain at ten weeks but the employees would be entitled to 60% of their average wage. Finally, beginning on January 1, 2021 and thereafter, employees could take up to twelve weeks of paid family leave and receive 67% of their average weekly wage.

To add to the burden to employers, these weeks of paid family leave could be taken in one day increments, such as a day a week for several weeks. This would create an incredible administrative nightmare for employers. It's difficult enough to find replacement employees but it is almost impossible to find them for one day at a time!

So now we were at the eleventh hour trying to get an on-time budget and we literally had no time to further negotiate paid family leave. Clearly, this was done intentionally to put the pressure on, and make it less likely that senators would hold out to change the agreement that had probably been worked out weeks before. Needless to say, there were not too many happy campers in that conference.

From the outset, it seemed likely that paid family leave would be a part of that budget. Not only did the governor have it in his executive budget, but the IDC had it as its priority. In fact, the IDC's leader, Jeff Klein, had a separate bill to require paid family leave. By agreeing to this provision the partnership between the republican majority leader and the IDC got stronger. However, the relationship between the senate majority leader and the republican conference members deteriorated. A budget that included both paid family leave and the $15.00 minimum wage was not favored by most of the republican conference members.

When we went back to the senate floor to start voting on the budget bills, I approached Jeff Klein, with tongue only partially in cheek, and told him that I wanted to be part of the IDC because they did better in the budget than the republican

majority members. He laughed, but I didn't. No wonder that New York is rated either last or next to last of all states for a favorable business climate.

Eighteen days later, the IDC's influence got even greater. That's because the republicans lost the special election to fill the seat vacated by the conviction of senator Skelos. The democrat candidate, Todd Kaminsky won. So for the rest of the session leading up to the next November election, the republican control was razor-thin.

THE PENDULUM SWINGS BACK- THE 2016 PRESIDENTIAL ELECTION

There are very few things you can say with certainty about elections, but one thing is quite certain, namely, that the pendulum will eventually swing back. And it swung back in the 2016 presidential election. Quite frankly, I doubted this would happen after President Barack Obama won the presidency so decisively for his second term. I truly believed, at that time, that he put together an unbeatable coalition, primarily those who not only approved of big government but depended on it for entitlements. The pundits opined after the Obama/Romney election, that Mitt Romney lost because of his famous statement to the effect that the democrats and Obama had 45% of the voters, who were receiving some type of government entitlements, in their back pockets.

I happened to believe that his statement was not far from the truth, but the media attacked Romney unmercifully for his "insensitive" comment. I thought Romney was a good candidate that would have helped bring the country back to a

more rational approach to government. He emphasized individual responsibility, but still understood that some entitlements were necessary and proper.

I have read extensively on government, and the successes and failures of government. One common theme is that a democracy doesn't collapse from threats from the outside, but rather dissolves from the inside. And I believed, and still believe, that once there are more individuals being taken care of by government than those producing revenues to support government, a democracy will not stand.

After the 2012 election cycle, I strongly believed that the country, as we knew it, was coming to an end, and that there was no way that an individual with a limited government philosophy would ever again be able to win the presidency of the United States. I continued to hold this belief in 2016 through the republican primary season at which time 16-plus candidates sought the republican nomination for president.

Quite frankly, my choice at the beginning of the process was Marco Rubio. I believed that a young face who was obviously very intelligent and articulate might bring a new, younger voter to the polls to break the democrat hold on young voters, and that he gave republicans the best chance to be victorious. As the primary season went on, one establishment candidate after another fell and the populist message of Donald Trump became louder and louder reflecting the feelings of republican primary voters.

I cringed from time to time as Donald Trump would make comments that seemed designed to be offensive to someone. I also cringed when I would see twitter posts by him inflaming one group or another. But what offended me even more was the republican establishment criticizing Trump and refusing to get behind him, especially former presidents and presidential candidates like the Bushes, Mitt Romney and John McCain. They obviously had forgotten that the party leaders and rank and file got behind them during their presi-

dential races.

What also was quite irritating to me was that republican candidates who were running for reelection either ran for the hills and would not comment about Trump, or would openly say that they would not support him. Some went further, and criticized him at every campaign stop.

Once Marco Rubio was out of the race, I made it clear that I was supporting Donald Trump. I'll never forget one rally of republican committee people held in Syracuse. There were electronic and print reporters at the rally when I stated that I was supporting Trump, and the reason was that we needed a change in the direction of the federal government. I also stated that there is no doubt that some things that Donald Trump had said were offensive, but that there were only two candidates, and that the other candidate would just continue leading us in, what I believed to be, the wrong direction. I concluded that it's about time that everyone understands that it is better to be offended than to continue in the wrong direction.

Needless to say the newspaper picked up on that comment and it was repeated over and over by many, including some residents of my senate district, who told me in no uncertain terms by email, that I was totally wrong. It's ironic that those who didn't want Trump to be offensive, had no trouble being offensive to me.

At the time, I was also on the ballot for reelection to my state senate seat. Fortunately, I had no opponent, but whether I had an opponent or not, I never hesitated to give my opinion on issues. I was even so bold as to put a Trump sign on my lawn. Well, actually, it was more than one Trump sign since many of them disappeared over time. But I was prepared with replacement signs to last all the way through election day.

Believe it or not, I actually got emails to my state senate email address from two neighbors of mine. I didn't know them personally, but they freely gave their names and addresses. Their messages were the same. How could I possibly

support Donald Trump and have his sign on my lawn? The messages went into great detail about how Trump was so offensive and I was wrong about Trump. They even demanded that I take the sign down. Rather than just ignoring them, I wrote both back the same message: "There are two candidates. I obviously support Trump. It is clear that you support Clinton, and I disagree with you. But I would never in my wildest dreams even think about writing you an email to demand that the sign of your candidate be taken off your lawn." I never heard anything more from them.

The reason why I had so many Trump signs is because I attended the republican convention in Cleveland, Ohio. In New York state, republicans select 3 delegates and 3 alternate delegates to their national convention from each congressional district as well a group of at-large delegates. I expressed my interest in being a delegate, and Tom Dadey, republican chairman for Onondaga County, accommodated me.

Interestingly, however, John Kasich earned enough votes in the primary to entitle him to one of the delegates in the congressional district in which I lived. I told Tom that it didn't matter to me which delegate I was pledged to on the first ballot, because I wanted to participate at the convention. As a result, I ended up technically being a Kasich delegate but as a practical matter it didn't make any difference since Donald Trump was going to, and did, win the nomination on the first ballot.

So my wife and I attended the national republican convention in Cleveland. This wasn't our first. We actually attended four. The first was in 1996 when Bob Dole and Jack Kemp were selected as the republican ticket. This convention took place in San Diego, California. It was absolutely beautiful and a lot of fun except for the speeches, which were quite boring. To give you a flavor of the event, the first people to grace the stage were four U.S. senators dressed in cowboy garb with a lot of stars and stripes. They sang "This is my Country" and the "Grand Ole Flag." And republicans wonder why we don't

appeal to the younger voter.

The other memory that I have is about Roy Bernardi, then mayor of Syracuse. I really got a kick out of how Roy was using the convention in order to promote himself. I hasten to add that I don't have any problem with that but it was sort of interesting, since I had never been to a convention before to see how that worked.

The instance I remember the most was when Roy ran into Jack Kemp, the eventual vice presidential nominee. He talked with Kemp for, at best from what I saw, a few minutes. Bernardi's aide, Jim Parenti did a great job sending out a news release to the local Syracuse media stating that Jack Kemp and Roy Bernardi met and discussed several issues. Quite frankly, the only discussion I heard was, "How are you." "I am fine, thank you, how are you?" However, the impression given in the news release was that Roy Bernardi was in high level discussions with the soon-to-be vice presidential candidate of the republican party.

In any event, it was an outstanding experience to be at the convention, especially it being our maiden voyage. We still have a photograph of the balloons coming down immediately after the nomination vote was taken, and my wife and I cheering. Unfortunately, that election didn't go so well.

The next republican convention I attended was in 2000. It was at this convention that George W. Bush and Dick Cheney were nominated as candidates for the republican ticket. It was held in Philadelphia, Pennsylvania, clearly a democrat city. What I remember most is how much security there was at the convention and how many protestors were trying to cause trouble. However, this convention was very exciting. My wife and I knew George Pataki very well, since George was first elected to the state senate the same year I was first elected. In 2000 he was one of the individuals who announced that he was interested in running for president. He obviously didn't make it. However, he was rewarded with a prime time speaking role, and he did an absolutely fantastic

job. It really made my wife and I proud that we knew someone so well who was so high on the national radar as George Pataki.

The media though, latched on to another convention speaker, Dwayne Johnson, aka "The Rock." He was the World Wrestling Federation's champion at the time. He later became one of the most successful actors in Hollywood. It was a reminder of an early lesson I learned in my first campaign – sometimes issues don't matter.

My wife and I also attended the 2012 convention, as a delegate and guest, when the nominees were Mitt Romney and Paul Ryan. The convention took place in Tampa, Florida, and like the others, our hotel was probably the furthest hotel from the convention center. The reason was simple. New York is consistently a blue state, always in the democrat party's column. The organizers of the conventions wanted to make sure that the key republican state delegates, that were really needed to win, were given prime locations to stay and prime locations in the convention center.

This was the convention where Clint Eastwood made a speech to an empty chair and spoke frankly to President Obama, who he pretended was seated in the chair. I thought it was amusing. Others did not think so, but it was certainly better listening to Clint Eastwood than to John McCain, who got a prime time speaking spot. All that kept going through my head was that one of the republican party's main problems was that it continued to select candidates whose turn it was to run for president, rather than the best candidate, who would appeal to more people. Watching John McCain speak at that convention, after having lost four years earlier, was like watching paint dry.

But again, as in the other conventions that I was involved in, it was really a great opportunity to speak with people throughout the country with similar philosophical underpinnings. Also, the events were fun. Seeing Mike Huckabee playing the bass guitar on stage at one of the parties was a kick.

The 2016 Cleveland republican convention was different. First, although Donald Trump had the sufficient votes from his primaries victories, there was still some uncertainly and excitement because some of the delegates still wanted to select an establishment republican candidate. Also, it was different logistically too. Since the presumptive republican nominee, Donald Trump, was from New York state, our hotel was in walking distance of the convention center, and our position on the convention floor was directly in front of the stage. My wife and I were seated in the fourth row, center stage.

In addition, the speakers were more diverse and interesting than the typical politicians that we heard in prior years. We got to go to the Rock and Roll Hall of Fame, which was outstanding since we could relive our youth and celebrate the kings and queens of rock and roll. Most of all, it was different because there was a feeling in the convention center that Donald Trump could actually win, since he had struck a chord with middle America and those that felt they had been left behind by the Obama/Clinton entitlement crowd.

One of the most enjoyable parts of the convention was when Ted Cruz spoke. There was a bitter rivalry between Cruz and Trump during the primary season. Each had said nasty things about the other and the wounds had not healed. My wife and I thought that Cruz would only have been allowed to speak if he was going to endorse Trump, so there was palpable excitement in the convention center when Cruz approached the microphone.

He spoke and he spoke and he spoke, and basically said nothing about Donald Trump. New York delegates, who were front and center, including yours truly, started getting a bit agitated to say the least. That agitation led to a chant "Endorse Trump, Endorse Trump..." This obviously shook Cruz up to the point that he stopped and looked down at us wanting to say something, but all he could think of was something to the effect of "settle down." This just got the crowd chanting louder, and when he didn't say that he endorsed Trump he was

literally booed off the stage. Again, this convention was like none of the others that we attended.

There were a bunch of signs in our area referring to Hillary Clinton, saying "Lock Her Up." There was even an individual, I'm not sure if it was a man or a woman, in prison garb carrying a ball and chain. When he or she appeared, the chant got louder "Lock Her Up! Lock Her Up!"

I got into the festivities more than I normally did. Before the convention, I went to Bergans, a clothing store on Salina Street in Syracuse. You can get just about any wild outfit you can possibly think of at Bergans. Joel Bergan told me his biggest customers were online consumers. He prided himself with having suits with broad stripes, hats that could be worn proudly on the corner of any red light district, and shirts and ties of every color and style. I purchased a red and white thick-striped shirt with a white collar, a wide white tie, white pants, red shoes and socks, and a red hat. I never had the guts to wear the whole outfit together but wore parts of it during various convention sessions.

The convention floor was jammed with television and radio personalities. One radio reporter from Albany saw me, took out his phone and videotaped an interview during which I explained I was a delegate and didn't want to be confused with someone having a street business in downtown Cleveland. It was shown back home and became quite a hit since my outfit was so outside of my usual conservative dress. But again, the convention was fun, much different from the more staged, planned, boring conventions of the past. In fact, many of our friends who were watching the convention told me it was easy to pick me out of the crowd, up front in the New York delegation, with my red hat. Needless to say, I got ribbed about it too.

Each morning the New York state republicans held a breakfast in our hotel and the speakers were great. They included Newt Gingrich, Rudy Giuliani, Steve Forbes, John Bolton, and Senator Ron Johnson of Wisconsin, who was in an

extraordinarily close race, that he fortunately won.

The speakers at the convention regular sessions, including Donald Trump, clearly revved up the crowd, and we truly believed when we left Cleveland, that republicans had a good chance of taking back the White House. As the campaign progressed, as in most other races, there were many ups and downs. The lowest of the lows was when the Billy Bush bus recording was made public. The comments made by Trump on that tape, and the media's incessant airing of them, obviously didn't help in the quest for the women vote.

When Trump started taking on the media, calling them liars and worse, I thought it was a huge mistake. At first it was hard to believe Trump's statements that the media was in bed with Hillary Clinton. However, when the various reports were aired showing that primary debate questions were being leaked to Clinton's camp by media moderators, the public's eyes were opened. These reports were literally confirming what previous were considered to be outrageous statements by Donald Trump. There is no doubt in my mind that none of the other republican candidates for president would have ever taken on the media the way Trump did. And eventually he was proven to be right in many respects.

The news conference of FBI director, James Comey, where he, in effect, exonerated Clinton, even though others had been indicted for far less, was unbelievable. After citing the gross negligence of Clinton in the use of her private server in transmitting classified materials, FBI Director Comey's conclusion that there was no crime, was absurd. Was Trump right on the existence of a deep state, as well ?

There is no requirement in the law that an individual intentionally discloses classified information to be indicted. All that has to be proven is that he or she acted in a grossly negligent manner. To ignore the law and virtually exonerate Hillary Clinton towards the end of a campaign was truly unbelievable.

More remarkable however, was that after additional

emails were discovered on Anthony Weiner's computer, and after notifying Congress of this, Comey reopened the investigation, and then only one week later Comey again found no crime. Unbelievable! This was especially hard to believe considering that the FBI Director claimed the FBI reviewed more than 100,000 emails in that week. Why he said anything at all during the presidential election was just beyond explanation. Rather than exonerate Clinton, these actions of the FBI director demonstrated that there was a swamp in Washington that needed to be drained, which Trump had been saying all along.

It was difficult to believe that the polls were as wrong as Donald Trump was saying that they were in the final stretches of the campaign. Nobody thought that the polls could be so far off, including myself. But they were. I did believe that there was a strong underground vote for Trump, but I never expected it to be as strong as it was to put him over the top in states like Michigan, Minnesota, and Pennsylvania. But it was enough. During the campaign I stated repeatedly that there were many voters out there that would not admit that they were voting for Trump since many didn't want to be berated by the Clinton supporters. It was simply better to not engage anyone and just express your opinion forcefully by your vote.

Each year on election night, the local Onondaga County republican committee has a get together at a local hotel to watch the results. I normally didn't get a separate suite to watch the results with staff, friends, and family but in 2016 I did. However, I repeatedly left the room to go to the main ballroom to talk to the republican committee members and guests who were also anxiously awaiting the election results.

As the night wore on, no one wanted to leave. It's difficult almost to express the feelings that we were experiencing as states were turning red, one after another. It was a real high to watch the results all night long into the wee hours of the morning to the time when Donald Trump made his victory

speech.

I didn't get home until about 4:00 AM, slept for one hour, then took a shower and left for the airport. I had previously booked a flight to Florida. Frankly, I didn't feel tired at all since the adrenaline was still flowing. The only other feeling I had like the one I felt on this election night was on the election night when George Pataki won the governor's race. I was on a television news set being interviewed when it was announced that George Pataki had defeated Mario Cuomo. Seeing a friend become governor of the state of New York was truly exciting.

I just hoped and prayed that Donald Trump would do a good job. If not, that pendulum that keeps swinging, will swing back and hit republicans in their derrieres in 2020.

NEW YORK CONTINUES TO MOVE LEFT

Despite Donald Trump's victory, Hillary Clinton beat him in New York by about 2 million votes. That margin primarily came from four of the five boroughs of New York City - Bronx, Queens, Brooklyn, and Manhattan.

A leftward movement in New York continued. Where would a governor commute a jail sentence of a minimum of 75 years for robbery and murder? Well maybe California, but we don't have to guess in New York since Andrew Cuomo actually did it.

In 1981, there was a robbery of a Brinks truck in Rockland County, New York. This robbery resulted in the death of a Brinks guard, and two police officers. A few years before the robbery, Judith Clark joined the May 19th communist organization, an offshoot of the radical Weather Underground. Showing no remorse during her trial for these offenses, she spewed radical rhetoric repeatedly, which included referring to those killed as "pigs." In her sentencing, the judge found her not capable of being rehabilitated, and sentenced her to a minimum of 75 years in prison- time well beyond her life

expectancy.

When Cuomo's commutation was announced, needless to say, the family members of the three murder victims, Sergeant Edward O'Grady, Officer Waverly "Chipper" Brown, and Brinks guard Peter Paige, as well as the entire law enforcement community, protested loudly.

The commutation did not mean immediate release from jail but rather meant that the parole board could release her as early as her next hearing. Largely because of these protests, the parole board did not release Judith Clark on her first appearance. However, she still remains eligible for parole.

Only in New York, but probably in California, would a group organizing a six-decade-old New York City Puerto Rican Day parade select Oscar Lopez Rivera to honor. Rivera was the head of an organization called Fuerzas Armadas de Liberacion Nacional. This group sought independence for Puerto Rico. To reach that end, rather than simply advocating for independence, the group took credit for over 100 bombings in the United States, resulting in the death of six and injury to many others, including police officers. President Obama, just before leaving office, commuted Rivera's federal sentence, which was to be 55 years in jail.

In an attempt to enhance his claim to be the most "progressive" politician, Mayor Bill de Blasio quickly announced he would be attending the parade. To his credit, or maybe still smarting from his commutation of Judith Clark's sentence, Governor Cuomo announced he would not attend. The parade, and the honoring of Rivera went off, as planned.

So, although the country, with Donald Trump's election, seemed to be moving the pendulum to the right, New York state kept its pendulum moving further leftward. There are other examples. Shortly before Andrew Cuomo released his 2017 New York state executive budget in mid-January, he held a news conference with none other than Bernie Sanders

to announce his "free College tuition" proposal that would be in his executive budget. Observers of New York politics were unanimous in their belief that this proposal was made to capture the hearts and minds of the progressive wing of the democratic party; a wing that he believed he needed to put himself in a position to be at least considered for the democrat nomination for president in 2020.

Never mind that New York State residents were voting with their feet by moving out of New York state because of its high taxes, onerous regulations, and redistribution of wealth. In the past, during its redistricting years (every 10 years) the state of New York lost congressional seats since its population had grown at a smaller rate than other states. But in 2016, for the first time, New York State saw a net loss in population; not just in relation to other states, but a true net loss. In light of this flight from New York, it made no sense to give away more "free stuff," in this case, a "free" college education to be paid for by the already overburdened taxpayers of his state. But Andrew Cuomo seemed to be more interested in moving to Washington, D.C. than keeping people in New York.

Consistent with the 2016 budget negotiations, both legislative bodies rolled over to governor Cuomo and approved the "free" college education, to the great detriment of New York state taxpayers. Although there was a grueling fight by the rank and file in the senate, the senate failed to buck Cuomo.

The governor wasn't satisfied with his demonstrated ability to achieve what he wanted from the legislature. He also wanted the ability to select an inspector general whose job would be to oversee and investigate, if necessary, the economic development activities of the state government. Towards that end, he included a provision in his executive budget that would have given him that authority.

A little background is necessary. From the date that

the governor took office and announced his many economic development proposals, he relied heavily on the State University of New York (SUNY). SUNY, through Alain Kaloyeros, created organizations outside of SUNY to enter into contracts and administer those contracts for economic development. Through investigations by United States Attorney Preet Bharara and to a much lesser extent, by Attorney General Eric Schneiderman, Alain Kaloyeros, Joe Percoco, one of the governor's closest allies, and some contractors with whom they dealt, were indicted. As of the time the executive budget was introduced by Governor Cuomo, namely mid- January 2017, those cases were moving towards October 2017 trials. Needless to say, the general public, fueled by the media, was again demanding "reform".

Governor Cuomo's view of reform was to get the legislature to allow him to appoint an inspector general to oversee these contracts and investigate them if necessary. Talk about the fox guarding the hen house! Fortunately, the legislature rejected that proposal.

At about the same time, Tom DiNapoli, the comptroller of the state of New York, proposed a bill that would change the procurement process and give the comptroller more oversight over these contracts. I jumped on that bill immediately. Since the legislature was acting less and less as a check and balance over the governor, at least a check on economic development contracts by the comptroller would help. As a result, I introduced the comptroller's proposed legislation.

There were some legitimate objections to the bill, and after learning of them, I agreed to amend it. The comptroller agreed to the revisions, and the amended bill was introduced.

I made it abundantly clear in republican conference after conference that I wanted to pass this bill and I wanted to pass it early so that the assembly could do the same, allowing it to get to the governor's desk well before the end of session.

The reason was that if the governor chose to veto it, the legislature would at least have the time to override the veto before the end of session.

After it was reintroduced, I met with the assembly sponsor, Crystal People-Stokes, who seemed to be interested in passing it expeditiously as well. A few weeks later she amended her bill to be identical to mine. Representatives of the comptroller's office informed us that the assembly was interested in getting the bill done.

Unfortunately, time was running out in the session. I was able to again discuss the bill in detail in a republican conference the wednesday before the Memorial Day weekend. After I discussed the importance of not only passing the bill, but passing it early, John Flanagan opened it up for discussion. There were minor objections but only from two or three senators. The balance of the conference members who spoke expressed their desire to pass the bill.

But rather than committing to put the bill on the calendar, John Flanagan began moving to discuss other issues that needed to be discussed. I literally jumped out of my seat, emphatically stating that I wanted an answer, one way or another, whether we were going to put this bill on the calendar when we got back from the Memorial Day break. He hesitated and said that that was one of the four things that he wanted to discuss. Quite frankly, I don't think that was his intent. But after refocusing, he did make a commitment that as soon as we returned from the break he would put the bill on the senate calendar for a vote.

An interesting thing happened on Sunday of that weekend. I got a call from Andrew Cuomo. He wanted to talk about the comptroller's procurement bill. Needless to say, I already knew that he definitely did not want it to pass since it would curtail his ever-expanding powers. He started out by asking me if I was going to put something in the bill to deal with the

"stipend issue".

Briefly, the "stipend issue" was a matter that arose a couple of weeks earlier. Legislators, both in the senate and assembly, who are heads of committees or are leaders, are entitled to stipends. The highest stipend, $46,500, is for the majority leader of the senate and the speaker of the assembly. My stipend for deputy leader and Joe Morelle's stipend for his parallel position in the assembly was $34,500. Flanagan, had adjusted senate stipends so that the IDC and its members in leadership positions were also given stipends, as were some republicans who were not chairs of committees. However, the total amount of stipends did not exceed the total amount authorized by law.

Moreover, these stipends were fully disclosed by Flanagan in the senate's financial reports. When the brouhaha started, a senate counsel gave a legal opinion indicating that these actions were wholly lawful. But as you might expect, the press had a field day with it and some democrats were asking for investigations.

I asked Cuomo what the stipends had to do with oversight of contracts by the comptroller. His exact words were "everybody is talking about it." I couldn't quite understand the logic, and I told him it doesn't matter what people were talking about since the issue about stipends was not relevant to the procurement bill. He then asked me if I had known about it and if I thought it was legal. I told him that I didn't know about it until it was reported in the press, and that the republicans had a legal opinion that it was done lawfully.

He wouldn't let it go. He wanted to get a commitment from me that I would change my bill in order to include the stipend issue. He was obviously trying to pressure me to not pursue the bill because there is no way he could have believed that I would add a totally irrelevant amendment to a piece of legislation that both houses wanted to pass.

Cuomo then claimed I was playing politics. Amazing! An accusation that I was playing politics from a man who never took a breath without assessing how his every word and action would affect him politically.

I told him that I wished that this conversation was taped since no one would believe how ridiculous he sounded, linking stipends to a procurement bill and accusing me of playing politics. Come to think of it, he probably was taping the call.

The conversation lasted for at least ten minutes. Cuomo kept going around in circles. He finally said that he could ask the attorney general to do an investigation. I said that was his prerogative, and that he should do what he wanted to do, but that I was not going to change the bill. That ended the conversation.

To keep the majority leader in the loop, I immediately called Flanagan to explain what happened and emphasized that I wasn't going to change the bill. I again told him that I wanted to get the bill passed the following week. He seemed appreciative of my call and he didn't say anything that would lead me to believe that he had changed his mind about putting the bill on the calendar to be voted on when we got back from the break.Two days later, I got a call from Rob Mujica, the former chief administer of the senate finance committee, and current budget director for the Andrew Cuomo administration. Rob's move from the senate to the governor's office was no great surprise to me since he had become close to the governor, even while he was an employee of the senate.

The call came when I was in the Baldwinsville public library waiting to participate in a Memorial Day parade. Rob told me that the procurement bill was "not the solution." I responded that the governor appointing his own inspector general to review his economic development actions clearly was not the answer. I then asked Rob what he had in mind as an

alternative. He literally told me he would have to think about it.

However, he also brought up the New York state fair director position. At the time, there were rumors that the governor was going to appoint a new director, and relieve Troy Waffner, the acting director, of his position. Right after the rumors first surfaced and continually thereafter, I made it clear publicly that it would be a horrible move since Waffner was doing a great job.

I also had called the commissioner of agriculture, the direct supervisor of the state fair director, and explained my position. He was well aware of my strong support for Troy Waffner, because he was present each year at the opening day of the fair when the governor cut the opening day ribbon. At each of these events I told the governor, face to face, that Waffner was doing a wonderful job and he should be made director, rather than remaining merely acting director. The governor never responded to me. This call from Mujica came after my many positive comments about Troy Waffner in the press and the phone conversation with the commission of agriculture.

Well you guessed it. Mujica asked me about who should be the state fair director. He obviously knew who I wanted as director, and knew I had been advocating on Waffner's behalf, and that I thought that appointing a new director to replace Waffner was a terrible idea.

I confirmed what he already knew and explained my feeling that Troy Waffner had done an incredibly good job and deserved to be named state fair director. Just to be clear, Troy is a Democrat, and previously worked for democrat senator Dave Valesky. So my position had nothing to do with partisan politics, it had to do with keeping good people in positions in which they were doing a good job.

It was obvious to me that Rob was trying to get me to back off the procurement bill in return for the possible nam-

ing of Troy Waffner as fair director. However, I didn't bite. Rob definitely knew that I wouldn't bite since he knew me very well having worked closely with me when he was the senate finance secretary and I was chair of the senate finance committee.

After these calls the governor kept pounding away against the procurement bill despite substantial support for the bill that would have put some checks and balances over the governor's almost unlimited discretion over economic development dollars.

When we got back from the Memorial Day break, we had our usual republican conference. In spite of the commitment that Flanagan made to do the procurement bill, he decided not to put it on the calendar for a vote. In no uncertain terms, I told him he had committed to doing the bill but, almost on cue, two senators stood up and said they recalled no such commitment by the majority leader. Fortunately, the sole democrat in our conference, Simcha Felder, stood up to speak, which was significant since he rarely spoke in conference. Simcha made clear that there was, in fact, such a commitment. Despite this, the bill was not voted on that week. That left only three session days left to pass the bill.

Interestingly, on the weekend before the final three days of session, the IDC leader, Jeff Klein, put in a bill. The bill called for the governor to appoint someone to review economic development contracts, which was virtually the same proposal that the governor made in his proposed budget. It was very obvious that the governor had gotten to Klein. Who knows what he promised him.

The only powers that I was attempting to give to the comptroller were the powers that he previously had and that the legislature foolishly, in 2012, had taken away from him. The reason they were taken away was that the governor argued that it was slowing down procurement contracts. So for

Klein to put in a bill allowing the fox to guard the hen house made no sense to me other than possibly a perceived political benefit from doing so.

Since the senate and assembly bills were identical, the comptroller's oversight bill could pass the senate and the assembly in the last week of session, if there was a will to do it. As you might expect, the legislative leaders of each house and of the IDC didn't have the will, so the proposed legislation died.

To his credit, Flanagan did put this bill on the calendar during the 2018 legislative session and it passed overwhelmingly. Unfortunately, the assembly did not take up the bill. So, the governor retained his power, and he continued his "progressive" movement to the left, while New York residents continued their rapid movement out of the state.

WHERE DO I GO FROM HERE?

My frustration had become palpable. Knowing that the state was accelerating in its movement in the wrong direction, I only had three choices. The first choice, was simply to not run again. I had been in elected office for over 40 years, and I know I would not be faulted for packing it in. However, every bone in my body told me that I had never quit before, and I shouldn't quit then.

The second choice would be to mount a challenge against John Flanagan and seek the position of majority leader of the senate. I believed that such a challenge could possibly be successful since three senators who voted for Flanagan indicated to me that they had made a mistake in doing so. Moreover, two senators that voted against me, Mike Nozzolio and Hugh Farley, retired and were no longer in the senate. Their replacements, Pam Helming and Jim Tedisco had philosophies close to mine and it would be quite possible that both would vote for me. However, politics is an interesting game, and although you can trust some people who give you their word, you can't trust them all. This is especially true when the sitting leader holds all the cards such as making committee assignments and allocating resources.

In addition, if there was to be a vote, it would have to

be a vote to change majority leaders during an election year. With the slim majority that the republicans held, such a vote would result in turmoil and could contribute to the loss of the republican senate majority for a very long time. If that happened then the move to the progressive left would be able to proceed unabated.

Moreover, I thought that even if I was to become majority leader, I would still have had to convince a majority of the republican senators that we would need to be much more aggressive to accomplish real checks and balances and resist the leftward movement in state government. Judging from my observations of some of the members of the republican conference, getting the support needed to do so, by no means would have been a certainty.

It became obvious to me that the only real way to try to change the direction of state government was to change it from the top – and that would be by beating Andrew Cuomo in the November, 2018 election.

Beating an incumbent governor would obviously be a daunting task, but it becomes even more so when you consider that the incumbent is a democrat, in an overwhelmingly democrat state – a state that gave Hillary Clinton two million more votes than it gave Donald Trump.

Additionally, it would be more difficult for an upstate republican to win such a race since the population is concentrated downstate. Moreover, to date President Trump had not endeared himself to the majority of New York state residents. And, being a republican who voted for Trump at the republican convention, and who supported him during the campaign would make it very difficult for me to win a race against Cuomo. But never say never.

George Pataki took a shot at Mario Cuomo. No one, including myself, thought that Pataki could beat Cuomo, but he did. He was an upstater but was an upstater from Peekskill, New York, which is not the same as being an upstater from central New York. What Pataki had going for him was

that, at the time, there were such negative feelings about Mario Cuomo. People thought there was a need for change. I don't know whether the negative vibes about Andrew Cuomo were as intense as they were against his father when Pataki ran against him, but there was a very negative feeling about Andrew in many parts of New York.

When I campaigned for George Pataki in central New York, and introduced him to people, no one had any idea what a "Pataki" was, let alone who he was. However, the campaign buttons with the name Cuomo on it, crossed out in red ink, accurately reflected the sentiment of New Yorkers---anyone but Cuomo. Although Pataki won by less than 200,000 votes, he won. Could history repeat itself for me?

So I started to make some calls to individuals who I respected and trusted to get honest opinions. People who were close to me thought it would be a great idea and thought I should do it. My wife, thought I was crazy, but she already knew that well before then. The one person that gave me the best advice was Joe Bruno, the former majority leader of the state senate.

He suggested that I should make this decision in two parts. First, I should travel around the state to various republican functions, so that the party regulars could get to know me and learn something about me. He thought that if I could speak at some of their events, they would get a feeling for me, and at least decide if I knew what I was talking about, and whether I appealed to them.

He suggested I do this until the end of 2017, which would give me about six months to make the rounds, and then I could evaluate the situation. The actual committee vote for the republican party nominee for governor wouldn't take place until the end of May of 2018 but by the end of 2017, I should have a pretty good idea whether or not I had a chance of getting the nomination. Obviously without the nomination, I was going nowhere.

At the time I spoke with Bruno there were other

candidates that were considering the governor's race. Rob Astorino, who had run against Cuomo during the last gubernatorial election cycle, no doubt would be one of the potential candidates. Rob, was in a difficult race for re-election as Westchester County Executive at the time. Obviously, he was consumed with that campaign and could not really discuss the governor's race. However, assuming he won reelection, he would be a formidable candidate.

Also out there testing the waters was Dutchess County Executive Marc Molinaro, a former New York state assemblyman. Marc was a young, articulate candidate who seemed to be very close to me on the issues. However, Harry Wilson was the leading contender. He was a successful businessman who turned around failing businesses. He also previously ran statewide against comptroller Tom DiNapoli and ran an excellent race. He, would still have some statewide name recognition. Moreover, Harry pledged that he would contribute one million dollars of his own money to the campaign. And as you know, dollars are the life blood of a campaign.

Harry Wilson also had been traveling around the state making speeches for over a year before I even thought of the possibility of running. No doubt he would have substantial support from rank and file republicans and from republican state delegates to the nominating convention.

As a result, even getting the nomination would be an uphill battle, but, there simply was no downside in taking Joe Bruno's advice and getting out there from July through at least the end of 2017 and evaluate at that time.

By labor day of 2017, I had traveled to events in Lewis, Yates, Livingston, Fulton, Saratoga, Oswego and Erie counties. At some events I was the main speaker, and other events I was given the opportunity to speak for a shorter time. The reception was good, because in upstate there were substantial negative feelings about Andrew Cuomo and his policies. However, it was impossible to gauge who actually would support me as opposed to the other republicans traveling around the

state, testing their own support. Moreover, I had yet to attend republican events downstate.

The word that I was exploring a gubernatorial run got out very quickly. Some learned of my intentions through newspaper articles, and through interviews on television and radio. One important interview was on the statewide Spectrum channel with Liz Benjamin. Another was with radio show host Bob Lonsberry on WSYR in Syracuse. At the outset, these two interviews got the most attention.

Fortunately, through labor day, the reports were even-handed and factual and I couldn't ask for anything better than that. However, what I learned during the first few months of my travels, was that New York is a big state, with many counties and a lot of roads that I hadn't traveled. Clearly, if I became the candidate, it would be a grueling campaign, much more demanding than any other campaign in which I had ever been involved.

Because of that, I religiously kept up my exercise regimen. I may have been seventy years old during this first leg, but I was still in good shape. I was easily able to keep up the pace of the statewide travel while continuing to perform my duties as a state senator.

No doubt my age would become an issue in the campaign, but fortunately, we had a President of the same age. And more importantly, I took great care of myself. In fact, I sometimes went a little overboard.

I played full-court basketball at the YMCA until I reached my mid-sixties, and continued to play in my high school alumni basketball game until I hit seventy. In fact, I challenged the president of LeMoyne college to a one-on-one game in August. It probably wasn't such a bright idea. The game was played before the incoming freshman class at Lemoyne. The President, Linda LeMura had been a Division I college scholarship basketball player and was a "kid" in her 50s. And, she was good!

She also had the home court advantage since every

time she scored a basket, hysterical cheering broke out in the gym. Whenever I scored a basket, I would hear a chorus of boos.

The game was tied, and whomever made the next basket would win it. Despite my best efforts, Linda won - but she cheated. As she was driving towards the hoop, the women's basketball coach came out on the court and set a pick, so Linda was able to go around me and make a layup. The place erupted. I protested, with tongue in cheek. I haven't heard how my protest went, but it probably made more sense that she won before her home crowd, since judging from the boos, I may already have lost a lot of votes.

Running for state-wide office would be tough, physically and mentally, so you had to stay in shape, but still have some fun too.

SEEKING THE NOMINATION

P rior to labor day, there were a lot of articles concerning my possible run for governor. However, most of them were local. For example, Mark Weiner of the *Syracuse Post-Standard* and Robert Harding of the *Auburn Citizen*, both wrote about my potential candidacy. As time went on there was more interest. In addition to *Capitol Tonight*, hosted by Liz Benjamin, several other political talk show hosts had me on their programs as well. An important radio host, Fred Dicker of TALK 1300, had me on his statewide broadcast on several occasions, as did Steve Penstone of Finger Lakes Radio. They seemed genuinely upbeat about my candidacy.

Since the greatest challenge was downstate, after labor day my pace accelerated and concentrated in the Hudson Valley and New York City. By mid-September, the potential GOP candidates still included Harry Wilson, Rob Astorino, and Marc Molinaro, but both assembly minority leader, Brian Kolb and former gubernatorial candidate, Carl Paladino began to be mentioned.

Harry Wilson was still the odds-on favorite. When Wilson ran for comptroller I remember seeing him on CNBC TV talk-

ing about complex financial issues that plagued the state. He was extremely knowledgeable, articulate, professional and genuinely motivated to meet those challenges.

Unfortunately, with the heavy democrat enrollment advantage and strong support by the unions for DiNapoli, Harry didn't win, but he had run a very competitive campaign. He clearly was the darling of the GOP and the candidate the GOP wanted to run against Andrew Cuomo. However, by the fall, Harry wouldn't commit to a run for governor.

Rob Astorino had run a credible race against Cuomo four years earlier but in the fall of 2017 he was in a knock-down, drag-out battle for reelection for his Westchester county executive seat. There were those who tried to convince him not to run for reelection but rather to go directly to the gubernatorial race, but Rob decided to run for re-election. If he had won the election, he would have been in a prime position to be selected the republican nominee in 2018. However, as it turned out, he lost.

The only reason Carl Paladino was mentioned was because he had run against Andrew Cuomo in 2010, having won a primary against Rick Lazio, the designated republican candidate. When he ran he was a complete disaster. Paladino put his foot in his mouth every time he spoke and seemed to believe that picking fights with reporters would enhance his chances. He got killed by Cuomo.

Assembly minority leader, Brian Kolb eventually announced he was considering a run for governor. Since he was an upstater, living in Ontario county, he would be one of my main opponents, with both of us fighting for the upstate vote.

Because of the importance of downstate, I took a many trips to New York City. My first meeting on Septemeber 18th was with George Pataki. At the time that Pataki was seeking the republican nomination for governor, Ralph Marino, the then senate majority leader, hated Pataki and did everything

he could do to get senators to support another potential nominee for governor, conservative party member, Herb London. When I indicated to Ralph that I was going to support Pataki, he reminded me of what he had done for me and tried to change my mind.

As a young senator, my first committee chairmanship was for the veterans' committee. As a veteran, I was honored to get this committee. However, within a year's time senator John Sheffer from the Buffalo area announced that he was leaving the senate to take a position at the University of Buffalo. This left open a vacancy for the chair of the tourism, recreation and sports development committee. Since I had been a high school and college athlete, I thought this position would be perfect for me . If appointed, I knew that I would enjoy it and do a good job.

Mike Nozzolio, who came to the senate the same year that George Pataki and I did, also expressed an interest in that committee. I called Ralph Marino and informed him of my interest and he told me of Nozzolio's interest as well. So I suggested to Ralph that he pick five sports that Mike and I could compete in, and whomever won at least three of the five competitions would be named chair. Ralph laughed heartily, which he rarely did. He must have liked the joke but, I was dead serious. The competition didn't happen, but Marino gave me the committee chairmanship.

Marino reminded me of this when I told him I was supporting Pataki. I told Ralph that I appreciated what he had done for me but I truly believed that Pataki was the better candidate, and I followed that up with substantial support for him in central New York. In the early stages of his campaign in central New York, Pataki's entourage consisted of one or two of his aides, and my wife and me.

In fact, during campaign stops, this small group would have dinner at Joey's restaurant in Syracuse. It was a lonely group,

but once Pataki won, everybody in the world attempted to join the after-election dinner, some of whom didn't help in the campaign until the very end when it looked that Pataki had a chance. As Mel Brooks said in his movie, *History of the World Part I*, "It's good to be da king."

In any event, I met with George in New York City, and the first thing he told me was that he thought that Marc Molinaro would be the best candidate. I told him that I wasn't there looking for his support yet but simply to inform him that I was in the mix for the nomination and that we would see what developed.

He asked me how I could possibly justify many of my votes in favor of budgets as a member of the senate and expect to be taken seriously about being critical of Andrew Cuomo's policies. I told him that no one could dispute that I fought harder than anyone to change the governor's budgets and that I had some successes. You had to fight the fight, as hard as you could, but you also had to govern and ultimately pass a budget rather than having gridlock like was happening at the time in Washington. Pataki's response was "good answer." I replied that it may have been a "good answer" but that it was also the truth.

The meeting ended shortly thereafter. Talking to him reminded me that no one possibly thought that he could beat Mario Cuomo, just like the general public now thought that Andrew Cuomo was invincible. I emphasized to every audience that I spoke to thereafter that the race was winnable and that no one thought that Pataki had a chance, but he won because the time was right. I had the sense that the public was in the same mood as when Pataki won, and wanted "Anybody but Cuomo."

I had this sense because people from all parts of the political spectrum expressed to me their strong dislike for Cuomo and many of his policies. Stephanie Miner, the mayor

of Syracuse for eight years, who years earlier had worked for Mario Cuomo, despised Andrew Cuomo. Stephanie, as mayor, was very outspoken and stated clearly her disagreements with Andrew Cuomo during her time in office, despite the fact that she began his first term as co-chair of the state democrat party!

If there is anything that Andrew Cuomo doesn't like, its someone who disagrees with him at all. Stephanie had no problem expressing her disagreements, and Andrew didn't like it. During her time in office, Cuomo ignored Minor and showed her who was boss by running everything he did in central New York through the republican Onondaga county executive, Joanne Mahoney, who smiled and nodded at his every word.

Stephanie was and is a progressive democrat, so I knew the progressive wing of the democratic party was not enamored with Andrew Cuomo. I thought that there would be a progressive primary opponent and someone, maybe Stephanie or actress, Cynthia Nixon, would seek the working families party line. In my mind the threat from Cuomo's left would give progressive and liberal voters an option – to vote on the working families party line. They clearly wouldn't vote for a republican candidate, but the votes on that line would be peeled off from the Cuomo democrat line to give a republican at least a chance to win in November.

While in New York City in mid-September, I also went to see John Catsimatidis. John is an accomplished businessman who had been close to Mario Cuomo and had also supported Andrew Cuomo on many occasions. He was also the host of a radio show in New York City that was listened to by many interested in politics. I had a good talk with him, but, obviously, he didn't give me any great hope that he would be a supporter. However, I did ask him if I could at least be a guest on his radio show. He was non-committal but I was pretty

sure, at some point, he would interview me, and he ultimately did.

The interesting thing about politics is that the longer you are in it, the more people you get to meet, and the more people you have a chance to make impressions on, good or bad. When I went to Catsimatidis' office, I was greeted by his attorney who was a former state supreme court judge. He was very cordial and complementary of me. He reminded me that when he went through the senate judiciary committee for senate confirmation that I was the chairman of the committee, and he told me how gracious I had been to him during this process. That was great to hear. Who knows, maybe he would be helpful.

My final stop in the city was the Empire Club reception where I spoke. The Empire Club is an organization of republicans who help finance republican candidates. It's an arm of the state republican committee. My speech seemed to be well received and this appearance accomplished what I wanted it to accomplish – to get more people to know who I was and what I stood for.

Even though New York City was of special importance, I still had to go to other counties throughout the state and in the early part of September I did just that. I attended a constitution day event put on by the Ontario county republican committee. With Brian Kolb potentially in the race, it was important for me to be there, even though the chairman of the Ontario county republican party worked for Kolb. I obviously knew who her preference was for governor and that it wasn't me, but I had to touch all the bases.

Around this time I also attended a barbecue in Tioga County and said a few words there. This was very fertile territory for GOP candidates because Andrew Cuomo refused to approve hydrofracking in the southern tier of New York and the local residents were not happy with that decision.

I also spoke at the "Cayuga Strong" rally put on by the Cayuga county republican committee. Since Cayuga county was in my senate district, I expected support from them when push came to shove, but you can't take anything for granted.

While traveling around the state, hopefully getting better known, I knew that if I was going to be serious about the gubernatorial race, I would have to get a campaign team together. I spoke to many potential team members during September, including Jeff Buley, legal counsel for the state republican party, who I had known for years and who I respected. Other stalwarts at the state party level were Jim Thompson and Ori Jacinto. They both gave me ideas about fundraising and securing the nomination. I felt it was extremely important to stay close to the state committee without getting too close. I knew that I had to remain at arm's length because Ed Cox, the state GOP chairman, had not been a strong chair, and there were country chairs who wanted to take him out. So I never got too close to Cox but I didn't want him as an enemy either.

In mid-September, a former senate employee of mine, Benedicte Doran, called me and told me that a political operative by the name of Brad Gentile, of the East Hill Group out of Washington, DC, wanted to speak with me about my run for the GOP nomination for governor. I had never heard of him or his group but Benedicte told me that he had done good work for congressman John Katko during his last campaign. Quite frankly, I thought that Katko ran an excellent campaign and I was eager to meet with Brad. We met on September 25th.

I also learned that Gentile and his colleague, Stephanie Valle, had done political work for Chris Gibson, a former congressman from the Hudson valley who had been very seriously considering a run for governor. For whatever reason, after he left Congress, he changed his mind and took a college teaching position. The fact that Gentile and Valle were close

to him and had started the process of organizing a gubernatorial campaign for him, would be a strong positive.

Brad and I first spoke in generalities. However, he agreed to put together a campaign plan, a summary of what he thought he could do for my campaign and an estimate of the costs. I though he was impressive and someone who could be helpful in a statewide campaign – a type of campaign that I had never contemplated, let alone run before.

In early October, I received the proposal and decided to hire Gentile and Valle. The timing was perfect in my mind since the campaigns of the other potential GOP nominees were starting to move forward.

Unfortunately, that plan didn't work out, so I eventually hired Mike Lawler and Bill O'Reilly (not formerly of the Fox News Network). Lawler was to coordinate the campaign and O'Reilly was to manage the communications. They were both excellent. Mike knew everyone in New York politics and had run the Astorino campaign for governor four years earlier. Bill was the best political communications person I'd ever run across, and they were both fun to work with. The race was serious business but you had to have some laughs so as not to go crazy.

One of the most bizarre occurrences happened during this period. In mid-October, Kolb and Molinaro made a joint announcement that they were in discussions to form a "joint republican ticket" to challenge Cuomo. No one had any idea what that meant. Was Molinaro going to be on the governor's line, and Kolb on the lieutenant governor's line, or vice versa? When asked about this, Kolb literally said that it didn't matter because they were both in it to serve the public. Wow!

The only thing that made any sense was that they would help each other along the way and see how things played out, but who knows what was really on their minds. What was clear was that a few days later, Marc Molinaro filed

with the state board of elections to open a campaign account which is the first formal step in making a gubernatorial run.

Other than reading what was going on with the other candidates, I simply continued going around the state visiting as many places as possible, including Rockland, Orleans, and Alleghany counties.

I did newspaper interviews in Alleghany and Monroe counties and also was interviewed by two TV stations in the Rochester area and attended a republican event in Monroe county. The main speaker at the event was Judge Jeanine Pirro, of the Fox Network, who I had known since the Pataki administration.

This Monroe county event turned out to be a foreshadowing of things to come. Prior to the event, Monroe county republican chairman, Bill Reilich, would not return any of my calls, but he gladly accepted a check from me reserving two seats at this dinner. When I arrived I asked him if I could get a brief speaking role to continue my efforts to get people to learn about me. He refused.

Just before the event started, I spoke for a while with Jeanine Pirro and then asked Reilich if he would at least introduce me. He agreed to, and did so. I was there to be seen and heard, so after her speech, I asked Jeanine some questions during the question and answer session. I thought they were good questions but the answers were pretty vague. At least I got a chance to be seen and heard.

I was also interviewed by Bob McCarthy, of the *Buffalo News* the following week and attended an event in Niagara county, which went very well since Rob Ortt, a state senator and supporter of mine, informed the audience of his support for me before I was introduced. In October, I also attended an Orange county brunch and had another interview with Liz Benjamin on *Capitol Tonight*. Both of these were highly worthwhile. So, by the end of October, I had visited fifteen counties

and had spoken at most of them. I felt that this effort was definitely moving me forward in the race, and I was getting energized.

THE HILL AND
THE VALLEY

As November rolled in, the speculation was about who was in and who was out. The first definite statement came from Rob Astorino, the GOP candidate for governor four years earlier. Rob had lost his reelection bid for county executive of Westchester county. Many speculated as to what the reasons were and most came to the conclusion that it was President Donald Trump's unpopularity in the suburbs around New York City. There were many other political talking heads that pontificated about other reasons but their reasons were not as important as the result of his loss, namely that he had no chance of securing the republican nomination for governor again. Rob realized that and quickly announced that he was not a candidate in the 2018 gubernatorial race.

My favorite comment from the political prognosticators, and so called experts, was that he never should have run for reelection and should have just gone for the nomination for governor. Some also said they personally urged him not to make that county executive run. Sure, take credit for the wins and, as to the losses, argue that if he listened to you things would have worked out.

I have always felt, that once you lose a race, (in this case the 2014 race for governor) it is almost impossible to come back and run in the same race another time. In other words, once you are a loser you are considered a loser - one of the cold facts of politics. But, Astorino would have been an excellent candidate.

Harry Wilson, who no doubt was still the front-runner for the republican nomination, stated that he would make his decision before Christmas. I indicated initially that I would let everyone know what I decided by the end of December. Molinaro said the same thing.

In mid-December, Brian Kolb officially announced his entry into the governor's race. No doubt, his reasoning was that he wanted to be the first to announce, and get some momentum while the other potential candidates were still deciding. I thought that was a great strategy but there was no way I was going to make a decision on running for governor until I knew what Harry Wilson was going to do. He was a lock for nomination if he said "yes."

Right after the first of the year Harry announced his long-awaited decision --- he would not run. Surprisingly, a few days later, Marc Molarino also announced he would not run. He stated that with his family obligations, which had to come first, the time was not right for him to run.

Molinaro's exit from the race really didn't prompt a lot of comment. Quite frankly, it seemed like no one really cared that much about it. However, a lot of people cared about Harry Wilson not running. The leaders of the republican party were beside themselves. Thinking that Wilson was the only one who could possibly win, the chairman of the party, Ed Cox, in no uncertain terms, expressed his disappointment that Wilson would not be in the race.

Once Wilson was out, I definitely made up my mind that I was going to run, but I couldn't announce quite yet since

I had to file the necessary papers to establish a statewide committee to become a formal candidate. I also had to finalize my campaign team and my arrangement with political consultants Mike Lawler and Bill O'Reilly, and with individuals who were financial experts at raising money for a campaign.

I also met with Ed Lurie, a former state senate employee, who had also at one time led the senate campaign committee. Ed had helped a lot of state senate candidates in his day, and also helped to run statewide races, including a race for attorney general against Eric Schneiderman. His candidate had been John Cahill, who did extremely well in the campaign. In fact, Cahill had been mentioned on more than one occasion as a gubernatorial candidate once Harry Wilson dropped out.

It became obvious to me that once Wilson dropped out the GOP leadership was actively looking for another candidate of their own to run for governor. I knew I had to get going, so I decided on announcing my candidacy for governor on January 30, 2018 in central New York. I filed the necessary paperwork the day before.

So, as of the date of my announcement the candidates that were in were Brian Kolb, myself, and two other individuals who had been traveling the state expressing their interest in running, namely, Joe Holland and Joel Giambra. Neither one of these candidates seemed to me to be taken too seriously, so for all intents and purposes, it was a race between Brian Kolb and myself.

Amazingly, ten days later, on February 9, 2018, Brian Kolb dropped out of the race. He described his dropping out as a moment of revelation as he left his home in Canandaigua. Oh brother! No specific reasons were given for his exit.

Even though he was formally in the race for only 26 days, Kolb had been racking up commitments from republican county chairs in both central and western New York. As

the minority leader of the assembly, he had the full support of both current and former assembly members. Some of these assembly members were chairs of republican county committees.

Prior to the formal announcement of my candidacy, I continued to travel the state giving speeches and familiarizing myself with the committee members. I traveled to Steuben, Broome, Oneida, Otsego, Delaware, Schoharie, Albany, Rensselaer, Ulster, Westchester, Kings (Brooklyn), Manhattan, and Suffolk counties. New York is a big state. I also had TV and radio interviews throughout the state promoting my candidacy, all of which seemed to be getting good results.

The day after I formally announced my candidacy in Onondaga county to a full house of wonderful people who had supported me over the years, I went on the road again and made a speech in Dutchess county. Marc Molinaro, who was the the county executive of Dutchess, was present in the audience. Little did I know at that time, that despite my gaining traction after Kolb left the race, Molinaro was being encouraged by the party leadership to reenter the race.

In February 2018,everything seemed to be going my way. I participated in a debate in Buffalo put on by the Erie county republican chairman, Nick Langworthy. The debate was between myself, Joel Giambra and Joe Holland. I was extremely well received and I was highly complimented by Langworthy. I continued to travel the state speaking in Queens, and at the Hudson valley regional candidates' forum. I also attended a Manhattan GOP event where short-lived White House communications director Anthony Scaramucci spoke. I then spoke again to the Albany county GOP and participated in the CNY regional GOP screening meeting.

I was on the radio just about every day being interviewed by stations throughout the state. My prime statewide radio appearances were with Fred Dicker who by this time had

me on weekly, and Susan Arbetter, who had me on her show frequently.

I also attended the Finger Lakes candidate forum where I was praised by the chairwoman of the Ontario county republican Committee, Trish Turner. Since she was Brian Kolb's chief of staff in his district office, this made me feel quite good about my chances.

I then participated in the southern tier regional GOP candidate screening meeting and I attended the Rockland county executive's victory party where I sat with the chairman of the Rockland county GOP. By this time, I also had the endorsements from almost all of the senators in the republican senate conference, including John Flanagan.

What I really needed was some of the big counties to come out in my favor. In early February, we were on the verge of having two of those endorsements – John LaValle from Suffolk county (which had about 10% of the weighted vote needed for the nomination) and Bill Reilich of Monroe county (who had about 6% of the weighted vote). By this time, I had commitments from about 15% of the committee leaders. LaValle and Reilich both told Mike Lawler on a Friday that they would make an endorsement of me on Monday. This was huge since if they and the others, who promised to endorse me did so, by mid-February I would have had over 35% of the committee vote and 50% was needed. I was near the top of the hill.

So I kept working hard. I went to a Poughkeepsie republican dinner, where I was the main speaker, and also went to Washington, D.C. for the Republican Governor's Association conference. There, I spoke with some GOP governors and members of their staffs, as well as with big donors in the national GOP.

Other events included the Orange county GOP candidate forum, and the Queens county GOP executive committee

meeting. It was going wonderfully, but the big county chairs not only failed to follow through with their commitments for written endorsements, but also, despite my repeated calls, wouldn't call me back.

Well it didn't take me too long to figure out why I couldn't get return calls from LaValle and Reilich, and also Joe Mondello, the Nassau county GOP chair who had another 10% of the weighted vote.

At about this time, Nick Langworthy, the chairman of the Eric county republican committee suggested to other chairs that there be a straw vote taken as to who should be the republican gubernatorial candidate. His reasoning was that since the formal nominating process would not take place until the end of May, holding a straw vote earlier, would help the candidate start off much earlier with his campaign. The date he set for the straw poll was March 2nd, at a GOP meeting in Saratoga Springs, which had been scheduled to select the republican U.S. senate candidate.

This made a lot of sense to me. If you were going to beat an incumbent governor who had over $30 million in his campaign treasury, starting sooner would be a good thing. I have no idea what authority Langworthy had to take the lead on this and whether the state GOP Chairman Ed Cox was involved, but the idea gained traction with other chairs.

The ground rules, as set forth in a Langworthy letter to the county chairs, were that only county committee people who were physically present at the March 2nd meeting could vote, and that they could only vote for someone who had by then announced his candidacy.

Obviously, that looked really good to me since all the major candidates were now out of the race, which left Joe Holland and myself, Joel Giambra having dropped out a couple of weeks earlier. Since I was gaining many of Kolb's supporters, it looked to be positive for me.

Unbeknownst to me, there had already been substantial movement by some of the chairs, led by Langworthy, LaValle and Reilich to get Marc Molinaro to rejoin the race. I heard some rumblings about that but nothing that I could confirm.

I went to Saratoga for the March 2nd meeting and attended a GOP cocktail party the evening before. It became obvious that something was up. People that indicated that they were supporting me were a little laid back. LaValle was not even present, but had sent someone who said he was going to vote for Molinaro. Then I learned that Molinaro was going to show up the following day for the straw vote.

Also attending was Chris Gibson, the former congressman who was mentioned early as a candidate for governor but decided to take a teaching job instead. That he was there made little sense to me but as things were developing it appeared Gibson hadn't completely lost hope of becoming governor. I speculated that the reason that he dropped out was that he didn't think he could beat Andrew Cuomo, and that he would simply wait four years to see what happened.

Gibson was the speaker that evening and made a rousing speech about how Andrew Cuomo could be beaten. He didn't mention Molinaro by name but after speaking with him it appeared to me that he was going to back Molinaro.

I then began asking questions about the process that would be followed the next day. Ed Cox, the state GOP chairman told me that he had no idea how the process would be conducted and that it would be entirely up to the county chairs. What a leader! In fact, the county chairs were then powwowing about just that. The rumor was that Molinaro was going to be allowed to speak even though he had dropped out of the race and still was not an announced candidate.

As far as the voting procedure was concerned, there was talk about allowing chairmen who brought proxies from

other committee members to vote these proxies, contrary to the letter from Langworthy which stated that only those that attended would be able to vote. This helped explained why I couldn't get a straight answer that night, and why I couldn't get one the following morning.

That morning, Molinaro issued a news release saying that he was going to attend the meeting and announce that he would reenter the race if he won the weighted vote. Needless to say, I was incensed. I again asked Ed Cox if Molinaro was attending and whether he would be given an opportunity to speak. Cox said he didn't know about Molinaro and still wasn't sure what the rules were going to be at the meeting. Sure.

It was most interesting to me that Molinaro did not appear at the hotel where everyone gathered either on the night of March 1st or in the morning of March 2nd until it was time for him to speak. It was rumored that he was at a Starbucks coffee shop down the block on March 2nd – apparently getting ready to make a grand entrance.

In any event, just before the meeting was supposed to start, I saw a former employee of mine, Joe Burns and the state republican party attorney, Jeff Buley, in the front of the main room. I asked Buley in the presence of Burns what the rules were going to be, and he said that the chairmen were going to have a closed door meeting before the vote to agree on the rules. I then glanced at Burns. Since Joe left my office, he, on my recommendation, became a deputy counsel for the New York state Board of Elections making a very good salary. Thereafter, he moved to Buffalo near his close friend Nick Lanqworthy. I was told he stood up in Langworthy's wedding and had been given a very high paying job on an Erie county authority.

I looked Burns in the eye and asked him what was going on. He said he wasn't sure. I reminded him that I asked him what was happening about the straw vote a week or so prior

to the March 2nd meeting, and at that time he also told me he had no idea what was going on. This was, no doubt, untrue. It would have been impossible for Langworthy to orchestrate this symphony overnight and highly unlikely that Burns didn't know about it.

So the party chairmen went into a room, conferred and ultimately decided that only those present could vote, but that Molinaro would be allowed to speak and of course he would be allowed to speak last. They also decided that none of the candidates could be present in the room when the others spoke.

I went first, and read aloud Molinaro's press release. I then commented, in no uncertain terms, that the rules for this event had been substantially changed. I reminded them that only announced candidates were to have been allowed to participate in the straw vote and that Molinaro, even according to his own news release that morning, still had not announced.

I also then compared Molinaro's credentials to mine. I explained I had an engineering degree from Syracuse University and a law degree from Duke Law School and that Molinaro had a two year community college degree. I explained that Molinaro had no other jobs in his life other than elected office positions, and I contrasted that to my many years of law practice and many experiences in volunteer and charity work.

At about this time, Sue McNeil, the Fulton county chair, jumped up and said that I should stick to the issues. I shot back that these are the issues. What you are voting on in this straw vote is who would be the best candidate to run against Andrew Cuomo. I continued that I had been running around the state challenging Cuomo on every one of his actions and bringing the campaign to him. I made clear that the only way the republicans could beat Cuomo is to go right at him and fight it out, and I was the candidate that could do just

that.

I even mentioned Langworthy and his ground rules for this meeting that were obviously set aside for the ultimate goal, namely to endorse Marc Molinaro. I explained that I had been involved in many competitions, political, sporting and otherwise but I had never participated in an event where there were no rules or where the rules were changed at the last minute. It wasn't the warm and fuzzy speech that most would have expected but at this point, I knew that the nomination was wired for Molinaro, and I simply wanted to speak my mind, and I did.

When I finished speaking there wasn't one question asked. Later I learned that Joe Holland spoke and had only a few questions asked of him, but when Molinaro gave his presentation, the floor was open to questions that lasted over half an hour. The fix was definitely in.

After I spoke, I immediately went to my car and left. I learned later that Molinaro overwhelming won the straw vote but still did not announce that he was a candidate for governor. He stated that he would announce his candidacy sometime in the future. That time didn't come until one month later.

One of his comments in his announcement really said it all to me. He announced that he was going to run a campaign like "a quiet conversation" on the issues. The only quiet conversation that Andrew Cuomo had ever had was when someone stood in front of him and was lectured about what he wanted that person to do. You couldn't beat Andrew Cuomo with a quiet conversation and the republican delegates at the Saratoga Springs event knew that when they took the vote. So it looked like a handful of powerful committee chairs were going to get their way at the formal republican nominating convention in late May.

I stated repeatedly at all of my appearances throughout

the state that I wouldn't run a primary because a republican could not win statewide with a split party and I stayed consistent with that position as I was interviewed by numerous news stations. By this time, I was on with Fred Dicker on a weekly basis. He seemed supportive of me and critical of the GOP.

In analyzing the situation, my only hope was to gain the conservative party endorsement which would give me some leverage at the republican convention the end of May. A republican could not win the race without the conservative party endorsement. I hoped that the tail might wag the dog in this instance.

So on March 18th, I got in my car and drove to Brooklyn where I spoke at a conservative party brunch. I sat at a table with Gerard Kassar and Mike Long, the Brooklyn and state conservative chairs respectively. Also at the table was my senate colleague Marty Golden, who had publicly supported me. It went very well and the Brooklyn conservative party endorsed me.

Immediately following that event I went to Queens Village to attend its republican Lincoln day dinner. I sat at a table with the Queens county republican chair, Joann Ariola, who was obviously giving me the cold shoulder, a direct contrast from when we met earlier in my travels.

Probably the most memorable part of this trip to the city was a phone call I received from Ed Cox at 9 a.m. I thought it was kind of unusual to get a call at 9 a.m. Sunday from him. He was very excited and during the call said he had a wonderful idea that he wanted me to hear. He said that I should run for attorney general. I immediately said, "no". He said, "at least hear me out, you have to hear my reasons." I told him I didn't care what his reasons were since I simply was not interested. He persisted again asking me to let him explain, which I did.

What he told me was that I should run for attorney general and that I could win that race against the incumbent Eric Schneiderman, and after I won the race, I could run for governor. I replied, "are you delusional? By November, I will be 72 years old. You're suggesting that I should run for attorney general so that in the future I could run for governor? Do you really think I will be able to run for governor when I am 85?" Unbelievably, he persisted until I told him again, "NO".

Coincidentally, the evening after I attended the Brooklyn conservative brunch, there was an event for the state conservative party in Albany, which I attended. Marc Molinaro was there. We just said "hello". He was circulating throughout the room with a smile on his face, posing for photographs with various conservative party members. It looked like he had his ducks in a row and had been gathering a lot of conservative support.

At the event I spoke with Mike Long, who was pleasant, as he was at the brunch the day before, but he was obviously standoffish. I tried to explain to him why I should be the candidate because I not only had the qualifications but also had the skills to go after Cuomo on issues. Again, he was standoffish.

I also spoke with the conservative party chair of Cayuga county, Greg Rigby, who had not yet publicly pledged his support to me even though Cayuga county was in my district. He also looked nervous as I pled my case to him. It obviously was not looking good at all. I knew definitely that I was going nowhere when I approached Shawn Marie LeVine, the secretary of the state conservative party, who was always cordial and honest with me. I began pleading my case but she appeared uncomfortable and totally unlike herself.

One of the guests of honor at the event was Cardinal Timothy Dolan. He mingled among the crowd, and when he got to me, we had a short conversation and took a photo to-

gether. We knew each other from prior events that he and I had attended in Albany. I explained to him that if I became governor, his life would become a lot easier. He knew what I meant in that, since I spoke my mind on various issues including being against an unlimited statute of limitations for child sex abuse crimes. He abhorred the bill and knew that I was firmly against it.

I asked him to pray for me, not realizing that he would extend his hands over my head and pray for me at that moment. He was sincere, but he obviously had no say over the process or the outcome.

My radio appearances continued and I remained honest and forthright about my intentions. I continued to state unequivocally that I would not run a primary, despite everything that had happened. But to be truthful, I woke several mornings after the March 2nd event and thought seriously about a primary challenge, partially because I didn't think I was treated fairly, but most importantly because I knew that Marc Molinaro could never beat Cuomo and that I would at least have a better chance. We needed to take Cuomo out.

April was uneventful but May certainly was not . On May 7, 2018 the press was abuzz about allegations from several women about attorney general Eric Schneiderman. These women alleged assaults on them and various forms of physical abuse. Amazingly, one of his female acquaintances who was a woman of color, spoke of Schneiderman's assaults on her and his references to her as his "brown slave."

Others made similar allegations about Schneiderman's physical and sexual abuse against them. Why is it always the one who cries out the loudest as a champion and protector of women, who is the worst offender? What a total hypocrite. Nothing came close to this bombshell since Elliot Spitzer got caught with his pants down.

I frequently debated Schneiderman on the senate floor

when he was a member. He was a sanctimonious, arrogant person, who looked down his nose at everyone because of his belief that only he walked on the moral high ground. So, quite frankly, I was not saddened by his downfall.

Within hours of the press reports of his infractions, Schneiderman resigned. Amazing. I particularly liked his first line of defense, in a press release before his resignation, wherein he said: "In the privacy of intimate relationships, I have engaged in role playing and other consensual sexual activities. I have not assaulted anyone. I have not engaged in unconsensual sex which is a line I would not cross." Sure Eric, you would never do any such a thing. Then why did you resign a few hours later?

Schneiderman's resignation wasn't the only thing he had in common with Eliot Spitzer. Neither were prosecuted! Governor Cuomo referred Schneiderman's case to democrat Nassau county district attorney, Madeline Singas, to investigate the women's allegations for possible prosecutions. The allegations included "choking, hitting and slapping" them; threatening to hit one woman whom he called his "brown slave" unless she consented to finding a woman to have a threesome with; and threatening to have their phones tapped and have them followed.

D.A. Singas concluded in November, 2018 that the "women were credible but there were legal hurdles" to prosecuting Schneiderman. Not surprisingly, she never explained those legal hurdles. And no one from the press ever demanded that she explain. The only "#metoo" moment in this whole scenario by those who were suppose to have supported this movement was that Schneiderman could say to Spitzer – "me too, I didn't get prosecuted either."

Getting back to the governor's race, Dave Catalfamo was the spokesman for Marc Molinaro before Marc first dropped out of the race. I had known Catalfamo well when

he worked for George Pataki in his administration. As soon as Molinaro first dropped out of the race, Catalfamo contacted me and wanted to sit down and talk. When I spoke with him, he gave me certain pointers that would help me in my pursuit of the nomination for governor. I listened to him and he left. This meeting seemed of no consequence other than possibly leaving the impression that he was going to support me and was looking to possibly help.

When Molinaro released his statement on March 2nd in Saratoga Springs to the effect that if he won the straw vote, he would reenter the race, it was written by Dave Catalfamo. Dave was back in with Molinaro. Bouncing around isn't a problem for many in the game called politics.

Well, only a day after Schneiderman resigned, Catalfamo, as Molinaro's spokesman, sent out a tweet saying that I should be the republican candidate for attorney general. When I next appeared on Fred Dicker's show, he seemed to be encouraging me to run for that position, or at least he was positive about it. He mentioned that even Molinaro's people were trying to get me to enter the race. My comment, again probably not appropriate or politically correct, was that "Catalfamo was the same person that participated in the wired nomination process, why should I ever trust or consider anything he suggests?"

Oh well. What you see is what you get. I informed Fred Dicker and all those listening to his program that I had absolutely no interest in running for attorney general, and I would not do so.

Well, when I said "no" there was talk of John Cahill entering the race. Cahill was a name that was mentioned as a potential gubernatorial candidate when the party was looking for someone to run after Wilson dropped out. He decided against it. Now, he became an instant front-runner to become the republican attorney general candidate. Quite frankly, he

would have been a good one, but he decided not to do it.

The republican ticket continued to be filled prior to the republican convention, when on May 20th, Marc Molinaro announced that he would have Julie Killian as his lieutenant-governor running mate. Julie is an extremely bright, well-educated, and capable individual. However, I was surprised that he selected her in that she never won a significant race. In fact, she lost her last two races for a state senate seat. Although I was very excited that she was our senate candidate, her selection as the lieutenant governor candidate did not enhance the electability of the Molinaro ticket.

Also, Killian was from Westchester county which is adjacent to Dutchess county, where Molinaro was the county executive. So much for regional balance. So much for western New York, or central New York, the north country or the southern tier. However, Molinaro and Killian were formally nominated at the republican state convention on May 25, 2018.

It almost sounded to me like the GOP was trying to lose this race. You have a gubernatorial candidate whose highest level of education was a community college degree, and who had no work experience other than in elective office. The lieutenant governor candidate was extremely well-educated and an outstanding person, but she hadn't won a significant race and lived in a county adjacent to Molinaro's home. But hey, you never know. George Pataki won when the feeling of voters was "anybody but (Mario) Cuomo."

I began to think about Fred Dicker's theory that he raised when I first started appearing on his talk show. He felt that this whole group behind Molinaro was tied to Al D'Amato who was the power behind the successful George Pataki campaign. And, Al D'Amato had already endorsed Andrew Cuomo for re-election. It was no surprise to me that he would do so, in light of the fact that his lobbying firm, Mercury Enterprises,

was one of New York's top-grossing lobbying firms. Maybe Dicker had been right. Who knows?

Well, as someone said "It ain't over until the fat lady sings." Well the fat lady by then had finished her song to me. I hit the valley. So what was next? Retirement.

THE FINAL CHAPTER

Troughout the time that I attempted to get the republican nomination to run for governor, I repeatedly said that if I did not receive it, I would not run for the senate again. Despite being crystal clear about my intentions, many people still thought I would run. They were wrong. I realized that after 41 years in elective office, if I didn't get the GOP nomination to run against Andrew Cuomo, it was time for me to retire.

Once it was apparent that I wouldn't get the nomination, I never looked back. It was time to do something else, or do nothing else, whatever I ended up deciding.

However I didn't want to leave without attempting to fill my seat with a good and a strong candidate. That candidate turned out to be Bob Antonacci, who was the Onondaga county comptroller. Bob was from a good working family and had a good work ethic. I thought that he was a fighter and we were on the same side on most issues.

I thought for some time that I would like him to succeed me. In fact, about eight years earlier the legislature was redrawing state senate district lines. My district boundaries were going to be changed substantially. In fact those working on the redistricting had taken most of the City of Syracuse away from me and replaced it with half of the City of Au-

burn and four western towns in Cayuga county. In addition, in order for the numbers to balance for all the senate districts, they intended to remove the town of Onondaga from my district.

I objected, since Bob Antonacci lived in the town of Onondaga and I wanted to keep open the possibility that he could run for my seat if he was interested when the time came. The senate redistricting committee made adjustments and kept the town of Onondaga in my district. I didn't know exactly when I was going to retire but I knew it was likely to happen within the ten years before the next redistricting, and that turned out to be the case.

When the time came, some eight years later, Antonacci was interested and he had the relatively easy task of getting the nomination. However, the county executive, Joanie Mahoney, did not want Bob Antonacci as the candidate. She first backed Rick Guy, a very conservative attorney, who I had served with on the Syracuse city council years earlier. Guy happened to be Mahoney's chief of staff's brother-in-law.

Rick really didn't have much of a chance. He had put his name in for many open seats as they became available, and never seemed to catch fire. The other candidate was Joe Carni. My wife and I were good friends of his parents and we had known both of them for many years. However, I just believed that Bob had a better chance of winning than Joe Carni and Carni, in his twenties, still had a long political future if he didn't get this nomination.

Joanie Mahoney switched to backing Joe Carni when it became clear that Rick Guy would not be the candidate. But Joe had the good sense to see the writing on the wall and he eventually dropped out of the race and supported Bob Antonacci.

I did everything I could for Bob and the other senate republican candidates, including maxing out in the amount of

campaign contributions I gave to Bob, and providing a large contribution to the senate republican campaign committee. In addition, I did a commercial endorsing Bob, and was in some of his campaign mailers supporting him. I also recorded a robo call, at his campaign manager's request (and against my better judgment) just before election day, urging a vote for Bob.

The race was tighter than I thought it would be, with Bob winning by less than 3,000 votes. His opponent, John Mannion was a teacher and an active member of the New York State Teacher's Union (NYSUT), the most politically influential union in New York. The union and its members donated hundreds of thousands of dollars to Mannion's campaign and had the workers to not only assist during the campaign but also to get out the vote on election day.

As for the governor's race, I had little to do with it. That wasn't because of my reluctance, but it was because Marc Molinaro rarely sought my help, and when he sought it, he sought it through others. In fact, each time that I was asked to appear at a news conference that he held in central New York, I was asked by republican county chairman, Tom Dadey. When I went to Molinaro's news conferences, I spoke favorably on his behalf and echoed his messages. I explained the reasons why we needed a change in Albany and a new governor to lead that change.

I did meet with him once when he requested to see me in Syracuse, but it was a short meeting with little substance to it. I also went to an Onondaga county republican committee clambake, at which I received an award. Molinaro was there, but he didn't approach me – he had one of his campaign staff come up to me to tell me that Marc was there. I briefly talked to him shortly thereafter.

At that event I also said good things about Molinaro and the need for all of us to work together to win. And I meant

it, because it was necessary to change direction in New York. Cuomo had to go.

Other than the above, I heard literally nothing from him or his campaign until the last few days of the race. I got a text from him about four days before election day that alerted me to the fact that there was a poll done by Siena College showing that he was only 13% behind Cuomo, which was a substantial difference from the well over 20 % deficit that was reported up to that time.

His text was followed by a voicemail indicating that his internal polls were showing that he was really only 5 or 6 percent down. I found that very difficult to believe but "hey, you never know". George Pataki did it and no one believed he would. The second part of the message was that he was asking for a donation of ten thousand dollars. I ignored the text, and I ignored a phone from him later that day, no doubt to follow up on his ask for money.

The final result a couple of days later was that Molinaro lost by 1,265,000 votes, or by 22 percent. So much for the accuracy of "internal polls", or for honesty, whichever was the case.

Bob Antonacci won, but the republican senate majority got hammered. The republicans lost seven seats. A few were close, most were not. The seat formerly held by republican Tom Croci was now to be filled by a democrat, and republican John Bonacic's seat was not retained either. In addition, long-serving republican senate veterans, Carl Marcellino and Kemp Hannon, were beaten, and Elaine Phillips could not retain her seat in her first re-election attempt. Similarly, Terrence Murphy, shockingly, lost as well. Finally, Bill Larkin's seat, which he vacated by retirement, was won by a democrat. It was not only won by a democrat, the republican candidate got killed.

When the remaining republicans met to reorganize for

2019 and to elect a minority leader, to add insult to injury, the democrat who previously conferenced with republicans, Simcha Felder, did not show up. As a result, the republicans would have eight fewer people in their conference during the 2019-2020 term.

This was a total disaster for republicans of the state since the republican senate was the only potential check over the New York City democrat governor, and New York City democrat-controlled assembly. Soon the state would be totally run by democrats from the city.

The next election in 2020 will be in a presidential year, and traditionally, republicans have not fared well during those years in the senate races. We usually just barely held on. So the chances of regaining a republican majority in 2020 are very slim. Moreover, shortly after the 2020 elections, the state senate and assembly will do redistricting – which redistricting by the democrats in the senate would almost certainly result in it being almost impossible in the future for the republicans to regain the senate majority. In fact, it is likely that the senate will turn 2 to 1 democrat as the assembly has been for many years. It will be interesting to see how much the democrats advocate for "independent redistricting" after 2020. Not much.

The republicans also lost three congressional seats – the seats formerly held by Dan Donovan, John Faso and Claudia Tenney. As you'd expect, there were immediate calls for the removal of republican state chairman Ed Cox. Eventually, he resigned in mid-2019 and was replaced by Nick Langworthy of Buffalo. You remember him. He helped orchestrate the republican gubernatorial nomination for Marc Molinaro.

On November 16, 2018, John Flanagan called a meeting of the republican senators who would be part of the republican conference beginning January 1, 2019. The purpose of the meeting was to select a leader of the senate republicans,

albeit a minority rather than majority leader. Flanagan's opponent in this race was Cathy Young. Some senators called or texted me before going to the meeting and expressed that Cathy was seeking their support arguing that it was essential that the republicans have an upstate member as minority leader. I really got a kick out of that since Young advocated and voted for Flanagan when I sought the position. Apparently Young's upstate/downstate argument didn't work since Flanagan was elected minority leader of the senate by a 12-9 vote.

Depending on your political and philosophical leanings, the 2019 legislative session was either a disaster or a gift from heaven. Legislation that was stopped by the senate republican majority was easily passed by both democrat controlled houses, and signed into law by the governor.

This legislation included, but was not limited to: legislation mandating that insurers cover all FDA-approved contraceptive drugs and devices; legislation called GENDA, which added "gender identity and expression" to the civil rights law thereby prohibiting discrimination against an individual's expression of gender; legislation to decriminalize possession of small amounts of marijuana; legislation granting government financial assistance to illegal immigrants to attend college (Dream Act); a law that permits illegal immigrants to obtain state drivers' licenses; a law that expanded rent control in New York City, which included provisions, applying outside the City; a law that would allow migrant farm workers to unionize; legislation that will allow adults who were allegedly abused as children to sue the alleged perpetrator during a one-year window, no matter how many years ago the alleged abuse occured; a law that permits early voting and same-day voter registration; legislation that liberalizes criminal justice procedures in ways such as limiting a judge's discretion in ordering bail, and the Reproductive "Health" Act that allows abortions to be performed by non-

doctors and permits late term abortions up to the date of birth.

Again, these laws are good or bad, depending on your point of view. By now, the reader knows mine. In any case things have changed and will continue to change in New York state. The pendulum keeps moving back and forth and the New York elections of 2018 have brought the furthest swing to the left ever in the state.

For me, this is the final chapter in my 41 years in elective office. The only thing I know for certain is that just when you think things have been decided by the electorate, things in politics begin to change again. But someone else will be in the middle of that change since I am retired.

****

Now you have it. You now know how to get there and you know what happens when you're there. So, do you want to be a Senator, or a member of the school board or of a city council --- or a governor or President of the United States? Although you might not have long-term goals in the political arena, you should get involved – whether it be as a candidate or someone supporting a candidate.

I've met some of the most interesting people from my years in politics. They include military heros, religious leaders, music legends, sports hall of famers, political leaders, Presidents, and movie stars. I've also met some of the most wonderful people, that few would know, who have successfully championed causes that have positively affected our state and nation.

And I've met many who are not so good. But that's true in all

walks of life. The main reason we hear more about politicians is because they live in a fishbowl and are much more vulnerable to criticism. But the only people who don't get criticized are those that don't do a damn thing.

Yes, we are probably in one of the most divisive times in our political history, but good people can make things better.

There are few greater highs than helping to solve problems; or passing legislation that positively affects people; or helping to stop bad legislation that would harm people. There are lows too, but the highs greatly outweigh the lows.

We're all in this together. Now it's your turn!